THE
DIARY OF
A TEENAGE
DIRTBAG
1999-2003

Claire xxx

THE
DIARY OF
A TEENAGE
DIRTBAG

1999–2003

CLAIRE LE DAY

Matador
Unit E2 Airfield Business Park,
Harrison Road, Market Harborough,
Leicestershire. LE16 7UL
Tel: 0116 2792299
Email: books@troubador.co.uk
Web: www.troubador.co.uk/matador
Twitter: @matadorbooks

ISBN 978 1803132 730

British Library Cataloguing in Publication Data.
A catalogue record for this book is available from the British Library.

Printed and bound in Great Britain by 4edge Limited
Typeset in 11pt Minion Pro by Troubador Publishing Ltd, Leicester, UK
The cover was created using artwork from Claire's original teenage diaries

Matador is an imprint of Troubador Publishing Ltd

For my daughters: it's still 'as I say' not 'as I did'.

PRELUDE

30TH JUNE 2019
LISTENING TO 'TEENAGE DIRTBAG'
BY SCOTT BRADLEE'S POSTMODERN JUKEBOX

Just as long as no one *actually* reads this book, everything'll be just fine.

I kept a diary for a decade and wrote in it every night when I went to bed, meticulously documenting every excruciating detail of my adolescence. It immortalised all those secret thoughts I'm glad I never voiced and slept on for some perspective. All the extreme feelings I'd rather forget are still there, in black and white, taunting me with my douchey past.

The cliché tells us that there are two kinds of people in this world: the monsters that leave a wet towel on the bed and those that arrange their towels with some dried lavender from the garden. This book has been written by both of them and they are (entirely predictably) both me, just twenty years apart.

The decision to pursue this project was made when my brain was addled by two maternity leaves spent cooing, not sleeping and rewatching the entire back catalogues of *Made in Chelsea*, *Love Island* and *Gossip Girl*. At the point when I was able to quote, word for word, Chuck's proposal to Blair... *Life with you could never be boring...* I wondered if I ought to consider a better use for my time. And just like that, in the glimmer of a sleep-deprived moment and the dazzle from a Tiffany diamond on the Upper East Side, this book was born.

Until I started dusting off the volumes in my childhood bedroom, I had never actually read my diary. I had (apparently) lived it, but that didn't stop me from feeling like I was reading the inner workings of someone else entirely. I am completely unrecognisable and every thought process and toe-curling action feels like more than just a lifetime ago. It feels like a person ago. I do not believe myself capable of thinking and doing as I did, for, unbeknownst to me, I'd completely erased most of my adolescence from memory. This is why we don't understand teenagers. We simply forgot and conned ourselves into thinking, *We were never like that*, or possibly worse: *I used to be cool*. But the truth is that we don't actually remember what it was like to feel alone and stuck in hormonal limbo. If these words hadn't been penned in my distinctive swirling scrawl, I would avidly refute the notion that this was my past.

There's obviously some Darwinian phenomenon that has allowed me to live my life believing I'm a good person by simply forgetting all the shitty things I did, as a teenager in Scotland during the late 90s and early 00s.

ONE

ANGUS

18TH SEPTEMBER 1999
LISTENING TO 'BETTER OFF
ALONE' BY ALICE DEEJAY

*It was Edinburgh in the late 90s; the Blur/Oasis battle was
over (Oasis won), the 'millennium bug' was going to gobble
us up and I was meeting a boy. I was thirteen and I felt
compelled to write my very first diary entry to document
the life-changing events that took place in the Princess
Street branch of McDonald's on a murky autumnal day.*

I HATE stupid, smelly, immature boys!

Jane and I had our 'date' with Angus and two of his friends
today. It didn't go very well. We'd arranged to meet at McDonald's
and then planned to go into town. I'd been so excited, planning
my outfit and topics of conversation all week.

1

I wore a white crop top, Miss Selfridge capri pants, platform trainers and a thick layer of Natural Collection orange foundation. My eyebrows were bang on trend and 'barely there'; my eyeshadow a garish, metallic blue and my scent an overwhelming combination of CK One and Impulse 02. Hellllllooooooo, millennial. I arrived through the golden arches feeling utterly irresistible and like a member of All Saints. My mother tried her damnedest to sabotage my look by forcing me to throw on a turquoise M&S fleece before leaving the house (although I feel compelled to highlight that fleeces were still considered legit urban outerwear in 1999).

Angus is in the year above, cool-ish and not bad looking. I met him the other day when I went to pick up Chloe (*my sister*) at her friend's house, and Angus was there. He's her older brother and he offered me a drink and a Tunnock's Teacake while I waited. We were just sat there when I was super brave and coolly asked him if he would like to go for lunch with Jane Lasker and me (and he could bring a friend too) on Saturday. He looked a bit surprised, but said, 'Err yeah, ok.' (!!!!!!) What if he becomes my boyfriend?!

Jane Lasker was my best friend at the time. I was never one of the lucky ones who had a consistent best friend and I rotated through them with every adolescent phase hoping the next one would be THE one. I envied the duos that held strong throughout the awkward years, navigating hand in hand through childhood and becoming adults together. There comes a point in every girl's life when playing with mud and practising handstands in the garden simply doesn't cut it anymore. Sadly, this turning point happens at different times for everyone. My primary school friends had just reached puberty ever so slightly earlier than me and so they promptly ditched me. They were older than me and had the legs and boobs that got the fourteen-year-old boys flocking while I awkwardly covered my puppy fat in an oversized Gap sweatshirt, pale pink bootcut jeans and a kangol hat. Something inexplicably hormonal and social had happened during the summer of 1999 and I was left behind, instantly friendless and uncool.

I went to St Catherine's, an all-girls school; the mere thought of it still leaves me cold. When we started back at school in August 1999, everything had changed and there was no doubt in anyone's mind that childhood, innocence and joy were to be left at the school gate before entering. St Catherine's was a place of ruin where evil flourished, and if you weren't thin, pretty and a total bitch, you were doomed. I suspect the fires of hell are still ablaze in the belly of St Catherine's as it continues to churn out high-achieving, beautiful psychos.

Fortunately, I wasn't alone, for Jane Lasker (although slightly cooler than me) was still awkwardly fringed, fleeced and wouldn't even have recognised makeup if she'd got stabbed in the eye with an eyeliner. We bonded instantly over our mutual immaturity and hatred of the mean girls at St Catherine's. We were desperate to hang out with boys, but we hadn't quite figured out how to achieve this yet, so we joined forces and went in search of boyfriends and popularity together.

I turned up at 2pm and Jane arrived shortly afterwards, but about thirty minutes later we were still just sat there like lemons waiting for Angus and his friends to arrive. I knew it was too good to be true. Boys never want to hang out with us. I think Jane thought I'd made up the 'date' with the boys and kept saying really annoying things like:

'Where's your fantasy boyfriend then, Claire? Oh, there he is! Oh no... he's still in your head.'... 'They were obviously playing a prank on you!'... 'I can't believe you really thought this was going to happen!'

She's such a biatch sometimes. We eventually gave up and decided to go and get a McFlurry downstairs and there they were! Angus with two friends, sat at a table for three and facing the wall! Soooooo rude! Their stupid table choice meant that we were kinda left to weirdly hover behind them as they ate their burgers. Jane and I were getting really bored because they were being so insociable (*spelling, cringe*) and horrid. They weren't even talking to us! We finally left all together and went to HMV, but the boys had still hardly said a word to us! Jane and I decided we were going to leave cos they were being complete sods so we went up to them and we told Angus we were leaving because they were being so insociable (*gahhhh!*) and I thought Angus was gay! And we left.

Huge apologies to the LGBTQIA+ community but I was thirteen and in comparison to now, 1999 was still an equality and diversity vacuum. The cast of friends were merrily calling each other gay, our catwalks were full of emaciated, unhealthy-body-image-promoting women and the Spice Girls were revolutionary for the simple reason that they were women. Sex and the City was 'smashing barriers' and apparently empowering women to spend their entire adult lives with the sole goal of getting a man to fall in love with them. EVERYONE on TV was white and middle class and spent all their time swanning about, talking about their love lives while sipping coffees and garishly coloured cosmopolitans. So sadly, yes, 'You're gay' was considered an insult. It was a disgusting comment, but I do feel slightly vindicated as Angus did, in fact, turn out to be gay.

4

I'm so upset because we don't know any boys. I just wish I was popular. When I look back on this I'll probably laugh that I was such a loser. But it's not funny, future me!

Oh, and Angus told Jane to say that he was going out with someone so that I wouldn't be upset that he didn't ask me out. Massive KB! Even though I didn't even necessarily want to get with him! God, he's full of himself! I hate him so much.

KB'd (knocked back); abbreviation. To be
KB'd. Archaic term from the millennium.
To be turned down for a date or sexual
encounter.

20TH SEPTEMBER 1999
LISTENING TO 'UNPRETTY' BY TLC

So who do I fancy?

Charlie Harper – I first saw him at the dean dance last year and spoke to him for ages but didn't get his number. He does Cadets, which I've just started on Monday evenings at St Felix's, the boys' school. He's nice and tall.

A glowing recommendation indeed. Nice and tall? Move over Jane Austen, I've got it from here.

Charlie was a good egg though, and 'nice' was actually a fairly accurate description for fourteen-year-old Charlie Harper. He was vanilla: not very exciting but sweet and exactly the sort of stain-free flavour your parents would have approved of. In a world of smelly, monosyllabic, grunting adolescents he was well-mannered and attractive in a clean-cut way. He wasn't cool, but was tolerated by most given that he was good

5

at rugby and he had an older, badder brother. This just below average level of popularity made Charlie potentially bagable.

Tom Southall – He quite simply has the nicest smile in the whole wide world. He's really kind and funny and he knows who I am! He does Cadets too, but he is in the year above so we hardly get to do anything together. My mum teaches him French and says he's a real 'nice boy', which he seems to be. He smokes though, but I don't mind.

Ha! Tom Southall was absolutely anything but a 'nice boy'. He was charming and devastatingly cool, but he was the epitome of a bad boy. Everyone adored Tom and I was no exception. He sadly went from lovable rogue to 'drug enthusiast' over the next few years and I'd rather not know what happened to him in the end. I last saw him at a Hogmanay party, when we were in our twenties, smacked off his face with invisible pupils and a seemingly endless supply of Haribo. That smile though...

TWO

CHARLIE

27TH SEPTEMBER 1999
LISTENING TO 'SING IT BACK' BY MOLOKO

I really fancy Charlie Harper – he's sooooo cute! When I first started Cadets, he was the only one that didn't completely ignore me. I thought I was going to cry on the first day cos I was just sat in the classroom at St Felix's, with an ocean of space around me, and it felt like all the boys were talking and laughing behind my back. It's cos of my mum – I'm sure of it. I'm just 'Madame Le Day's daughter' to most of them. So I was just sat there trying to block out all the whisperings, when Charlie came and sat next to me.

'Hey, Claire. Just ignore them,' he said, pointing his thumb over his shoulder, 'they're idiots.'

And he gave me a cheeky wink. It was so sweet and I couldn't stop myself beaming at him. I wish someone like Charlie could be my boyfriend. I didn't realise he was one of Hamish (Mish)

7

Allison's friends though until tonight when my Mum told me. Hopefully Mish hasn't said anything bad about me. He says we're friends, but sometimes he isn't very nice to me.

I first met Mish, aged eleven, at Murrayfield Ice Rink's 'Wednesday Disco'. This was the only opportunity we had at the time to meet boys. Although we weren't actually too fussed yet, we felt like this was something we should want to do. Mish and I were sitting on the same bench tying our skates when I squeaked a weird 'hiya' at him one day. He somehow managed to surpass my level of awkwardness and said nothing before nodding towards the vending machine. We hobbled over on our skates and he rather gallantly bought me a packet of Skittles, which we shared. High on sugar and tween lust, we skated round to Boyzone's 'Love Me for a Reason'. By the time our parents came to collect us, Mish was my first 'boyfriend'. We had a few awkward 'dates' at the cinema before he brutally friend-zoned me.

'I don't want to be your boyfriend anymore. Let's just be friends.'

In retrospect, calling what Mish and I spent the next seven years in, a 'friend-zone', is preposterous. Mish was the worst 'friend' I think I've ever had. It was a long time ago and it doesn't matter at all, for I am mature and over it, but FUCK YOU, MISH! But we'll get there. We're still only children.

4TH OCTOBER 1999
LISTENING TO 'KISS THE RAIN' BY BILLIE MYERS

Charlie and I sat next to each other at Cadets today while we tried to put this huge gun back together. We spoke about the weekend's rugby, and I think he was impressed that I knew about rugby and had been to the game. This was the first game I'd been to see and I was keen to show off my new rugby knowledge (cos he's rugby mad). I'd asked Dad to teach me the rules over the weekend and I think I've got to grips with the basics. Charlie then talked for ages about the Autumn Internationals and I got a bit lost but, thankfully, I don't think he noticed.

We bumped into Mish when we walked out of school and he was acting super weird and kept tickling and poking Charlie.

'Come on, Charlie, tell everyone your secret! We all know your secret except Claire, come on, tell us... I bet Claire would love to know!'

Charlie then got really embarrassed and said he didn't have a clue what Mish was talking about. What if he fancies me? He has been really nice to me... I really hope he does! No one has ever fancied me before. I don't think Mish even fancied me when I was his girlfriend.

10TH OCTOBER 1999
LISTENING TO 'I'M KISSING YOU' BY DES'REE

I got up really early on Saturday so that I would be ready for my super exciting day ahead. We played hockey against Watson's and lost... AGAIN. I think my dad's getting a bit fed up of watching our games given that it's always raining and we always lose. I then hurried home and got my stuff ready for Kirsty's birthday sleepover (I packed my new *groovy chick* PJs, which I love!). Then I was off to St Felix's open day with Vicky – WOO HOO. I'm really hoping I bump into Charlie.

Kirsty and Vicky were also relatively new friends that Jane and I had made. We were forming a new 'semi-cool' friendship group where, in order to be part of the clan, you simply had to be distinctly average on all fronts.

When I got to the open day, I hadn't been there five minutes when I saw Charlie looking gorgeous! I didn't miss my chance and went straight up to him and said, 'Hiya.' We got to talking and started going round the school together. He's so dreamy... swoon! We went to the art block and he helped me try to make a pot. It was so romantic.

I clearly thought we were recreating the scene in Ghost. It would be fair to say that, at the time, my entire impression of what love should be, was based on 1990s romcoms and DiCaprio blockbusters. The fact that teenage boys didn't behave like these scripted dreamboats was a constant source of disappointment to me.

I saw Mish just before I left and he said Charlie was probably going to get a hard time for hanging out with 'a teacher's daughter'. Arghhh, it's so annoying. My mum being a teacher has absolutely nothing to do with anything! Surely Charlie doesn't care...

The sleepover was fab! Kirsty, Vicky, Jane and I watched *Candyman* while the others went upstairs cos they were scared. Haha! We stayed up all night and watched films then played truth or dare. My dare was, 'How much beer can you drink in a minute?' What a day!

Puberty was still such an abstract concept to me that I took refuge in the familiar comfort of an old-fashioned sleepover. They offered a rare opportunity for us to embrace our childlike side. We could regress and indulge in marshmallow-fuelled pillow fights and teddy bears, safe in the knowledge that there was no one 'cool' watching. They were also, however, an opportunity to practise being a teenager before fully committing to the cause and humiliating ourselves in public. We usually couldn't think of anything other than sneaking into the drinks cupboard and talking about sex though. I wanted to grow up as quickly as possible. Whatever it took. Horror movies and beer? Yes please! Throw in a 90s ouija board and I was definitely game. This Candyman viewing haunted me for years though. Even now, I can't think of much that would successfully convince me to say 'Candyman, Candyman, Candyma…'. AAAHHHHHHHHHHHH!

12TH OCTOBER 1999
LISTENING TO 'DRINKING IN LA' BY BRAN VAN 3000

I saw Charlie at Cadets yesterday, but he completely ignored me and then just said, 'Bye', (without even looking at me) as he walked out the door. I definitely thought he liked me before! What did I do wrong? I bet Mish was right and Charlie doesn't want to hang out with a teacher's daughter. It's so shit and unfair so I have decided to call him, and possible topics for conversation are:

- Rugby – revise upcoming games
- Blair Witch Project
- Teenage Ball

So I called him and I think it went ok. I got Jane to ring Mish after to find out what was going on and apparently they decided that Charlie and I will end up going out. YAAAAY! Then out of the blue she started having a massive go at me.

'You're using me, Claire. You used me for Angus and now you're using me again. Mish thinks so too! I'm just not having it!'

11

She then slammed the phone down on me. What the hell?! Why would she say that? I thought we were supposed to be best friends!

This was the first clue that Jane would eventually reveal herself to be a total fruitcake.

15TH OCTOBER 1999
LISTENING TO 'LITTLE DISCOURAGE' BY IDLEWILD

I'm head over heels in love! I called Charlie again today and he was so flirty (I think)! We were just talking about New Year's Eve (2000) when he said, 'You know how you're supposed to kiss someone at midnight? Well… I've got tickets to go into town and wondered if you might want to go with me?' I thought I was going to die of happiness! I also asked him if he was going to the Teenage Ball because I had tickets and he more or less said yes!

18TH OCTOBER 1999
LISTENING TO 'IF I COULD TURN BACK THE HANDS OF TIME' BY R. KELLY

I need to pull myself together! It's been three days since I called Charlie and I haven't stopped thinking about him. I've been told that there's a disco with St Felix's and I keep imagining him dancing with me, cradling my face in his hands and then kissing me. I am totally obsessed. I keep wishing that he'd ask me out. Every time I listen to R. Kelly – 'If I Could Turn Back the Hands of Time' – I think of him and me together… ahhh… swoon… sigh…

24TH OCTOBER 1999
LISTENING TO 'THERE SHE GOES'
BY SIXPENCE NONE THE RICHER

Jane and I were in town and saw these really cute guys. I kept smiling at one of them and then Jane dragged me away because 'I was being sad', and I suppose she was right.

25TH OCTOBER 1999
LISTENING TO '9PM (TILL I COME)' BY ATB

I finally did it. I asked Charlie out! I'd been excited about it all day today because I was convinced he'd say yes. I caught up with him after Cadets and I told him I had something to ask him that I had never asked anyone before. I must have gone bright red, I was so embarrassed. I told him I hoped he'd guess so I didn't have to say and he said he had a small idea. Then his exact words were:

'Look, Claire, if it is what I think it is, then I thought we were just friends, if you know what I mean.'

Oh.

It felt like a venue (note the unusual collective term) of vultures had just ripped out my heart. He may as well have just punched me in the face. I acted natural and just about gulped through a 'Yep… cool.' I wanted to say that wasn't what I meant, but I couldn't think of anything quick enough. It was too obvious anyway so I quickly changed the subject and asked him again about the Teenage Ball and he said, 'Maybe.' I then rang Mish and he said, 'Maybe', for the ball too. I'm really worried I'm not going to get any boys on my table.

30TH OCTOBER 1999
LISTENING TO 'DISCO 2000' BY PULP

SJ's Party

I was so excited to get invited cos everyone was going, but it was so crap in the end. Jane got completely smashed and I had to hold her hair back in the toilet. There was sick everywhere, it was so gross, and all she could manage to say in between her chunder chunks was, 'Oh, just fuck off, Claire, and leave me alone.' I did eventually *fuck off* after she said, 'I bet you're loving this!' Erm, no. Not really. I wonder why I'm friends with her sometimes.

Lucy Murphy and Sofia were pulling everyone. Polly Duff supposedly had sex with Andy Burns then she pulled Lucy away from the guy Lucy was pulling and started pulling him! What a slapper!

No one wanted to pull me. No one wanted me there. I don't really feel like anyone ever wants me anywhere. I wish I'd worn something different too. My mum had convinced me I looked really nice, but I knew I shouldn't have listened to her.

I vividly remember what I wore to this party and it was not the required teenage 90s party uniform of short, black and spaghetti-strapped. I was dressed for a five-year-old's birthday party with a broderie anglaise blouse, a knee-length blue and white gingham skirt, bare legs and my 1999 standard-issue Kickers.

Jane left early so I went and sat with the popular girls outside. They all just stopped talking and stared at me before Lucy said, 'Errr, sorry, Claire, but we were kinda having a private conversation.' I was so embarrassed I just said, 'Oh, sorry', and left hoping it was nearly time for my dad to come and get me.

Lucy Murphy and I had been 'friends' since birth, but she was popular now and I hadn't made the cut. Lucy's parents spent most of the early 80s, with my parents, drinking wine in their perms and shoulder pads. There was no doubt in their minds when Lucy and I were born at opposite ends of 1985 that we were to be the best of friends. We spent our whole childhood together with all the face-painting, cartwheeling, Brownies, sleepovers, makeovers, after-school clubs and ballet classes that it entailed. After the fateful 'puberty' summer of 1999, Lucy suddenly stopped calling us 'best friends' and transitioned us to 'special family friends'. Lucy then took her new role as mean girl very seriously, and I found not only being dumped but then bullied by my childhood best friend heartbreaking. I envied 'those girls' so much, with their blue hair mascara, Rachel Green hairdos and hipster (of the low-rise not bearded variety) pleather mini skirts.

17TH NOVEMBER 1999
LISTENING TO 'BEAUTIFUL ONES' BY SUEDE

I've just got back from the Cadets weekend trip with the boys and I had the best time! Charlie and I got on so well. On the last night we were all sat in the common room, playing cards and having a laugh. We decided to have a 'truth session' so I told them how I liked Tom Southall and thought he was hot, which made Charlie go weirdly grumpy. It seems they all fancy Lucy and Sofia etc (sooo predictable!). I still really like Charlie and later that night, I heard one of them say I was 'an absolute babe' and I'm fairly certain it was him. Wooohoooo!

18TH NOVEMBER 1999
LISTENING TO 'SANTERIA' BY SUBLIME

I was telling Jane about Charlie maybe saying I was 'an absolute babe' at school today when she said, 'I don't think so, Claire, he got with Vicky at the weekend and they're an item now. There's no way he's interested in someone like you.'

Oh.

It's so confusing. I *really* thought he liked me. Also: Someone like me?! Fat? Loser? Ugly? What does that mean? Jane seemed to really enjoy telling me too. She kept giggling about it saying I was 'disillusioned'. My God, she can be such a bitch. Does she realise how hurtful she's being?

20TH NOVEMBER 1999
LISTENING TO 'THAT DON'T IMPRESS ME MUCH' BY SHANIA TWAIN

My Fourteenth Birthday

I went to the cinema yesterday afternoon to see *The Sixth Sense* with Charlie and Mish. It's annoying that Charlie doesn't like me cos we get on so well! It was freezing so he wrapped his scarf around me and walked me home. He gave me the biggest hug outside mine and I thought he might kiss me, but he just pecked me on the cheek. I love him so much! He didn't talk about Vicky at all so I don't think she is his girlfriend. Phew.

My birthday party was amazing. We went to see *The Blues Brothers* and then we went home for my sleepover. We had a bit to drink – gin and Coke. Vicky didn't mention Charlie either, so I wonder if Jane had just made it up. Later on, I thought Kirsty was going to die choking on a mint. It was really scary but she's fine now.

Gin and Coke?! We were savages.

THREE

SOFIA, 'QUEEN OF THE BITCHES'

28TH NOVEMBER 1999
LISTENING TO 'YOU'VE GOT
IT BAD' BY OCEAN COLOUR SCENE

Friday Night Disco

6pm: I'm a bit nervous about the disco tonight and what Sofia might do to me. We had a huge fight at school today and I think I've gone and given myself an enemy for life. I hate her so much and no one else can see what a bitch she is! She's only popular because she has huge boobs and all the boys fancy her, but she is sooooo dumb and mean. Lucy worships the ground she walks on now too – it makes me sick.

Sofia was a horrible bully, but fortunately for me, not a bright one. She looked like Jessica Rabbit's human love child and if she'd stopped moving, she'd easily have been mistaken for a blow-up sex doll. She had enormous eyes, lips and boobs, and she pranced around looking glorious with her flicky, Sun-In-ed hair, a not totally unsuccessful 90s St Tropez tan and a sticky layer of Urban Decay lip gloss.

She had been held back a year and this only meant she was one year more developed and one year more practised at boys than the rest of us. This gave her spectacular confidence and made her the unrivalled Queen Bee.

So we were queueing for lunch today, when Sofia, Lucy and the other bitches just walked past everyone right up to the front. Sofia does this every day and no one ever says anything – it drives me nuts!! What makes her so special? I'd had enough and decided I wasn't ever going to get anywhere in life if people like Sofia get to be the winners. I stepped out in front of her and asked her what she thought she was doing.

She pushed me and told me, 'Move, saddo!' I said, 'No, why should you get to skip the queue?'

She screamed and spat at me then said, 'Am gonna kill you at the disco tonight! Am gonna rip your fuckan' skirt!'

I smiled at her and told her, 'I'm wearing trousers.'

This simple comeback, aged fourteen, is one of my all time faves.

11pm: I wore my black Miss Sixty trousers and a black top that I pulled through the neck to reveal my stomach.

Classy...

No one spoke to me all night after what had happened with Sofia. Even Jane kept her distance and just said she 'didn't want to get involved'. I spent most of the night by myself then Lucy came up to me and said, 'I just think you should know what you did to Sofia was really uncool. You really upset her and we all think you're a bitch now.'

Great.

6TH DECEMBER 1999
LISTENING TO 'YOU'RE GORGEOUS' BY BABYBIRD

Jane, Vicky and I arrived at school early and we had nothing to do so we went to the local shop and they dared me to buy a pack of ten Silk Cut and we had one each. I really liked it! Vicky had never had one before and burnt my fleece. Jane and I had another one later on, but had to put it out really quickly cos we thought a teacher was coming.

> *Is this really how my smoking story started? How disappointingly unglamorous. I recalled it happening in altogether different circumstances... the sun setting over the ocean in late summer, a bonfire crackling by my toes with some spunky Frenchman leaning in to light my cigarette with a wink. It took sixteen years to kick the habit because I was dared to smoke a Silk Cut round the back of the janitor's shed.*

10TH DECEMBER 1999
LISTENING TO 'SAVE TONIGHT'
BY EAGLE EYE CHERRY

Sofia is totally out to get me. She spat at me when she was walking past me in the corridor so I said, 'Fat cow.' She then launched into how much she hated me and wanted to hit me so hard that I'd die. Lovely.

I'd completely forgotten about all this spitting. How disgusting. The thought of seeing anyone spit at an actual person now makes me recoil in horror.

18TH DECEMBER 1999
LISTENING TO 'FLYING' BY CAST

The Teenage Ball
Jane, Kirsty and Vicky got ready at mine before Charlie and the boys arrived for dinner. Charlie looked sooo cute in his kilt. We had a really cool time all together and then my dad gave us a lift to the ball. As soon as we arrived, Charlie and the guys went off to hang out with the other boys. What's the point in having a table if no one ever sits at it? Jane just sat there and kept saying, 'This is really lame, Claire.' As if it were my fault!

I am still really annoyed that Mish last minute decided to go on Lucy's table with Sofia etc rather than mine. He's such a fickle popularity hunter. He'd promised me he'd come on my table, but was completely happy to dump me the second he got a better offer from the 'cool girls'. I looked for him once we'd got there, but he wasn't around.

Jane and I danced a bit together and then this really ugly guy called Neville asked me to dance. I wanted to die more than dance with him, but who says no? Sofia would have said no. He seemed sweet though just DISGUSTING to look at. Did he think we were well matched? Urgh. So I danced with him and I could see everyone giggling at us. I was so embarrassed.

19TH DECEMBER 1999
LISTENING TO 'TUBTHUMPING'
BY CHUMBAWAMBA

Got the goss about Mish from my parents at dinner tonight. Apparently he'd snuck a bottle of vodka into Lucy's house and drank loads trying to show off in front of the girls and then vommed on Lucy's parents' brand new carpet. Lucy's dad had then driven him home. Ohhhh ohhhhh – knowing Mish's mum, he would have been in MEGA trouble after that. Ha! How embarrassing for him... In front of all the popular girls too? HAHAHA poor vommy Mish.

I've been invited to Dan Jeffries' house party tomorrow night. I am so desperate to go. My mum doesn't know whether to let me go or not...

I LOVE MY MUM, SHE SAID YES!

FOUR

DAN JEFFRIES

Dan Jeffries' House Party

Well, that was one of the best nights of my life! When Jane and I arrived we were given beer cans to drink. Yuck. Then I started to pull Dan, the guy who was having the party. He is so nice but a bit ugly. My mouth is all red and sore from pulling him so much. He kept saying how beautiful and sexy I was, and he totally felt up my tits.

> *Argh, cringe.*
> *Dan Jeffries was not 'ugly', but he had bad acne which was difficult to see past as the image-obsessed fourteen-year-old that I was. What Dan lacked in traditional looks*

*though, he more than made up for in everything else. He is
an amazing musician who has breathed nothing but music
(and fags) since the day he was born. He had a wicked
sense of humour and the most adorable, infectious chuckle
that still makes me smile fondly when I think of it. He lived
in his own little world; completely disinterested in who or
what was cool. Dan only cared about playing his guitar and
listening to Led Zeppelin with a fag permanently drooping
from his bottom lip. He went on to study music and played
in a multitude of bands over the years. He's now playing
music in the West End and still chain smoking like a trooper.*

Jane pulled Charlie and I could see her looking right at me
when she was snogging him! I could tell she was smirking, even
though I couldn't see her mouth. Ummm, hellooooo? She is
supposed to be my best friend and she knew perfectly well that
I still like Charlie. I'm so upset that she betrayed our friendship.
It feels like she just did it to show me how easy it was. I wish she
would be a better friend sometimes.

Andy Burns was being as sick as ever and trying to convince
me to give Dan a blowjob! He kept just giving me a little nudge
and a wink.

'Oh, go on, Claire! Suck him off! You'll love it.'

Gross! I would never do that. He's funny though. I'm pretty
sure he was joking. He says 'lads' a lot.

*Andy Burns really was the ultimate 'lad' in a way that stopped
being even the slightest bit acceptable after American Pie
had its heyday. Teenage Andy 'Lads Lads Lads' Burns has
not aged well. He was a decent enough guy though, despite
his obsession with discussing the lewdest and weirdest sex
acts in existence. All my sex slang and sex terminology has
come from Andy 'Lads Lads Lads' Burns. Over the next four*

years, I grew to admire his unabating cheerfulness, forever unfazed by everything around him. He was always the first to buck me up, make me smile and snap me out of any whiney teenage mindset I'd got myself in. He grew up with three sisters so despite spending most of his time spouting the most outrageous filth, he was completely harmless and surprisingly respectful towards women (although I suspect he may have had the odd drink thrown in his face over the years). Everyone liked Andy Burns and he transcended all social circles. Other than having marginally less hair and a more comprehensive repertoire of vulgarisms, Andy was the same at thirty-four as he was at fourteen (which may not be the compliment I initially meant it to be!). You'd want Andy 'Lads Lads Lads' Burns to arrange your stag do, but possibly not marry your sister.

22ND DECEMBER 1999
LISTENING TO 'MOVING TOO FAST' BY ARTFUL DODGER

I called Dan. It was really good. He was really nice and he asked if I wanted to meet up tomorrow… woo hoo!

What a literary masterpiece this is turning out to be.

24TH DECEMBER 1999
LISTENING TO 'BORN SLIPPY' BY UNDERWORLD

So my date with Dan actually went really well. We went to McDonald's and he paid for my lunch – so sweet. Then we decided to go to the cinema and see the new James Bond film,

The World Is Not Enough. It was ok. After the film we bought a packet of fags and went to sit on the turning thing in the park.

A roundabout, Claire?

We chatted for ages about music. There is NOTHING he doesn't know! I kept telling myself I could get over his looks cos he is amazing otherwise. It was seriously fucking cold though, so he walked me all the way home with his arm around me. It felt wonderful and for the first time it felt like someone was actually into me. I couldn't believe it. I loved spending the day with him, but when we got to my house we pulled and I didn't really enjoy it. He tasted of stale fags and just kept poking his tongue in and out my mouth. I've decided to start smoking so I can pull him and not notice the difference. I was going to anyway.

Doh!

28TH DECEMBER 1999
LISTENING TO 'STEAL MY SUNSHINE' BY LEN

I was at Jane's house last night with Dan and three of his friends. Jane got so drunk and pissed right in the middle of the street! I don't think she minds but I saw her naked butt! Jane then pulled Dan's best friend and kept saying to me, 'Don't let me pull him again, Claire, I'm too drunk...' So when she next went to pull him I tried to stop her and she slapped me in the face and screamed at me, 'Fuck off! You can't control me!'

What the hell is her problem? All of Dan's friends really fancy her too – it's so annoying. Jamie Ross spent twenty minutes crying in the bathroom over her. I don't get it.

Dan and I had a great time though. He told me he really fancied me and I'm starting to really like him. How COOL is that?! I just wish I fancied him more. I had so many fags and made a gorgeous drink with gin and Red Bull. Yummy!

Horrific.
    Jane is clearly a lunatic and how I can't see this yet is beyond me. I was just so desperate to share my adolescence with someone, that my best friend was a sociopath and I didn't fancy my boyfriend.

1ST JANUARY 2000
LISTENING TO 'UNDER PRESSURE' BY QUEEN AND DAVID BOWIE

Happy New Year! I was quite depressed all evening because I had to stay in with my family. My mum said I was too young to go to any parties or into town, even though Dan and Charlie both offered me a ticket for the street party. It does make me wonder who I'd have gone with if I'd had the choice…

Mamie (*my grandmother*) fell down the stairs carrying champagne flutes just after the stroke of midnight and had to go to A&E to have her ear stitched up. She's ok, but it put a bit of a dampener on the party.

After midnight, Dan came round with some friends to say hi as they had just been in town, but left soon afterwards as Dan was so drunk. Apparently he'd drunk a whole bottle of gin. I'm not convinced…

Charlie and Mish arrived just as Dan was leaving and we hung out in my room for an hour listening to music. On their way out, Charlie gave me a big hug and kissed me on the cheek, whispering a 'Happy New Year, gorgeous' as he lightly let his hand stroke down my back. It made me tingle with excitement and it was way nicer than Dan's drunken, ginny, faggy snog and boob grope. Gross.

2ND JANUARY 2000
LISTENING TO 'LIVIN' ON A PRAYER' BY BON JOVI

I've just spent the day with Dan and all the boys. I really enjoy his company, but no matter how much I try, I can't bring myself to fancy him. Today I met three more of his friends and I know it sounds bitchie but I would much rather go out with any of them than Dan. When I talk to him on the phone, I think that I could fall in love with him. He's dead cool, so funny and pretty much the perfect guy. When I'm with him, however, I'm totally put off. The only exception is when he is playing music and I get transported into a fuzzy dream world.

I have a very clear memory of my fuzzy dream world with Dan Jeffries. I could see my future in which he becomes a world famous rock star. It involved Dan CONTINUOUSLY playing the piano to a film-style montage of our wonderful life together. This fake, alternative future with a man I didn't fancy who had a penchant for narcotics and a rock 'n' roll lifestyle, would no doubt have led to me slowly becoming addicted to pills, coke and booze. Fast forward twenty years and I'd be sprawled out on a grand piano, lonely and drunk in my massive house. I'd have the velvet curtains pulled shut with just the tiniest shard of sunlight sneaking through to accentuate the thick haze of cigarette smoke. I'd be stuffed into a sequined, fish-tailed ball gown and I'd permanently have a dirty gin martini on the go. It wouldn't end well for me, but I'd inadvertently have

pushed Dan into getting clean and marrying his second
wife – an evangelical vegan in her twenties. Probably.

I can picture myself growing old with him when he plays music.
It makes me adore him, but as soon as he's done playing the last
chord the dream is dead and he's back to being a spotty teenager.
He'll put his arm around me or hold my hand and all I'm thinking
is, *Yuck yuck yuck*, and then when he pulls me it's like, 'Oh man,
excuse me while I go and puke!' I don't want to dump him because
he is so nice and everyone thinks I'm cool now. If I dump him,
he'll tell his friends and they'll think, *Woah, what a fucking bitch!*

> *Oh, the shame.*
> *This blatant groupie mentality has never fully left me.*
> *It's astonishing that I haven't married a musician (or had*
> *an affair with one). I'm wise enough now to know that the*
> *temporary infatuation I feel when I see ANYBODY play*
> *music is simply that: temporary. I'm frequently horrified*
> *when I encounter band members after their set and the*
> *man (that was minutes earlier the love of my life and the*
> *reason I might leave my husband) turns out to be an obese*
> *seventy-two-year-old named Terry with food in his beard.*

4TH JANUARY 2000
LISTENING TO 'IMAGINE' BY JOHN LENNON

I hate myself soooo much. Jane had a party last night and I finally
dumped Dan. I told him it wasn't working and that I was sorry. I
then told him I wanted to stay friends, but he just said, 'Well, fuck
this shit', grabbed a bottle of whisky and stormed off. *Well, that's it,*
I thought, *I've blown my chance of keeping my cool, new friendship*
group. The thing is, I REALLY do want to be friends with Dan.

Dan was so upset. He got really drunk and spent the rest of the night telling me he thought he could fall in love with me. It was really awkward and I didn't know what to say. Thank God he didn't play the piano.

Later that night, Dan eventually passed out on the sofa. His friends had already started calling me a bitch for what I'd done to him. I was feeling so unpopular when Benny told me he was really pleased that Dan and I weren't together cos he thought I was 'the hottest girl ever'. I was so flattered (especially after an hour of abuse from the others) and a bit drunk – that I pulled him. It was only for a minute until I realised it was total madness and I really didn't like Benny at all! What was I thinking?! When I pulled away, I turned round to see I'd done it right in front of (a no longer passed-out) Dan. He was just staring at me then he cried. It was awful.

Benny would easily have grown up into a David Brent-esque character. He was dumpy, thin-lipped and nouveau riche. He thought he could buy friends largely thanks to the (unmentionable but common knowledge) fact that his dad was head of the Scottish Italian Mafia. Urghhh, it makes me shudder just remembering that kiss. What was I thinking indeed?

I felt terrible. Jane was really distant with me for the rest of the night. When I asked her what was wrong, she said, 'I just can't believe what a bitch you are.' She's so right. I am. I wish I hadn't pulled Benny. I can't believe I've been so insensitive to Dan. I spoke to Andy 'Lads Lads Lads' Burns tonight and he said all the boys are 'against me' because I was so harsh to Dan. I feel so guilty. I know I deserve it, but Jane is supposed to be my best friend and I overheard her tonight telling all the boys what a 'slut' I was. I mean, if either of us is a slut…

Ahhhh, Charlie is going to find out what I did too and he'll never fall in love with me now!

8TH JANUARY 2000
LISTENING TO 'WONDERWALL' BY OASIS

Jane stayed over at mine tonight and we watched *Cruel Intentions* then smoked some tea and banana skins. It was so cool.

I actually remember it being distinctly uncool as I initially rolled up a teabag, put it in my mouth and lit it.

11TH JANUARY 2000
LISTENING TO 'BARBER'S ADAGIO FOR STRINGS' BY WILLIAM ORBIT

Back to school and it certainly seems that the rumour mill has been active over the holidays. Everyone apparently thinks I danced topless at Dan's party and that's how I 'got him to go out with me' in the first place. I then supposedly had sex with Benny in Dan's bed and he caught us and dumped me. I mean, come on! Sofia seems particularly fond of these stories. Jane also seems weirdly happy about the whole thing and is making no attempt to correct anyone. Charlie apparently told her that he'd have gone out with me if I wasn't a 'pull Benny kind of girl'. GODDAMNIT! Jane also told me that Mish said I was a 'man' because I had really hairy arms. Oh God! How embarrassing. What can I do about them? Can I shave my arms?

This did actually result in me shaving my arms aged fourteen.

17TH JANUARY 2000
LISTENING TO 'LITTLE GREEN BAG' BY GEORGE BAKER SELECTION

I learnt today (from Jane of course) that Sofia is now apparently all pally with Charlie. That's just what I need! Apparently she's been telling him that I never stop talking about him at school and that I'm 'obsessed'. SHIT!

I decided I wasn't just going to lie back and take it so I went to see Sofia at lunch. I asked why she's been saying this as, if anything, it seemed that *she* was a little obsessed with me. She DID NOT like that. She said that Charlie and her are 'best friends' now and she is going to tell him not to talk to me anymore because 'You're a slut and no one wants to be your friend.' I said, 'Please don't, Sofia...' then panicked and added, 'or else!' She laughed in my face and was like, 'Ohhh, I'm soooo scared. What are you going to do, you fuckan' saddo?' So I poured a glass of water over her head and walked (ran) away.

Ten minutes later I was in the classroom and she came in carrying a full glass. She told me it was 'dirty bog water, her spit and loads of people who hated me's spit'. She threw it at me then launched herself at me as a group of girls were chanting her name. I grabbed her to push her and she threw her hands around my neck and we were both screaming, 'YOU BITCH! YOU BITCH!' She then grabbed a fistful of my hair and repeatedly rammed my head against a desk before someone finally broke it up. I'm really bruised and my scalp and head hurt so much. Why does everyone hate me?

FIVE

PSYCHO JANE

25TH JANUARY 2000
LISTENING TO 'BREAKFAST AT TIFFANY'S' BY
DEEP BLUE SOMETHING

Jane had another party at the weekend. It was waaay tamer than normal and most of the guys still hate me after what I did to Dan. I told Jane I thought this guy called Jonny was cute and she pulled him straight away. She definitely did it on purpose!

27TH JANUARY 2000
LISTENING TO 'YOU NEVER CAN
TELL' BY CHUCK BERRY

Grrrr! I lost a twenty deck of Marlboro Lights at school today. Or someone nicked them. Probably Jane. There's no way I could ever accuse her though. She's being really cold with me. I just wish we could be best friends again. I asked if everything was ok today cos it felt like I was being excluded from stuff and that she didn't like me anymore. She then looked at me in the most disgusted way possible.

'God, Claire, chill out. It's not always about you, you know. No one's excluding you. Get over yourself.'

Except her and the other girls ARE excluding me. I know it! I can feel those little glances at me followed by giggling. God, I hate this school.

2ND FEBRUARY 2000
LISTENING TO 'PRIDE' BY NO USE FOR A NAME

I was sat in English today, when I couldn't really read the text anymore. The whole centre of the page was a mass of black and white spots and zigzags. I tried to focus, but the more I tried, the more it made me feel sick. I went up to Miss Gray to try and explain.

'When I try to read, it makes me feel sick.'

She snorted and slid her glasses down her nose to stare me out.

'You're going to have to do better than that I'm afraid, Claire.'

So I sat back down at my desk. About half an hour later the whole right side of my head felt like it was going to explode and before I knew it, I puked all over my desk. *Is that better?* I thought. Miss Gray asked for someone to accompany me to the nurse and Sofia was all like, 'I'll do it, Miss. Poor Claire…' God, I hate her! Why isn't everyone else seeing what a two-faced bitch she is? I felt too awful to argue. When we were walking to the nurse she laughed and said, 'Haha, you stink, Claire!' I didn't have the energy to say anything back, but thought that if I was going to be sick again I would definitely get her in my sights first. Sadly I wasn't. When I got home, my mum said it sounded like a migraine. I hope that never happens again.

12TH FEBRUARY 2000
LISTENING TO 'THESE WOODEN
IDEAS' BY IDLEWILD

I'm so lonely. I genuinely feel like I haven't got a friend in the world.

13TH FEBRUARY 2000
LISTENING TO 'RISE' BY GABRIELLE

I'm feeling so low. Nearly every single person I know is going to John Miller's party. He is a friend of Dan's, so I haven't been invited/have categorically been told that I am not welcome. Apparently he hates my guts and I've not even met him. Sofia and Lucy and all their friends are going. Sofia will no doubt spread her lies and do her best to make sure everyone despises me by the end of the night. Jane was supposed to come to my house tonight, but then got a last-minute invite and she obviously opted for the party option. I actually don't mind not seeing her as she's been a massive bitch to me all week over such tiny little things. I wish I was going to the party though.

I've just finished reading *Of Mice and Men* and I'm still sobbing – it was so sad. God. I'm such a loser sat at home, reading and crying while everyone in the whole world is at the party. This party could have been my chance to become cool or show everyone that I'm not who they think I am. I'm not a loser! I just wish someone would give me a chance.

34

25TH FEBRUARY 2000
LISTENING TO 'KISS ME' BY
SIXPENCE NONE THE RICHER

I've just found out that I've been invited to SJ's party at the weekend – so excited! I'm definitely going to pull someone this time! I didn't think I would get invited as SJ is friends with Sofia, but I guess she doesn't really care and most people are going. Woop!

27TH FEBRUARY 2000
LISTENING TO 'PURE SHORES' BY ALL SAINTS

SJ's Party #2

> *When I think of teenage parties and all the debauchery that they entail, I think of THIS party. It was pure anarchy. I found my 'kiss list' at the back of one of the diary volumes (which will not be published!) and this party marked a turning point for me. According to the list I snogged ten people at this party. I felt like Claire Le Day had arrived.*

I had the most amazing, slapperish time at the party! I pulled so many people! It's gross, but I enjoyed myself and it's nice to feel liked. Everyone was there and I felt so much better and more at ease than at SJ's last party. Sofia was being so nice to me, which was weird. She told me that Jane has been bitching about me loads and I should be friends with 'her lot' instead… errr, what? So weird. She's probably plotting something, so I definitely need to keep my wits about me.

Apparently Andy 'Lads Lads Lads' Burns pulled fourteen people!

The only person who was acting weird was Charlie. He was such a dick to me. I asked if he was having a nice time and he said, 'It sure looks like you are', and walked away. Well, I was. Why don't you go and snog Jane again! He has no right to get on his high horse. He had plenty of opportunities to get with me and didn't take them. So what if I want to pull lots of boys that aren't him?

I then went on to list and describe each person I snogged. I want to curl up and die reading it all... Boy number 4 was called Dave, had cool spiky hair, was wearing a green hoodie and had been eating an apple... Boy number 5 touched my bum...

Astonishingly, I thought it more important to document every tiny detail about each snoggee rather than mention that one of the partygoers was thrown off the second-floor balcony. Screams started emanating from the front of the house as everyone rushed round to see a boy in a crumpled heap, lying suspiciously below the Juliet balcony. Carnage ensued as the police and paramedics arrived. He was stretchered off in a pretty bad way and the police then went through the arduous process of taking statements from drunken, hysterical teens. I remember Sofia running around, with her arms flailing through the air, screaming, 'OH MY GOD OH MY GOD!' But yeah, some guy tasted of apple when I snogged him. I know what you're thinking: grade-A storytelling.

1ST MARCH 2000
LISTENING TO 'PUSH' BY MATCHBOX 20

I really want to leave St Catherine's. It's like a coven. I can't bear the bitchiness anymore. Is this normal? Surely people aren't like this in the real world. This cannot be it. Jane has been snapping at me all the time, and it seems she wants to hang out with Kirsty and Vicky instead of me now. She keeps referring to them as 'her actual best friends'. If I ask what they're doing or talking about they just giggle at me.

'You wouldn't understand', or 'Nothing. You had to be there...'

I can't ask Jane if we're ok (which we clearly aren't!) cos she just goes on about how I'm being 'desperate and clingy' and it's not much fun to be around me if I need 'constant reassurance'. So I have to pretend that them ignoring me and leaving me out all the time is fine by me.

Sofia spent most of lunch chucking bits of food at me. I am so fed up of all this shite. I wish she would just leave me alone. It feels like everyone is turning against me. No one likes me. I'm just fat and sad and unloveable. Never mind unloveable – unlikeable. Dislikeable? Fuck's sake. I might as well add stupid to the list. Just being liked by someone would do right now.

2ND MARCH 2000
LISTENING TO 'DANCING IN THE MOONLIGHT' BY TOPLOADER

Jane couldn't stand to be around me today. We'd made plans to do something tomorrow night and I asked her what she wanted to do, but she completely ignored me. I was sat right next to her and she literally pretended like she didn't hear me! I asked again.

'Oh God, Claire, whatever you want to do. It'll probably be really boring anyway.'

I don't think it's boring when we hang out. I can't do or say anything right, right now. Why do I repulse her so much now?!

We were inseparable over Christmas and... oh, I don't know. I just don't get it.

In physics later, I eventually asked, 'Have I done something wrong?' She snapped a 'No! God!' at me. Vicky laughed right in my face and said, 'Just cos she's having a good time now...' Jane burst out laughing and made me look like a prat and a half. Before I knew it, Jane, Vicky and Kirsty were all giggling uncontrollably and pointing at me saying stuff like 'Aw, look at her! She still thinks you're "best friends"... how sad.'

I went to sit at another bench by myself... I felt so left out and I nearly cried, but I didn't want to give them the satisfaction. Fucking bitches.

I called Vicky tonight and convinced her to tell me why Jane was acting like a psycho bitch. Apparently Jane felt that we were spending too much time together and that we needed some time apart because I annoyed and suffocated her. I feel crushed, and what was left of my self-esteem has now evaporated. Why am I even surprised? I'm no fun. I offer nothing. I wouldn't be friends with me.

Ouff, teenage girls are MEAN.

6TH MARCH 2000
LISTENING TO 'HAVE YOU EVER'
BY THE OFFSPRING

Jane called tonight and told me she had never said any of that stuff. She didn't sound very sincere and I'm not sure if I believe her, but we went into town yesterday and she seems alright with me now.

I cannot believe I was so quick to forgive and forget. Why did I idolise her?

10TH MARCH 2000
LISTENING TO 'MIAMI' BY WILL SMITH

Jane and I went out again tonight. I was a little nervous to find out which Jane was going to come out, but I had nothing else to do and no other friends so I was quite grateful to hang out with her... God, I'm such a loser. We bought five Bacardi Breezers, drank all of them quickly and had such a giggle. She said, 'I'm so glad you've chilled out, Claire, and we can be best friends again.' *I've* chilled out?! Best friends?! I have ZERO idea what is going on, but hopefully things'll be ok with us now.

16TH MARCH 2000
LISTENING TO 'NO SCRUBS' BY TLC

Jane has been acting really strange with me again for the last week. She's got such an attitude problem and always manages to make me feel so insignificant. She called me tonight and said I've changed and I wasn't myself anymore. Apparently *loads* of people have noticed and they're all saying I'm trying to be like her too much, e.g. because of the way I cut my hair.

> *Bitch, please. I had absolutely no control over how my hair was cut at the time. I would go to my mum's hairdressers with a picture of Gwen Stefani and come out with a little me version of my mum's 80s power bob.*

She has long dark brown hair and a thick fringe and I have short blonde hair with a wispy fringe... whaaaat?!

'That's ridiculous, Jane! My hair is the total opposite of yours! Maybe you should stop paying so much attention to what *everyone* is saying all the time...'

'I'm finding it really difficult to deal with the way you're behaving, Claire!'

The way *I'm* behaving?! I didn't say anything and we said bye, but seriously? I think she's a bit of a psycho.

30TH MARCH 2000
LISTENING TO 'IRIS' BY GOO GOO DOLLS

St Catherine's is the most evil place on earth! I just can't stick it anymore. I never want to leave the comfort of my bed. I cried this morning, walking to school, I was dreading it so much. I nearly turned around and went home, but I CAN'T LET THEM FUCKING WIN. When I did eventually drag myself through the doors, I found that someone had stuck a piece of paper on my locker saying, 'FAT UGLY COW', with a picture of a hairy pig. I'll never know who it was, but karma will get them. Was it Sofia? Lucy? Jane? Vicky? Kirsty? It doesn't matter… Karma will get the whole fucking lot of them! It doesn't even make sense! Was it too difficult to draw a cow? Dicks.

2ND APRIL 2000
LISTENING TO 'SHE'S SO HIGH' BY TAL BACHMAN

The most amazing thing happened: Scotland beat England at the rugby Six Nations. WOOOO!

Well, it's very reassuring to see a small amount of happiness and normality. I can finally recognise myself in the above statement.

21ST APRIL 2000
LISTENING TO 'WHOLE LOTTA LOVE' BY LED ZEPPELIN

I think I can now officially put Jane in the 'will never be friends again' pile. On Friday night, a group of us went out to hang in the park. We bought some Bacardi Breezers, and Jane and Dan Jeffries brought some beers from their houses. Dan and I were laughing about something stupid (and completely unrelated to Jane) when she suddenly stood up, death stared the hell out of me, poured her beer on me and threw the empty can at my face. I was speechless and my jeans were completely soaked. I was really annoyed so I got the EMPTY beer can and threw it back at her before walking off. I'd had enough of her madness so decided to go home and shouted a final 'You fucking psycho!' as I walked away. She started screaming abuse at me and then ran full pelt up behind me and pushed me to the ground. I was just able to put my hands out, but bruised both knees and got loads of glass and gravel in my hands and in my chin. I was bleeding, covered in beer and a bit shocked. I looked up at her thinking she'd apologise, but she spat at me and stormed off, continuing to hurl insults at me like 'fake cunt' and 'fucking whore'. I don't think we'll be friends again now.

Jeez... What a psycho.

24TH APRIL 2000
LISTENING TO 'I GUESS THAT'S WHY THEY CALL IT THE BLUES' BY ELTON JOHN

It's Easter Monday and we're at school! So annoying. I haven't spoken to Jane all day and loads of girls are saying things like, 'I've heard that you were both as bad as each other. Shouldn't you just say sorry and get over it?' Umm, no! I have nothing to apologise for! Apart from being friends with such a mentalist!

1ST MAY 2000
LISTENING TO 'SULLIVAN STREET'
BY COUNTING CROWS

I am so upset. I missed out on the best-sounding party at Andy 'Lads Lads Lads' Burns' house at the weekend. I was told it was cancelled so I went to Glasgow with the family, only to find it was back on last minute, but it was too late for me. EVERYONE was there. I cried when I found out. My parents were all like, 'There'll be other parties. It doesn't matter.' They just don't get it.

All everyone has been talking about at school today was *the* party. It sounded so good! Jane's really pissing me off. She keeps standing near me and loudly saying things like, 'God, wasn't the party amazing?! I'd hate to have missed it. It's probably the best party I've ever been to! Everyone was there… it was amazing!' Piss off, Jane. THEN I found out she'd pulled Mish. I don't know why but that's really annoyed me. Maybe cos he's supposed to be my friend? Although I clearly don't have any friends, so why am I even surprised?

8TH MAY 2000
LISTENING TO 'DANCING IN THE
DARK' BY BRUCE SPRINGSTEEN

Cadets Weekend Trip Away
I sometimes think I should have been made a guy. Not in a transvestite or lesbian way but just in the way that my brain works. Everything is much much simpler with boys and I just get on with them so much better. I don't want to be one of those girls

who only has guy friends, but girls are so complicated – they're either overtly mean or secretly mean. My sister is probably the only girl I actually like.

I was paired up with Charlie for orienteering, which was actually quite good fun. I still fancy him a bit, but I've accepted that we're just friends now. He told me how Jane, Vicky and Kirsty had all been bitching about me at Andy 'Lads Lads Lads' Burns' party and he was confused cos he thought they were my friends. I wish I could say I'm confused too, but I'm wholly unsurprised. The fucking back-stabbing bitches!

After we set up our bashas, we had dinner round the fire. Tom Southall was there and cooked me up a sausage (no sexual innuendo intended… in *your* endo… hahahaha).

Well, it seems all that time spent with boys did my childish humour some good.

He is soooo cool and his smile just makes me want to explode. Plus he treats me like a complete equal. I know I should just try to like myself more, but it's hard when I feel like everyone around me is cooler than me and they all know it. There's just an agreement in Edinburgh that I'm a loser and there's nothing I can do to change it. But not Tom. He's either not heard or he's making his own mind up. He's one of the coolest people I've met and he likes me and talks to me in a normal way, like a normal person.

Finally.

I made him laugh when we were all quoting *Monty Python and the Holy Grail.* BEST. FEELING. EVER.

Anyway we had the night exercise and then everyone went to bed except Tom, Charlie, me and a few others. We decided to go for a walk and try to get across to this rock in the middle of the river. Charlie and the others chickened out and went back to the camp, but Tom and I crossed the river holding hands. My heart was racing and I couldn't tell if it was holding hands with Tom or potentially recreating *Deliverance* with one wrong foot. When we got there we lay back and looked up at the night sky through the trees. I can't explain how wonderful it was. I felt the happiness in the pit of my stomach. Tom had some dope so we smoked some on the rock under the stars. Not to sound too clichéd but it felt magical. The river was furiously loud, but it was the most peaceful moment of my life. I felt calm and accepted and happy. I can't remember what we talked about, but I remember lying there next to Tom Southall, chatting and belly laughing. I was completely myself that night and wished things could always be as easy as smoking weed on the river next to the man with a killer smile. I was so indescribably content. There's almost a part of me that wished it hadn't happened cos now all the other shit seems even more shit in comparison.

It was around the same time that I wanted time to stop that we got busted by Dan Jeffries' older brother, James (who is the flight sergeant). He understandably isn't a fan of me after how I had treated Dan and he was on a massive power trip. We were quietly lying down when out of nowhere came this screaming.

'CADET LE DAY AND JUNIOR CORPORAL SOUTHALL! GET BACK HERE IMMEDIATELY!'

I nearly fell off that bloody rock I got such a fright! We went back to our bashas, but it was impossible to sleep because it was so so so cold. A perfect night nonetheless.

THURSDAY 18TH MAY 2000
LISTENING TO 'LIFE IS A
FLOWER' BY ACE OF BASE

Now that Psycho Jane and I aren't friends, I've lost that whole friendship group and I feel like I haven't really got any friends at all. She lied to everyone about the night we fell out at the playpark and everyone believes her. She told them all that I was smashing bottles 'like a maniac' and when she shouted at me for littering I went mental and tried to 'attack her'. It was only in self-defence that she pushed me and I cut my hands on my 'karmic glass'. To be fair, that is no less believable than what actually happened. It's just a shame that Psycho Jane's bullshit is more convincing than the truth. I have only Dan Jeffries as my witness and I forgive him for not jumping to my defence.

I found a note that Jane, Vicky and Kirsty had written about me. I think they planted it for me to find. I could hear them sniggering as they watched me reading it. I've been crying all night about it. I feel so alone. I've kept it for the future so I can, one day, look at it and not care anymore. Hopefully I'll be strong and amazing and I'll read it and think, *I am so much better than them.* I will NEVER do anything like this to anyone.

<u>Why we hate Claire Le Day</u>
- bitch
- hairy
- fat
- bad skin
- gross hair
- thinks she's funny
- thinks she's cool
- stupid blue trousers
- slut
- orangutan
- tiny boobs
- smelly
- disgusting

Even reading it back now makes me want to cry. I'd love to say I don't care, but I still feel for teenage me. Modern-day me would CRUSH THEM though. I'm just glad that I was able to see a future where it didn't matter. We talk a lot about resilience these days and how teenagers have none, but I'm not sure I would have the resilience, now, to cope with what I did when I was fourteen.

SIX

HANNAH AND GRETCHEN

27TH MAY 2000
LISTENING TO 'WELCOME
TO PARADISE' BY GREEN DAY

Hannah is my new friend. I met her at tennis coaching down the road about a month ago. She is Australian, smokes and she is a lesbian. She's so cool. She's even got a girlfriend, Gretchen, who sounds pretty cool too. Hannah and Gretchen go to Margaret Campbell's School.

If I had known then, that I was about to let THE Gretchen into my life, I would have run away screaming. Ah, Gretchen. The Moriarty to my Sherlock. The Malfoy to my Potter. The Joker to my Batman. I was probably not entirely blameless in what went down over the years, but Gretchen is my life's villain. From the second Gretchen and I first locked eyes, fate took hold and we knew that we were destined to be adversaries forever. Maybe it's something to do with pheromones, but the instant hatred between us was undeniable.

If I dig (very) deep I tell myself that there was probably a reason she was how she was and I just never took the time to try and understand her. I never even once considered her perspective and there are, as always, two sides to every story. I will accept that, perhaps unfairly for her, this book only represents one (biased teenage) view of what went on between us.

There is maybe a parallel universe that exists where Gretchen and I meet under different circumstances and become best friends. A world where we love each other like sisters and whisper secrets as we sip hot chocolate and stuff our faces with fistfuls of toffee popcorn. But that was not to be; for in this world, she spun her wheel of misfortune and it landed on me. DING DING DING! Arch nemesis jackpot! Unlike Sofia, Gretchen was bright. She was a master manipulator who made my life hell for the next four years until I left for university.

Where's Gretchen now? I don't really know. She's either in prison, in an inpatient psychiatric unit, or she grew up and is living a completely normal life; married with 2.4 children and helping out at a soup kitchen on Sunday mornings. I'm nervous that she's going to read this and sue me for libel, but this was how I saw things at the time. In fact, Gretchen is the primary reason that I have anonymised the whole book as I'm slightly worried about what she'll do to me. She is almost definitely a very different person to her teenage self, and a small part of me feels bad that I have embarked on a one-woman character assassination, but hey… *shrug*.

If you asked Gretchen now what she thought of me, you would likely get one of two infuriating answers:

1. *'Claire and I hated each other. She made my life hell and bullied ME until I went to uni…'*

Or, perhaps far more aggravating:

2. *'Claire Le Day? Oh yeah, I'd completely forgotten about her! Yeah, we went to school together. I don't think she liked me very much, but she didn't have much of an impact on my life. I had more important things to worry about.'*

Gahhhhh, it was clearly that one! Even my made-up hypothesis about Gretchen has the ability to drive me bonkers!

28TH MAY 2000
LISTENING TO 'ALL STAR' BY SMASHMOUTH

Last night, Hannah and I went out with Gretchen and some of their friends from Margaret Campbell's. We went to the skate park and then Hannah came back to stay at mine. I don't know what she sees in Gretchen, who is mentally disordered. She is apparently anorexic (although she's nothing like the *real* anorexics at school). She cuts her wrists and Hannah told me that she's had to 'save her' from overdoses in the past by sticking her fingers down her throat. Hannah said Gretchen needs her and she could never break up with her cos she would probably commit suicide. I know I've only met her once, but I think Gretchen is really manipulative.

When we got back to mine, Gretchen rang Hannah in tears saying she couldn't trust her at my house and that she could sense

49

that I was a 'threat to their relationship'. She said she needed Hannah to stop being friends with me for them to survive. About an hour later she rang back and dumped Hannah. Wow. She is craaaazy. Hannah said this happened nearly every day. She didn't seem too upset and so we snuck downstairs and made some cocktails with white wine and nectarines. I was really sick.

I am not surprised. Mixologist extraordinaire working her magic once again!

I wonder what it would be like to kiss a girl. Hannah and her lesbian friends make it seem so normal, and I get on really well with them. I can definitely see that Hannah is hot. How do I know that I'm not bisexual?

8TH JUNE 2000
LISTENING TO 'ROUND HERE'
BY COUNTING CROWS

School is hell at the moment. Between Psycho Jane and Sofia I feel like I can never let my guard down. We went on a chemistry trip yesterday to the BP oil refinery and found out today that it blew up a few hours after we left. I bet Jane did something… the psychopath.

I'm spending all my weekends with Hannah, Gretchen and their friend Maggie.

Maggie was a rollercoaster of a friend. She was larger than life and I was always slightly jealous of her confidence and humour. To this day, I am yet to hear a better belly laugh than Maggie's. My God, that laugh… It was pure joy. She could get a room full of people on their hands and knees, gasping for breath with a quip and a twenty-second cackle. She was a big girl with bold clothes, a bright lip and a short shock of white hair. I loved Maggie McFarlane.

We eventually ended up at St Felix's together and we used to sneak out for cigarettes round the back of the local Co-op bins. She'd bring the gum and the Dior Addict lip gloss; and I'd spray us with Tommy Girl from my pink, pocket-sized atomiser before tiptoeing back into school. These cigarettes with Maggie represented that 'one on one' best friend time that I craved more than anything.

I absolutely adored Maggie, but she certainly put me through my paces over the next few years and was not always as wonderful as I viewed her. In the end though, I was the one who finally blew it.

27TH JUNE 2000
LISTENING TO 'IT'S MY LIFE' BY BON JOVI

Am I bisexual? This is probably the most absurd question I have ever asked myself. Hannah is so attractive that I keep questioning if I fancy her. I'm probably just being curious and experimental. There's definitely no way I'm a lesbian, and aren't bisexuals often just lesbians who haven't fully committed themselves to the cause yet? Hannah says she's 'bisexual', but she's clearly just a lesbian. God knows what Gretchen is. Some people would say that bisexuality is just greedy. Maybe I'm just greedy? Maybe I'm so desperate for a relationship that I think if I became bisexual it would open more doors? I bet bisexual people would hate me saying this. Perhaps I'm just craving any kind of affection that I don't care where it comes from. I'm probably imagining a 'grass is greener' scenario, but I should probably at least pull a girl one day to see.

6TH JULY 2000
LISTENING TO 'RAMP! (THE LOGICAL SONG)'
BY SCOOTER

Last day of school! Thank God. I appear to have survived (relatively) unscathed (and by 'unscathed', I mean not maimed beyond recognition).

We got our yearbooks and I look very average. Typical.

Sofia has been a mega cow all week and she told her older sister and her friends that I've been bullying *her*! She finds this kind of thing hilarious. They marched into the classroom at lunch today and screamed at me for what seemed like forever. They said I needed to watch my back and that they'd 'fuck me up'. They called me a 'fat nobody' who doesn't even deserve to *be* bullied by Sofia. Actually, it very much seems like I do (I didn't say). It's a fine balance between keeping some dignity and not inflaming the situation further. But I'm so fed up with being a pathetic, head-down nobody. I should have just kept my mouth shut though, but I couldn't stop myself. I can't remember exactly what I said, but it was along the lines of:

'Sofia's a dick and although I never have, she actually does deserve to be bullied. Anyone that believes her bullshit about me bullying her is clearly even dumber than she is.'

Then two of them grabbed me and held me down on the desk and the third one pulled my arm back, ripped the arm off my jacket and gobbed in my hair. I had my face rammed against the desk as one of them repeatedly flicked my cheek.

'Haha. Look at all that fat wobble! You're a fat ugly cunt, Claire. Next time you won't be so lucky.'

Sofia was sat there the whole time smiling and laughing. When they left I was just standing there silent and fighting back the tears. She hopped off the desk and patted my head.

'Oops. Isn't it funny how people just get the wrong end of the stick? You look like such a fucking loser right now, Claire! It's so funny! Imagine if you actually could bully me! Hahaha!'

I just about managed not to cry. Why does this kinda shit keep happening to me?! Am I really so hateable that people want to make me feel like this? I can't ever imagine knowingly making anyone feel as terrible as I do right now.

I then walked to St Felix's to meet Mum, but she was running late and I bumped into Tom Southall. He flashed me a dazzler. I honestly think his smile is better than Brad Pitt's, and it made me feel instantly better. He put his arm around my shoulders and led me back out the school gates.

'Come on, pal. Let's go for a fag. You look like you need it.'

At that moment no one could have said anything better to me. God, he's so cool. We had a fag and chatted. He told me I was 'a really cool girl'. Really? If so, then he is really the only person to think so! I'm a lot of things, but I don't think that 'cool' is one of them. If someone like Tom Southall was ever interested in someone like me, that would shut Sofia up.

I spoke to Hannah when I got home and her advice was, 'Why don't you just beat the shit out of her? Want me to?' I wish it were that easy. If only I had people like Hannah and Maggie at school with me.

SEVEN

YANNICK

15TH JULY 2000
LISTENING TO 'THE REAL
SLIM SHADY' BY EMINEM

I've arrived in the South of France and I miss my friends so much. Ha. *Now* I've got friends? Now I can't be there? I miss smoking. I miss freedom. There's nowhere I can go to be on my own. I am NON STOP with my parents and grandparents. I am simultaneously suffocating in a world of supervision and solitude.

My childhood summers were glorious and privileged, but I was too much of an ungrateful twat to appreciate them at the time. My grandparents lived in Paris, but had two small holiday homes in the South of France and in Brittany. The house in the south was in the middle of nowhere, up in the hills near Nice. There was a pool, but otherwise it was

54

really only somewhere for young children and stressed-out couples in need of electronic detoxes to enjoy. There were no people, no bars, no shops and no internet. It was an absolute nightmare for the grumpy, family-hating teen that I was. We would usually spend two weeks there before all heading up north for a month. Brittany, by contrast, was bursting with cousins, boys, bars, beaches, shops and activities.

I spoke to Hannah yesterday, and although I thought Gretchen and I were becoming friends because she was being so nice to me, Hannah told me she hated me. Of course she does. I was so gullible to fall for Gretchen's frenemy shit. Why am I so polarising? I have done NOTHING wrong to Gretchen. How can you just hate someone for no reason? Bitch.

26TH JULY 2000
LISTENING TO 'SET YOU FREE' BY N-TRANCE

I arrived in Brittany late last night and I got up early this morning to buy fags. I went and sat on the jetty, contemplating my life in the sunshine and smoked till I felt sick. This is my favourite place in the world.

31ST JULY 2000
LISTENING TO 'STAND BY ME' BY BEN E. KING

I met up with the twins, but they have their idiot Danish friends staying with them so it's not the same anymore.

I'd met the twins a few summers before. They are a pair of highly intelligent, half French/half Danish pocket-sized blonde bombshells. Hanging out with the twins certainly attracted a lot of male attention, but simultaneously rendered me completely invisible. They were adorably innocent and completely oblivious to the sexual power that they had over men. I found this naivety so endearing and such a breath of fresh air compared to the St Catherine's girls. We had absolutely nothing in common, but we liked each other and I was certainly grateful to have some drama-free, normal girlfriends.

7TH AUGUST 2000
LISTENING TO 'SCAR TISSUE'
BY RED HOT CHILI PEPPERS

The twins and I met a whole new bunch of people on the beach last week. The Marseille brothers (Les Marseillais – Ben and Seb), Marc and François are my favourites.

And they still are. I feel like I've grown up with them as they held my hand through adolescence like the big brothers I had always dreamed of. My whole body still aches with nostalgia when I think back to my summers in Brittany with François, Marc and Les Marseillais. They were some of the happiest times of my life and it makes me want to cry, now that it's over.

François is fabulously talented. He has a mass of curly brown hair, a character-building gap between his two front teeth and boundless energy. He was forever making up little songs and skits that kept us endlessly entertained – a natural performer. He moved to La Réunion island and worked as a physio for a while before sacking it all in to follow his performing arts dream. He is now the lead singer/songwriter of a band, a stand-up comic and the owner, manager and actor of an improv theatre company. François spends his life doing his dream job(s), trail running through paradise and drinking rum before going to bed in his beachside property with a big spliff and some exotic jawdropper that previously only existed in 90s Peter Andre music videos. Bastard.

Les Marseillais, Ben and his little brother, Seb, were raised as old-fashioned gentlemen. They represent, what I now realise to be, the elite of men. Poor Seb was subjected to years of listening to my repetitive tales of heartbreak as I got disgustingly drunk bemoaning yet another dickhead.

'Why can't I fall in love with a nice guy like you?!'

I'd then pour myself another dramatic glass of vodka and try to snog him. I was always dutifully returned home (unsnogged) and ever so fortunate to be worthy of his friendship. He was reliable, overlooked and utterly wonderful.

Ben actually looked like France's answer to Hanson with nipple-length blonde hair and an enormous, ripped, muscular frame (which was totally out of keeping with his age and average level of activity). He is nothing short of brilliant and even then, he was wildly passionate about the reptilian world. He was arrested aged twenty after being the first person in the world to successfully (and completely illegally) breed a rare species of frog in his Marseille apartment. His insane physique only improved with age and he looks like Thor now. He ran away to live in the jungle and became a world expert and pioneer in all things reptile, so sadly no one ever gets to see him in the flesh.

Marc and his family are all boat shoes, pearls and jumpers tied round their necks. Despite my limitless wealth of life-shaping, Marc-related memories, when I think of him, my mind weirdly goes straight to his white Fiat Punto. I reckon I spent half my adolescence in that car. Marc drove this car so recklessly that it leaves me cold to think of all the potential consequences that we miraculously managed to avoid. Drink driving was (is?) terrifyingly rife in France and these boys were, sadly, not exempt.

I think it was probably during the summer of 2005 that I was awoken in Marc's spare room by the loudest French drum and bass imaginable. I staggered out and saw Marc dancing around his kitchen, naked with a fag hanging out his mouth. He screamed in shock when he saw me and I then watched his face change as the memories from the night before came flooding back... the beers... the dancing... the rum... THE CAR!

This morning ritual of dread and slow realisation had become a worrying trend for the two of us by 2005. Fortunately this was a mere month before we met our future spouses and the jig was up.

So we ran outside to see a crumpled heap of a car. He grunted a brief 'Merde!', kicked the bumper, shrugged (in the most French-'bof'-way imaginable) and went back into the kitchen. He pulled out a tray onto which he put a brioche, confiture de mûres, a pack of Marlboro Lights and two large glasses of Pastis. He balanced the tray on one hand and held out the other to lead me out to 'breakfast' on his terrace – naked. He was a goofball. A damaged, drink-driving alcoholic, sure, but a goofball nonetheless. In retrospect, it was probably for the best that he married the most conservative Stepford Wife in Europe. She's essentially his mother (who incidentally has a double-barrelled first and last name) and the 'fun' stopped the second he said 'I do'.

They are all much older than me so I told them I was fifteen. I will be in November so it doesn't feel like too much of a lie. I'll probably never see them again.

Oh, Claire. Ha. How wrong you are. I had to come clean about two years later in a blaze of truth after the lie had become monstrously big and all-consuming.

So they had all been planning to go clubbing in Dinard last night and invited the twins and me. I really wanted to go, but there is no way I would be allowed:

A. into Yannick's car (he has just got his permit and will be driving)
B. out later than midnight
C. clubbing

So I told my mum that I was staying at the twins' house. There was no way I was going to miss out on this.

So the night started well. François, Les Marseillais, Yannick, Marc, the twins and I went to the prize-giving of the regatta and sat in the sunshine and drank Ricard. Yannick and Marc then drove to Dinard and I sat in the front with Yannick while François and Ben were headbanging to 'Get on Top' in the backseat. François is so funny...

We went to La Rhumerie (a rum bar) and I spent the whole night staring adoringly at Yannick.

Yannick was tall, dark, handsome AND charming. The fact that he drove simply blew me away. Not even my friends' older brothers back home were driving yet. This guy was next-level mature and I was awestruck. Fourteen... ahem... fifteen-year-old me couldn't get past being in the passenger seat with him... like an equal!

After drinking a lot of rum, Yannick and I were getting on so well! When we were walking back to the car, he took my hand and said he was very pleased to have got to know me... ahhhh swoon. Well, I'm very pleased to get to know *you*, Yannick, you gorgeous bastard you.

When we got back we went to the beach where we sat around a bonfire and people were passing round bottles of whisky and rum. Hoards of people kept arriving from all over. It was amazing and I went skinny dipping about three o'clock in the morning. I felt free and when I ran into the cold sea I thought, *Fuck you, Psycho Jane, fuck you, Sofia, fuck you, Gretchen! Life is soooooo great without you!* I then spent the night cuddled up to Yannick and he kissed me!!!!! I could have died happy right then and there! The twins and I left about 5am and went back to their house. Pretty sure I've got away with it... phew!

Marc and Yannick took us sailing today on Marc's dad's boat. It was the most incredible day and Yannick kept putting his arm around me and kissing me. I couldn't believe it! Someone like Yannick likes someone like me! It's mental.

11TH AUGUST 2000
LISTENING TO 'SOMEBODY TO LOVE' BY QUEEN

What the hell happened?!?! My lovely little fairytale life has gone very wrong indeed. We all went camping on the nearby island last night and I was really excited about my first full night of complete freedom. At first my mum was like, 'No way. Not even next year!', but she eventually said yes!! She's a hero really.

So we all walked across late in the afternoon when the tide was out. We set the tents up and then sat round the fire drinking rum punch and tequila shots. It was so idyllic with the sun setting over the sea, everyone laughing and the sand still warm from the hot summer day. Yannick was sat behind me with his arms draped over my shoulders as he kissed the back of my head and neck. Everything was perfect (but obviously too good to be true), when Ben got so drunk and Yannick left to go and look after him. He told me someone needed to hold his hair back. I was like, 'He can have my elastic', but Yannick just left and said, '*Pas cool*, Claire.' They were gone for hours. When I eventually found him, he was acting really weird with me. I was devastated as I sensed that it was all over already. I made my way back to the fire, but then stopped and sat with François, who was smoking a spliff. He asked if I was upset because of what Yannick had said. What had he said? François told me he'd overheard Yannick saying there was no point in continuing the relationship because I didn't bring anything 'new' to his life. Does he mean like in a sex way? He is eighteen after all… gutted.

So I had the worst night after that and all I wanted to do was go home, but I was literally stuck on an uninhabited island, at high tide without a boat. I had clearly been dumped, but hadn't even heard it from Yannick yet. I'll NEVER get a boyfriend like Yannick again. My loserness obviously shone through in the end. You can't hide it forever, Claire. You're not really cool. Did I think that the hot eighteen-year-old French guy was just going to fall in love with dumpy fourteen-year-old me?! Ha! Who was I kidding? I spent a lot of the night crying and François was trying to console me, but I could tell he couldn't be arsed. I was so embarrassed that I was being so pathetic and dramatic, but I felt crushed. I know we'd only been together for less than a week, but I couldn't help it. I'm sure the gallons of rum didn't help me keep it together, but I felt so stupid and naive that I'd let myself believe that someone like Yannick would ever fancy a fat saddo like me. Of course I didn't bring anything 'new' to his life. Stupid, tragic Claire.

On the beach today, I asked Yannick why he hadn't had the decency to dump me BEFORE marooning me on an island with no escape strategy.

'Claire, I'm sorry that you had to hear it from François. I always find it difficult to tell girls when I like them and the same when I don't. I'm really sorry I don't have the same feelings as you and I'm sorry you didn't find out from me and I made you cry. I hope we can still be good friends.'

I am so gutted.

EIGHT

TOM SOUTHALL

28TH AUGUST 2000
LISTENING TO 'RHYTHM IS A DANCER' BY SNAP!

Back in Edinburgh. Got a brand new mobile phone with Mum today – a Nokia 5210. It's so gorgeous. I'm actually so happy to be back in Edinburgh and I spent the morning smoking with Hannah, Gretchen and Maggie in Princess Street Gardens. Then I met up with Charlie and we went to the Filmhouse Café and I had two cappuccinos!

You rebel, you…

I can't believe I used to fancy Charlie. He's nice, but he's actually a bit of a loser, and after spending the last month with older French guys he seems so… young and geeky. I got my summer photos back today too. I love Yannick – he's so hot! Not as hot as my beautiful new mobile though.

2ND SEPTEMBER 2000
LISTENING TO 'OLIVER'S
ARMY' BY ELVIS COSTELLO

Just got home and I've had the most amazing night. It was the end of the Edinburgh Festival fireworks night and everyone was out. I watched the fireworks from Princess Street Gardens with Charlie and Mish, and they just sat there with Charlie's flask of hot chocolate, tutting at me smoking.

Tom Southall and loads of his friends were there too and I kept looking over wishing I was with them. Charlie and Mish were being really boring. I went and said hi to Tom and co and they said they were going to this new club opening called Frankenstein's (Frankie's) and asked if I wanted to join. Every time Tom smiles at me, my legs feel hollow and I have to stop myself from mindlessly giggling. I would have followed him anywhere! Take meeeeee! Charlie and Mish weren't keen and went home.

Lucy Murphy and the popular girls are friends with me again now... ish. I'm not as popular or cool as them, but at least they're not ignoring me all the time anymore. I called Lucy before Mish and Charlie left and went to meet up with her and the other girls. Sofia was there, but we just ignored each other and there wasn't any drama.

Apparently I just needed a summer to catch up with everyone, although why I still wanted to be friends with these girls is baffling.

I convinced the girls to go to Frankie's and we all got in! I think they were impressed when Tom came over to say hi and he'd got me a test tube shot. They were like, 'OH MY GOD, Claire! You're friends with Tom Southall! He's so hot!'

I felt pretty smug…

We all bought a drink and then danced for the rest of the night – it was incredible. It was the first time I'd been in a club! Oh God, my phone bill is going to be huuugggge – my mum's going to kill me.

5TH SEPTEMBER 2000
LISTENING TO 'I WANT TO BREAK FREE' BY QUEEN

URRGGHHH, I'm so fat! I need to eat less. I've literally just spooned half a hazelnut tree's worth of Nutella into my mouth.

Hannah came round after school and we were supposed to play tennis, but we couldn't be arsed so skived off and she smoked all my fags. Gretchen and her had ANOTHER huge fight on the phone. She was apparently going to 'do something stupid' if Hannah didn't go and see her straight away. So Hannah left. It's so annoying. I'd have called her bluff years ago.

10TH SEPTEMBER 2000
LISTENING TO 'HEROES' BY DAVID BOWIE

I stayed over at Lucy Murphy's house last night and it was just like the old days. I love being friends with her again, but wouldn't ever be best friends with her now. I think she feels bad about how she treated me last year, but neither of us talk about it and we just pretend it didn't happen.

Apparently her parents check all the levels in their spirit cupboard because of Frank (*Lucy's older brother*) so we made a cocktail with a couple of drops from each bottle. It had about thirty different spirits in it and we poured a glass each. It tasted absolutely disgusting so we downed it and we were both sick.

If I screw my eyes up really tightly and think back to this night I can still taste the most fetid, bilious concoction ever created. The Tia Maria, the Cointreau, the Gordon's Gin, the Bacardi, the Warninks Advocaat, the Chambord, some Aberlour, the Stolichnaya, some Baileys and a final flourish of random homemade plum Eau de Vie. Jesus... the curdled poison. That was bad.

16TH SEPTEMBER 2000
LISTENING TO 'FREESTYLER' BY BOMFUNK MCS

I went to this amazing party with Hannah, Maggie and Gretchen. I pulled this hot guy and then Hannah and I went back to her house, watched *American Pie* (again!) and smoked 5,428,093 fags. Life is pretty great sometimes.

18TH SEPTEMBER 2000
WAAAASSSSSSAAAPPPPPPP?!?!?!?!?!?!?!
 WAAAAAAAAASSSSSSSSAAAAAAPPPP?!?!?!?!?!

22ND SEPTEMBER 2000
LISTENING TO 'RHYTHM OF
THE NIGHT' BY CORONA

I've had such a crazy night. Hannah, Gretchen, Maggie and I bought some drinks and we went down to the canal with loads of their friends from Margaret Campbell's. I accidently got majorly drunk and I was so sick. I'm such an idiot.

Getting quite as drunk as I did was in fact a genuine accident. I was just starting to get a sense of my alcohol 'limit' which, at this stage, was approximately four alcopops (Bacardi Breezers or Smirnoff Ices). This would allow me to have a good night without getting 'too drunk'. If you were really lucky, you could buy one (much cheaper) big bottle rather than four small ones and this was the case on the night in question. Lucky me! I thought as I picked up one big peach-flavoured bottle for £3.99 from the dodgy corner shop in Cannon Mills. The price felt about right so I didn't really feel the need to inspect the bottle any further.

We went and made ourselves comfortable on the edge of the canal and started a game of truth or dare. It was my turn and Gretchen dared me to down my bottle in one. *Why not?* I thought. *I'm planning on drinking it all anyway... You're on, Gretchen!* Everyone was cheering and I felt like a frickin' hero... for about five minutes. I then vividly remember standing up and walking over to Hannah when my legs stopped working and the ground jumped up and bit me in the face. I could taste blood, but felt no pain as my body no longer belonged to me. I proceeded to spend the next hour vomiting and slurring like a twat.

It was only later that I realised that my bottle of peach-flavoured 'alcopop' was in fact a bottle of Archers Peach Schnapps.

Urrgghhh. Even to this day my stomach lurches if I smell anything peach-flavoured. I do wonder if Gretchen had noticed my mistake...

27TH SEPTEMBER 2000
LISTENING TO '7 DAYS' BY CRAIG DAVID

I'm so upset. I spoke to Mish for the first time in ages and he told me that 90% of the boys at St Felix's call me 'Fat, Hairy, Man, Beast etc'. He said that even Charlie and Tom Southall were saying that. Why does everyone hate me?
MUST
STOP
EATING.

Piss off, Mish, you little bitch! It's only now that I can see that it was him all along. He was the bad guy. He was always there, lurking in the background, feeding me negativity. It was always him, chipping away at my confidence, spreading nasty little lies and rumours... Mish was Keyser Söze.

Not that it should really matter, because body confidence has nothing to do with your actual body, but I was in no way fat or hairy or manly really. It's weird how some insults take off. I was a slim size 10/12, but like many other teenage girls, I was comparing my dysmorphic body image to unrealistic levels of 'perfection'. It was at this fragile age that 'fat' was the go-to insult and St Catherine's instilled a belief that there was really nothing worse than being fat. For nearly two years I went to lunch by myself because most of the other girls simply didn't eat. A can of Diet Coke for lunch was the go-to. But I was hungry! So I'd sit there day after day feeling guilty for being so 'weak'. Stupid normal appetite. The more I heard people call me 'fat', the more I believed it. I was eating more than everyone after all, so it made sense. I loathed my body and I felt 'fat' for most of my teenage years. I used to stand in front of my bedroom mirror, pulling at bits of skin and sobbing every night before I went to bed. So many of my diary entries started, 'I'm so fat! Diet starts tomorrow!' Or 'Feeling like a huge disgusting whale.'

People that know me as an adult probably wouldn't believe that I had such poor self-esteem. I LOVE ME. I love food. I love eating. I love my healthy body, the laughter lines and the pregnancy stretch marks. I even love my post-breastfeeding, spaniel-eared excuses for boobs. I'm thankful for all of it. I am disgustingly confident now to the point that I have most likely gone too far the other way. I'm the sort of person that might text you when I'm in a taxi to meet you.

`I hope you're ready. I look AMAZING tonight.`

Where was I when I was fourteen? When I needed me most?

1ST OCTOBER 2000
LISTENING TO 'HITCHIN' A RIDE' BY GREEN DAY

Gretchen and I totally 'connected' at a party last week and she said I was a 'blonde version of herself' and that's why we've clashed so much in the past. I was so glad that the drama was over… FOR ABOUT FIVE SECONDS! I then pulled a guy called Malcolm and out of nowhere Gretchen called me a 'cheap tramp'. This led to Hannah and Gretchen having a massive fight and then splitting up (again!). Hannah left with me and told me not to worry cos Gretchen probably liked Malcolm and thought everyone was a cheap tramp.

The next day I rang Malcolm:

'Hey, it's Claire.'

'Hey.'

'How are you?'

'Alright.'

'So... um... you have fun last night?'

'Twas alright.'

'So I wondered if you wanted to go for a coffee today?'

'No thanks. I'm knackered.'

'Yeah, you sound quite tired.'

'That's cos I am. Bye.'

'Oh [embarrassed], ok, see you then.'

'Bye.'

I rang Hannah, mortified, and she said that he'd apparently always fancied Gretchen and she'd just found out that Gretchen and Malcolm pulled after we left. He also told everyone that I was 'easy' and gave him a handjob, but he didn't even come. Gretchen magnanimously spread the word and that I was denying it cos I couldn't give handjobs. Arrrggghhh!!! THAT DIDN'T HAPPEN!! I only pulled him. He probably didn't even say anything about the HJ and it was all Gretchen. I wonder if Gretchen and Sofia would get on? They'd so be besties. They would dance around some kind of Claire anti-shrine singing I hate Claire songs, drinking my blood and stabbing my fat voodoo doll.

14TH OCTOBER 2000
LISTENING TO 'GOOD RIDDANCE (TIME OF YOUR LIFE)' BY GREEN DAY

I went out with Hannah and the boys from Margaret Campbell's last night. She was in need of cheering up as she just found out that Gretchen has been cheating on her with Malcolm for months! I guess that explains a few things...

We went to the Globe and I had four shots of Goldschlager and four shots of green Apple Sourz! Tom Southall bought me a shot and I nearly choked on it when he smiled at me and ruffled my hair. If only you could bottle that smile.

There were tonnes of people out last night including William Macleod. He's in Tom Southall's year at St Felix's, but I don't think they're friends. We've been texting a bit since then and we're kinda friends now. It's weird, I always thought he hated me. He's so funny.

Meeting William Macleod marks the turning point in my adolescence. It would probably be more accurate to say that William Macloed WAS my adolescence. Everything changed after I met him (although this doesn't properly happen just yet). Ahhh, William… the class clown, the hopeless romantic and back then, my world. He had big green eyes, a cheeky grin and an infuriatingly childish sense of humour that had me hooked. He was my first everything and like all firsts, it felt truly epic. I'd be a different person today if I'd never met William-bloody-Macleod.

18TH OCTOBER 2000
LISTENING TO 'LADY (HEAR ME TONIGHT)' BY MODJO

My God – Gretchen is doing my fucking head in! Hannah keeps getting pissed and ending up back in bed with her. The on/offness is totally confusing and I can't keep up. Gretchen keeps trying to 'kill herself' cos she loves Hannah so much. Why don't you fucking well do it then, Gretchen?! Argh, I don't mean that really. Obviously I don't want her to die, but you'd think something more than a cuddle from Hannah would reverse her serious plans to end her life. They obviously got back together tonight and Hannah told Gretchen about my concern that 'she was making a huge mistake'. Thanks a fucking bunch. Gretchen has been non-stop sending me hate texts since telling me to butt out of her life etc. Well, Hannah is making a huge mistake. Gretchen is a total nutjob.

11TH NOVEMBER 2000
LISTENING TO '36 DEGREES' BY PLACEBO

I went to a party with Hannah, Gretchen, Maggie and their school friends tonight. It was amazing, but Hannah was crying because her parents were splitting up and she has to move back to Australia with her mum. Gutted.

Mum had a huge go at me cos she thinks I'm stealing money to fund my 'smookeen ahbeet'. She made me cry and the worst thing is I haven't. I obviously told her I didn't smoke, but I fund my 'smookeen ahbeet' with babysitting money. Thank you very much.

Tom Southall said he would come to my birthday party! I'm so excited. He's such a sexy beast! I wish I could get a guy like him. All his girlfriends are so beautiful. I wish I was prettier or thinner or boobier or had longer legs. Anything. I'd take anything – just to give me a shot.

19TH NOVEMBER 2000
LISTENING TO 'CHURCH ON
SUNDAY' BY GREEN DAY

My Fifteenth Birthday Party
Well, that was a fucking catastrophe. I was soooo excited all week. I'd only invited about fifteen people and I was determined

for it not to turn into an SJ-style party. I wasn't even calling it 'a party'. No smashing the place up and getting thrown out of windows, thanks very much. It started pretty well. We were drinking Smirnoff Ices downstairs, people were smoking outside and it was all good.

Tom looked mega hot and put his arm around my waist and gave me a long kiss on the cheek when he arrived. He then left his arm there for ages when I was talking to other people. I could hardly speak, I was so distracted. It felt like every other sense was numbed and all I could feel was his burning hot hand around my waist. Hannah, Gretchen and Maggie were all sat outside and I felt a bit left out of their trio tonight. Gretchen didn't even say hi or happy birthday or anything when they arrived. I didn't really want to invite Gretchen at all, but it would have been way more of a headache not to. Lucy Murphy insisted on bringing Sofia 'cos you guys are so similar and she really likes you!'. Hahaha! Bollocks! Both those statements could not be further from the truth, but given that I already felt obliged to invite Gretchen I might as well have all my frenemies round. What could possibly go wrong?!

We were all having a good time, but the doorbell kept ringing with tonnes of people I hadn't invited. I wasn't letting anyone in cos I didn't want stuff to get out of control, but it was starting to go mental out there. There were probably fifty-plus people outside the house cos word had spread about a 'house party', and cos loads of people had brought friends anyway there were nearly thirty at the party already. I was getting really stressed when Gretchen took me aside.

'You need to chill the fuck out, Claire, it's not cool. This party is really lame at the moment anyway. Surely you don't want everyone to say your party was shit...'

'I'm not sure it's shit, Gretchen.'

'Oh, it is. It would be so much better if you had some more guests...'

'Noooooo...'

She then barged her way past me to the front door (ignoring my protests) and LET EVERYONE IN! It was a total disaster.

The house was instantly trashed and there was nothing I could do to stop it. I shouted and pleaded and begged people to stop and leave, but I was invisible and my pleas just fell on hundreds of drunken, deaf ears. The original Victorian banisters were broken, the fridge was in pieces and there were cigarette burns everywhere. Not to mention the broken glass and the millions of empty cans and bottles strewn throughout the house.

Tom Southall eventually helped me get loads of people out and then was trying to help me clean up when suddenly he pulled me! It was so unexpected. He was coming out of the kitchen when he suddenly just pressed me up against the door and said I looked fit, before pulling me. I was pinned up against the kitchen door and it felt incredible. Before I knew it, we were making out on the bed and I gave him a BJ. I've never done that before and I'm not sure what possessed me to do it. I don't even know if I did it right.

Before he left, I asked, 'Was this just a one night thing?'

'No. But it's not a "going out" thing.'

Oh. I'm so upset. I feel a bit used and like he's totally messed me around. Am I never going to be 'a going out kinda girl'? What's so wrong with me?! I can't believe I gave him a BJ! Maybe all those years of wrongly being called 'slut' has actually turned me into one?

Gretchen and Hannah left, and Maggie and I spent about an hour trying to clean up and glue everything back together. We were tucked up in bed shitting bricks when we heard my

parents come home then suddenly a huge boom from my dad...
'CLAAAIIIRRRE!!'

He'd sat on a solid oak toilet seat that someone had somehow managed to break in two. My pathetic attempt at gluing it back together was obviously pointless and the glue was still wet. I'm grounded for two weeks.

MY. PARENTS. WENT. APESHIT.

24TH NOVEMBER 2000
LISTENING TO 'MR JONES' BY COUNTING CROWS

I saw Tom at Cadets on Monday and he acted like NOTHING had happened. I'd texted him on Sunday, but he hadn't replied.

> Thnx so much 4 helpin me tidy up. My parents obviously went apeshit & Im grounded. Hope u got home ok. C u tomoz. X

Then I found out that Sofia fancies Tom. Well, that's just great! There's no point in me even trying to compete with her! He'll clearly like her more than me. Would you prefer the flat-chested, fat-arsed, stumpy-legged 'man beast' or the big-titted, blonde goddess? I couldn't resist texting Tom:

> Y arent u replin 2 my txts? U probably kno by now dat I like u & I have 4 ages but when i pulled u on sat I REALLY thought u liked me 2 but u clearly dont! U got my hopes up & it hurts! TB!

TB is text back. He didn't.

25TH NOVEMBER 2000
LISTENING TO 'MUSCLE MUSEUM' BY MUSE

Gretchen has been sending me hate mail since my party. Just the usual aggression and hatred. I try not to care, but she is MEAN. I'm not even sure why this time. I'm the one that should be furious as it was all her bloody fault my house got trashed in the first place! My mum had said she wouldn't ground me if I said who was responsible, but my life wouldn't be worth living if I grassed up Gretchen. She's definitely the sort of person that will end up with a GBH conviction. Or murder. If this is her at fifteen, I'm not sure I want to see her at thirty. Despite my wholly undeserved loyal silence, she emailed tonight:

> You're such a fucking slut. Maggie told me what you did with Tom. You massive whore. There's no way he likes you. Probably just tried his luck cos you're so easy. You should probably stop being friends with us because no one really likes you and everyone bitches about you as soon as you have your back turned. Hannah is only nice to you because she feels sorry for you.

28TH NOVEMBER 2000
LISTENING TO 'I GUESS THAT'S WHY THEY CALL IT THE BLUES' BY ELTON JOHN

> Tom finally texted back: Listen Claire. Im really sorry bout the other night. It

wasnt cool of me. Hope we can still be friends.

13TH DECEMBER 2000
LISTENING TO 'WARNING' BY GREEN DAY

I made up with Psycho Jane at a party tonight. We were sat at opposite ends of a sofa (not talking) watching Hannah and Gretchen have (another) massive fight. I haven't spoken to her since the incident with the 'karmic glass' at the playpark. It's too tiring to have her as an enemy though and my hatred towards her has kinda dissipated over time. It appears I have bigger Gretchen-sized fish to fry now anyway.

So there we were, sat in silence as Armageddon was unfolding before our eyes. Hannah said, 'I just can't keep doing this with you. It's over. For good', and stormed off. Gretchen was left there crying when she turned to me.

'What the fuck do you think you're staring at, you fucking cunt?!'

'Yeah yeah, Gretchen. Take it all out on me…'

She marched off and Jane looked over to me and she was laughing. What a psycho.

'Why do you put up with that shit, Claire?'

I shrugged. What makes her think I put up with it?

'Probably the same reason I put up with your shit for so long.'

We both laughed and that was that. Friends again. Her and Dan Jeffries are going out now. I wonder if that's all she wanted the whole time and that's why she was always such a wanker to me? Either way I don't care anymore. It's all in the past (but maybe not totally forgotten). I'm not going to let myself get embroiled with her too much again. She's clearly still a bit of a psycho and I can only deal with one Jane, Gretchen or Sofia at a time.

1ST JANUARY 2001
LISTENING TO 'STAN' BY EMINEM FT. DIDO

BANG! I just felt like being a little cringeworthy and starting the year off with a bang! Got back to Edinburgh and I could not be happier. I've just spent two weeks with my grandparents in Paris and although it felt loooooong, I feel like it's done me some good.

I met up with Jane as soon as I got back and we walked around and she gave me the goss from Hogmanay. It sounded amazing; I'm so jealous.

2ND JANUARY 2001
LISTENING TO 'PRETTY FLY (FOR A WHITE GUY)' BY THE OFFSPRING

I have a new friend! A BOY friend! Andy, who lives next door, and I are *actual* friends now. I've just got into bed after a hilarious night at his. We met properly just before Christmas at a neighbour's drinks party and found out we actually got on really well. It's so much fun having a friend next door!

So tonight, we sat in his room, drinking screwdrivers and watching *Gladiator*. We were both really drunk and then (so dangerously now I come to think of it) crawled out of his bathroom window up onto his roof. We just sat there smoking, under a blanket, and looking out over Edinburgh. Had it not actually been romantic, it would have been insanely romantic.

'You're alright, Claire. I always thought you were a bit of a loser, but you're alright.'

'Thanks... I think. You're alright too. I always thought you were hot, but...'

He winked at me and put his arm around my shoulders as we chuckled together. It felt like a perfect friendship moment.

Next Door Andy and I have been friends for over twenty years. He's one of those guys whose looks peaked when he was sixteen, but that gave him just enough confidence for it never to matter again. Andy genuinely believes that EVERYONE has fancied him at some point. It's maddening to admit it now but he is not wrong, for I too was once part of this mass infatuation. It was only a little crush when he first moved in next door in 1997. I was still playing with my Tamagotchi and sharing my bed with twenty soft toys so it really shouldn't count. I was eleven years old and completely in love with Malcolm Kennedy from Neighbours, so credit to thirteen-year-old Andy, my standards were on point. He used to play basketball in his back garden and as soon as I'd hear the first bounce of that ball I would rush up to my bedroom to ogle him. I'd blast out some 'cool' music ('It's All Coming Back to Me Now' by Celine Dion from memory) and teeter on my window sill in the most alluring pose I could muster. I'd spend hours 'reading' and admiring him adoringly. Seduction 101 basically.

After a few months of me making him fall in love with me from afar, our schools had a joint disco at St Catherine's. I spotted him almost immediately and thought, Right, Claire, there's that cute guy from next door, go and ask him to dance. This is your chance. This was a particularly bold move as we were still at the age when boys and girls segregated themselves to opposite sides of the gym hall. No one would even dream of a solo mission without backup. I crossed no man's land and clearly and confidently asked him to dance.

I was sporting a rather unfortunate bowl-cut hairdo at the time, which made me look like Donny Osmond circa 1969. I have never suited a fringe anyway (although

I still regularly convince myself that I'll look like Claudia Winkleman and give it another go every couple of years), but I remember this one being particularly offensive.

So anyway, my ugly duckling looks, the persistent puppy fat and my antiquated hairdo made Next Door Andy explode with laughter at my proposal. He then spent the next ten minutes impersonating a stuttering version of my 'do dooo y-y-you w-w-want to d-d-dance' and shaping this awkward hairdo with his hands. I've never fully forgiven him for this, although he denies this ever happened. It took me nearly a decade to reattempt 'The Claudia' and three years before Next Door Andy and I spoke again.

5TH JANUARY 2001
LISTENING TO 'RE-REWIND (THE CROWD SAY BO SELECTA)' BY ARTFUL DODGER FT. CRAIG DAVID

I did a teeny tiny bit of revision today, but basically fuck all as I couldn't be arsed. I went round to Next Door Andy's and we had a beer and a cigarette as I helped him pack for skiing tomorrow. I met Psycho Jane tonight and we went to Negociants and drank Baileys and lime.

How did we even come up with such filth? Baileys and lime?! Lime cordial or a slice? Wouldn't it curdle? Why would someone even serve that?

We then went to Frankie's and drank mudslides and a test tube before going to meet the St Felix boys at Oz Bar. It got raided by the police because of all the underage drinking and we had to go home. It was quite funny though. Andy 'Lads Lads Lads'

Burns got carted off by the police for arguing with them and then screamed an 'up the revolution' and punched the air as he got thrown into the back of the police car.

Obnoxious little shit.

NINE

WILLIAM MACLEOD

5TH JULY 2019

Me: What did you think of my intro?

William: It's ok, but you talk too much about what you're like now rather than what you were like then.

Me: I know. I just find it so difficult to objectively say what I was like as a teenager.

William: Fit, provocative and a bit of a bitch.

14TH JANUARY 2001
LISTENING TO 'THERE SHE GOES' BY THE LA'S

I went to Psycho Jane's house last night and her parents were out so we invited loads of people round. It turned into a bit of a party and I texted William Macleod and asked if he wanted to come. I was actually quite excited when he arrived and I then spent most of the night chatting with him, sat on the kitchen floor. He's really quite cute and he made me laugh so much. After everyone left, William stayed behind. We were on the sofa chatting away and watching TV, when we pulled for hours and then he poked me. We talked all night until 8am and he stroked my hair as I rested my head on his chest. I felt so comfortable around him; like I'd already known him my whole life and it felt like he *knew* me. He'd just look at me and I'd think, *Yeah... you get it.*

> *Well, 'poked' is clearly the most disgusting word of the millennium. There is a reason I never felt able to 'poke' someone on Facebook. Ewwwweeeee, it's so gross. It's up there with other literary delights such as 'moist', 'smegma' and 'felching'. My husband and I weren't entirely sure what felching was so we had to google it. I wasn't convinced with his 'Is it not when you wipe your cock on a posh curtain or something after you've had sex?' It is not. Apparently that's 'zuffling' (a surprisingly sweet-sounding word). Where's Andy 'Lads Lads Lads' Burns when you need him?*

After I got home, William was all I could think of. I was completely infatuated. I could still smell his aftershave in my hair and it's left me wanting more! It actually feels like someone is pinning my chest down with a heavy boot when I think of him. In a good way. I want William Macleod in my life.

    Text to William: What would you think if
    I had something going on with you?

What an oddly phrased message.

83

He kept sending really weird texts saying he wasn't sure because he really liked me, but he thought we both fancied other people. So eventually, after getting totally confused with the whole thing, I sent him a text to say:

```
I'm going to make this clear and simple
for your tired little head. Do you want to
go out with me — Yes or No?
```

```
He replied: Yes
```

It was beautiful and simple and my heart leapt.

I spoke to Hannah later on and she told me that William and Gretchen have been friends for years. Noooooooooooooo!!!!!!! Fucking Gretchen?! How do they even know each other?! Fucking Edinburgh. Apparently she's already been saying things like, 'Are you only in it for the sex, William?' and 'You must be getting really desperate now, William.' How have I circled my way back to Gretchen again?! How have I ended up with this 'slut' reputation?! Admittedly yes, what went down with Tom Southall was a bit slutty, but I'm probably the only person who hasn't had sex! Gretchen spreads so many rumours about me it's impossible to keep up with them. I hope William can see past her lies.

18TH JANUARY 2001
LISTENING TO 'AFFIRMATION'
BY SAVAGE GARDEN

I don't think I've ever been so angry in my whole life! I want to smash Gretchen's head in! I've been trying to call William all night, but he's out and Hannah said he's at *her* house. I know what she's up to, and just before I checked myself with my Gretchen paranoia, Hannah told me she's trying to get him to dump me. I fucking knew it! She just wants to have William all to herself, but she'll make out like she's just looking out for poor vulnerable William. The bitch.

Gimme a chance, William. I'm not who she says I am.

Gretchen was probably equally as disappointed to discover William's new girlfriend was yours truly.

```
Text from Gretchen's friend: I heard
you're always meddling with Hannah
and Gretchen. Well you're going to be
spitting teeth for a week by the time
I'm finished with you. Back off or watch
your back.
```

20TH JANUARY 2001
LISTENING TO 'DEMONS' BY
FATBOY SLIM FT. MACY GRAY

I went out with William and his school friends last night. It turns out his best friend is Angus ('You're gay' McDonald's Angus!). I really picked him, didn't I? Gretchen AND Angus?! I'll find out he's Sofia's cousin or something next (he's not, I checked). We went to the Blind Poet and we actually all got on really well. I do wonder if Angus is genuinely gay though. He describes himself as 'mincing this' and 'mincing that' A LOT.

I've been thinking about William all day. Is this what love feels like? It feels different to lust, but then what do I know?! Can you be in love after only a week? Shakespeare certainly seemed to think so and he could be regarded as a bit of an expert on matters of the heart. So I'll go with yes, I am in love. William (Macleod not Shakespeare) is the first thing I think of when I wake up and then when I go to bed all I can hope for is to dream about him. I can imagine my life with him. I know it makes me sound like a world-class psycho, but it doesn't even feel that excessive and I think he feels the same. I do wish I liked him slightly less though cos I'm clearly going to end up so hurt.

23RD JANUARY 2001
LISTENING TO 'LUST FOR LIFE' BY IGGY POP

Finished exams finally! William came babysitting with me and gave me a mix tape. IT'S AMAZING! My lips hurt so much from kissing him all the time. He told me he wants me to stop smoking though. Umm, yeah... ok... sure, whatever, William.

Psycho Jane has stopped speaking to me again. It's exactly the same as before and the whispering has started again. What now?! She's such a capricious little bitch.

28TH JANUARY 2001
LISTENING TO 'VIDEO KILLED THE RADIO STAR' BY BEN FOLDS FIVE

Spent the evening at William's. I can't believe we've been together two weeks already! It feels like years though. I can't get over how much I like him. I'm completely obsessed with the boy. Hannah came round after I got home and apparently Gretchen said she wanted to be friends with me again. I'm super suss, but life is so much easier without her against me.

3RD FEBRUARY 2001
LISTENING TO 'PHILOSOPHY' BY BEN FOLDS FIVE

I went to Hannah's and started drinking with her and Gretchen before we went to the Blind Poet and met William, Angus and the rest of their friends. It was the most hilarious night. I nearly told William I loved him… phew! So glad I didn't, although I think I might (love him not tell him). Angus told me he was bi – AHA! I knew it! Everyone got super drunk and we went to ABBAR. But just when I thought, *This is nice. Everyone's getting on…* I clocked Gretchen all over William! She was sat on his crotch with her breasts in his face and playing with his hair. What is she playing at? Does she like William or is she just fucking with me? I totally lost track of time and then William walked me home and I got home about 2.30am – Mum and Dad were not happy bunnies.

6TH FEBRUARY 2001
LISTENING TO 'SUGARHIGH' BY COYOTE SHIVERS

William came and met me after school and we walked back to mine. I felt a bit smug when the girls saw my *boyfriend* come and pick me up. We spent the evening listening to his mix tape and pulling. I could do this every single night. FOREVER.

9TH FEBRUARY 2001
LISTENING TO 'THE DAY BRINGS' BY BRAD

The Pink Passion Party
Lucy Murphy, William and Angus came for a drink at mine before we went to the ball. William looked so handsome in his kilt. I'll never tire of him. We had the most amazing time once

we got there. Everyone was there, although Mish and Charlie were being weird about me going out with William saying stuff like, 'We just didn't think he was your type, Claire', and 'We're just surprised that you would like someone like *him...*' Well, it seems he is my type and I do bloody well like him, thanks for your concern, boys. If I didn't know better I'd say they were jealous that my attention is off them. But I know better.

I then spent the whole night dancing with William – it was dreamy. I really REALLY love him so much. At the end of the night I decided I was going to tell him I loved him. We were sat at one of the tables and I was sat on his lap. We were quietly watching everyone else and I just felt like the happiest person in the world when he said, 'You know I love you, right, Claire?' I thought I might explode. I just said, 'I love you too', and he held me so tightly. Ohhhh God, this is going to be horrendous when it all goes wrong.

14TH FEBRUARY 2001
LISTENING TO 'IF YOU'RE GONE' BY MATCHBOX 20

I love William. He makes me laugh so much. I could spend the rest of my life laughing and joking with him. I totally get it when people talk about getting a 'warm feeling' when they're with someone. I get that when I'm with William. Just thinking about him makes me smile. He bought me the Matchbox 20 album for Valentine's Day.

I cheated in the RE exam today. I fucking hate RE. I point blank refuse to spend a single second of my time learning any Jesus crap. I just don't want it in my head squeezing something useful out.

I went round to Hannah's house after dinner cos she was so upset. Gretchen had actually beaten her up cos she'd found out about Hannah kissing another girl. She had a huge black eye and a massive bruise across her back. I am finding it more and more difficult to be sympathetic though. Surely she is knowingly entering into this masochistic relationship? I am totally unsurprised by Gretchen's behaviour, so why is Hannah so shocked EVERY TIME? Although it does seem that when it comes to Gretchen, absolutely no one can see what I see.

17TH FEBRUARY 2001
LISTENING TO 'DOLL' BY FOO FIGHTERS

Over one month with William! It feels like forever and he has become my everything. We just spend hours sitting together and listening to music. If we're not together, we're talking on the phone. We never run out of things to say and I could talk to him about nothing for the rest of my life... Weird, but why not? He has become my best friend and I love him more than I ever thought possible.

20TH FEBRUARY 2001
LISTENING TO 'BRICK' BY BEN FOLDS FIVE

AHHH, William and I had a fight last night. He was acting really weird when we were at his friend's house. Apparently I'm different when we're around them and I don't pull him as much. I think I just find PDAs unnecessary and cringey. He apologised afterwards, but things didn't quite feel the same and I felt different when I looked at him. I feel so angry and frustrated. I can't bear the thought of losing him, but I'm also not sure I want to be his girlfriend anymore. Do I fancy him enough? Mish says he's 'punching'. Is he? I wish he'd never said that cos that's how I'm seeing it now. Mish has actually made me love William less... the total fuckhead.

22ND FEBRUARY 2001
LISTENING TO 'LIKE A PRAYER' BY MADONNA

I've been so confused about the whole William thing. We were so happy and I felt so in love, but then people (Psycho Jane, Mish, Hannah, Next Door Andy...) kept saying how I could do better. It got into my head and it was making me see him differently. I was roaringly drunk last night in Frankie's and decided to break up with him. I'm not even sure what made me do it. I suppose I decided I didn't really fancy him and I wanted the freedom to get with other hot guys. Madonna's 'Like a Prayer' came on mid-breakup and it felt all weird and wrong. He was completely heartbroken and staring at the floor.

'But I don't understand. You told me you loved me *yesterday*! How can you change your mind so quickly? I think we're perfect together – you're making a mistake.'

It did not feel good, but as soon as I'd started, it was too late and I felt like I had to follow through. I couldn't exactly just stop and say, 'Oh no, I've changed my mind. Forget I said anything!' Although maybe that's exactly what I should have said. He started crying and walked away, and I ended up running home crying and hysterical. What have I done?! What a fucking disaster.

24TH FEBRUARY 2001
LISTENING TO 'EVAPORATED' BY BEN FOLDS FIVE

I have made a HUGE mistake. I love him. What was I thinking? Was I testing myself? I feel like I've lost my soulmate. I am totally miserable without him. I texted William the lyrics of Foo Fighters' 'Walking After You' but changed some of the words to *I want you back* and waited all night for a reply.

He rang me tonight after my text and I begged him to get back with me. He said he adored me and he knew he could never live up to Yannick, but he wanted to give it another go.

Ohhh yeah. Urghhh, I remember. I'm so embarrassed about this. I had lied to William about having had a whirlwind summer romance with Yannick before losing my virginity to him in a perfect, totally unrealistic Hollywood fashion on a beach one night. Yannick had then represented everything that William believed he could never be. Yannick would always be 'my first' and all William could imagine was this experienced, handsome, older French guy who had swept me off my feet for my first summer of love. I'd lied on our first night together at Psycho Jane's, never thinking that it mattered or that there would be any ramifications. I don't even really know why I lied. It was probably to show off and make myself seem mature and sexy. Who knows.

4TH MARCH 2001
LISTENING TO 'TRY A LITTLE TENDERNESS' BY OTIS REDDING

It was Lucy Murphy's birthday night out at the weekend. We got ready at hers and bloody Sofia was there. I think she's finally realised that I couldn't give a shit about her anymore, so she's almost given up on giving me a hard time. She was wearing the shortest skirt I have ever seen and yet had the gaul to cough a 'slut' at me when we were getting dressed. I just laughed at her.

'Thanks for your concern, but as long as you're nearby, I'm confident I'll never be the biggest slut in the room. I'm not sure if you are in fact going for the whore look tonight, but if so then very well done, Sofia, you look like trash.'

She just snarled a 'fuck off'.

It feels great not to care about her anymore. She can't hurt me!

We went out to Frankie's and I got totally whammied. I then made the most stupid mistake ever: I kissed a guy called Doug. He was at the bar and when I was ordering drinks, he came up and offered me a fag and a drink. He kept saying I was 'really fit' and then when he moved in to kiss me, I just didn't pull away. He was really hot! I regretted it as soon as I'd done it. What was I thinking?!

I spoke to William when I got home and although I wanted to be honest with him, I was afraid that if I was, he'd break up with me and I couldn't bear to lose him again. Unfortunately a few people saw and told William about it today. He called me up really upset and I had to deny it. I got 'upset' that he'd think that of me. I wish I'd just told him now, but I thought it would crush him. I also thought I'd lie and it would then just fizzle out and I'd learn my lesson.

7TH MARCH 2001
LISTENING TO 'DANCING WITH MYSELF' BY BILLY IDOL

ARGHHHHHHH, this 'Doug Guy' thing has become such a huge deal now. Because William chose to believe me despite his friends telling him I'm definitely lying, he has now fallen out with them over it. They're furious with me cos I've essentially made him ho before bro. They can't believe William believes me and neither can I if I'm honest. Why would tonnes of people make up a story about me snogging some guy? Ahhhhh – I'm a monster and I'm now having to play the poor persecuted victim. Fuck. What a mess. I've made my bed of lies and now have to sleep in my filthy, cheating whore sheets. I feel so guilty, but I can't tell him now as it has completely spun out of control. William is the only person who believes me. I feel terrible. Gretchen seems to spend most of her free time now sending me MSN chats saying I'm a dirty slapper and I'm just taking William for a ride. Argh, she's so right.

TEN

FIRST TIME

18TH MARCH 2001
LISTENING TO 'WONDERFUL' BY EVERCLEAR

I drew a very good picture of some onions in art yesterday. Onions are pretty tricky. I'm not sure if I want to be an artist or a doctor, but I probably need to work a lot harder if I want to get into medicine.

I went out with William and Angus to the Blind Poet and drank long vodkas before William and I went back to mine and watched *Return to Paradise*. It was such a sad film. He saw me bawling my eyes out with snot and everything!

23RD MARCH 2001
LISTENING TO 'KRYPTONITE' BY 3 DOORS DOWN

I'm having the shittiest time at school. Everyone is just calling me 'slut' for cheating on William with 'Doug Guy'. Sofia is having a fucking field day. Luckily, I usually meet up with Hannah or William after school, which makes things better. I can't wait to start at St Felix's after exams and leave all these bitches behind. I had the house to myself all night, so I spent hours on the phone to William and had a fag in the kitchen.

Such a badass.

26TH MARCH 2001
LISTENING TO 'KATE' BY BEN FOLDS FIVE

All I can think about is shagging William. I wonder if it'll happen soon.

30TH MARCH 2001
LISTENING TO 'TINY DANCER' BY ELTON JOHN

Got some new FCUK trousers with my mum today. They are so cool.

Psycho Jane and I went out with William and his friends to Negociants tonight. They still all hate me cos of the whole 'Doug Guy' thing. Angus is the only one that's civil with me. Jane obviously doesn't have my back and I heard her tell William he should 'watch himself' with me.

2ND APRIL 2001
LISTENING TO 'TEENAGE ANGST' BY PLACEBO

I went to William's today, but he had to revise so I watched *Road Trip* and had lunch with his mum. It was actually a really nice afternoon. Then I went into town, bought the Foo Fighters CD and a really cool silver choker.

9TH APRIL 2001
LISTENING TO 'HIGH' BY FEEDER

I went to Glasgow with Hannah and her mum and we went to see Feeder at the Barrowlands. It was FUCKING AMAZING! I love Feeder. I rang William when they played 'High' so he could listen down the phone cos that was the first track on the first mix tape he ever made me.

12TH APRIL 2001
LISTENING TO 'NEXT YEAR' BY FOO FIGHTERS

I spent the entire day sat upstairs in Costa smoking with Hannah.

Outcome: I think I'm ready to have sex with William.

Mum and I went to get my new phone, a Siemens C35.

14TH APRIL 2001
LISTENING TO 'SHINING LIGHT' BY ASH

William and I had the most incredible night together at our friend's house. We had sex for the first time – TWICE! We stayed in her brother's room and it was a little awkward because we were on the bottom bunk so whoever was on top kept hitting their head on the wooden slats from the top bunk. The Batman bed sheets weren't exactly what I'd envisioned for my first time either, but it was amazing and perfect. It was both our first times, although he thought it wasn't mine cos of my STUPID STUPID lies. The lie has gone too far for me to tell him the truth. I wish I could have told him it was as special to me as it was for him. No more lies. When did I become such a liar?

This actually haunted me for years and I contacted him thirteen years later (a few weeks before my wedding) to confess. I felt the overwhelming selfish need to get married with a clean slate so I just called him through Facebook Messenger and spat it out.

'It was my first time too... errr... I just wanted you to know that it meant as much to me as it did to you.'

'What?! That's random. Why did you lie?'

'I was fifteen and I was a dick. Sorry.'

He was clearly a little confused by my first contact in over a decade and not particularly a) impressed with my lies, b) enamoured with me calling out the blue with a sudden need to offload my adolescent guilt.

'Err, ok. You sound so English now...'

Ouch. Touché. The words no Scot ever wants to hear.

22ND APRIL 2001
LISTENING TO 'BLACK & WHITE PEOPLE' BY MATCHBOX 20

William had a party last night. His friends still hate me and I can't say I blame them. They're constantly telling William I cheated on him with 'Doug Guy' and I feel obliged to stick to my story. It's exhausting. I'm such a cheating, lying bitch! We all pretend it's fine when Will's around and then as soon as he's out the room they either totally ignore me or cough things like 'whorebag' or 'slut' and all laugh. It's so horrible. I wish I'd never snogged that bloody 'Doug Guy'. Psycho Jane also gave me a hard time about 'Doug Guy' and said I should tell William. It's too late now! Why can't we just let it go? I'm pretty sure Jane snogged a random last night too and she's still with Dan Jeffries. The fucking hypocrite. I told William I loved him again last night. I haven't said it since we got back together. I just wish it could be the two of us. We'd be so happy if there was no one else around.

24TH APRIL 2001
LISTENING TO 'FIT BOY + FAINT GIRL'
BY 3 COLOURS RED

I hate St Catherine's so much. Two girls from the year above who I hardly know came into my class and gave me a bollocking for 'cheating on lovely Will'. They told me that if I ever hurt him again, they would 'fuck me up till I was eating through a straw'. Then they pushed me really hard against the lockers and spat on me. No one said anything. Psycho Jane looked like she was smiling and Sofia just sat there grinning. How am I reliving this nightmare again and again? Although I guess this is my fault this time. I couldn't stand to stay in school another second longer so I went home with a 'headache'. Not a complete lie, just a slight exaggeration. William brought me Maltesers after school to cheer me up. My dad is super suss about my 'headache'.

Having a lawyer and a teacher as parents was basically like living with the world's best human lie detectors. My dad wasn't 'suss', he knew EVERYTHING.

30TH APRIL 2001
LISTENING TO 'MONKEY WRENCH'
BY FOO FIGHTERS

> Got a delightful text from Tom Southall:
> What the fuck do you think you're playing
> at? Just had to meet with headmaster about
> drugs. I know it was you — did you tell
> your mum? Just fuck off. Ps. You're fucking
> scum for what you did to William.

How nice. Why am I always enemy number one? What business would I have telling my mum that Tom's doing loads of drugs. EVEN if I did (which I didn't!) she would never tell the headmaster cos she likes Tom and hates the headmaster.

William and I had a huge fight cos he got all weird asking if sex was different/better with Yannick and did I like him more… blah blah blah. Argh, it's so annoying. I told him I loved *him* and to leave it, but it really pissed me off. This insecurity is not sexy. I wonder if I made a mistake getting back with him. I'd have to be extra sure this time. There are no third chances. God, if I dumped William again, I really would become Edinburgh's most hated person. If I think things are bad now…

1ST MAY 2001
LISTENING TO 'WALKING AFTER YOU'
BY FOO FIGHTERS

> Email from William:
>
> Hey Claire,
>   I sent you a text this morning to say

99

sorry but no reply. I'm so sorry about yesterday and getting jealous about the whole Yannick thing. It just majorly gets to me when it really shouldn't. I ran out of school so I could write you this email. I'm sitting in Costa now and have spent £1 on 20 mins — what a bargain! I'm listening to walking after you which always makes me think of you. If we ever break up, I don't think I'll ever be able to listen to any music as everything reminds me of you! I know you hate this cheesy bullshit and I'm not surprised, it's quite dire but hey I'm that sort of guy. I love you Claire and when you said it to my face you made me the happiest guy in the world. It's all I ever want. I suppose these fights come from insecurity but sometimes I feel like you only want to go out with me because you can't be friends with me. Sometimes I think you don't love me like I do you. I can't imagine losing you and I wish I didn't need reassurance from you cos I know you hate it and I'm probably pushing you away. I know you liked Yannick and I can't do anything about that. I have loved finding out what you're really like. You're nothing like what you show the world. I wish everyone could see what I see. You're the most caring, funny and beautiful woman I know and you're my girlfriend. That's all I need. That was all i wanted to say. I love you Claire, even through these fights. Love

you more than you could possibly imagine.
William xx

2ND MAY 2001
LISTENING TO 'YOU'RE MY EVERGREEN' BY FEEDER

5pm: I think William's right. Am I just going out with him because I would lose him completely if I broke up with him? Does he love me more than I do, him? I feel like I should like him more. But then, surely it can't always feel the same as the beginning. Maybe this is normal? It's killing me because I really want to, but I just don't think I fancy him enough. But I do love him. I think.

11pm: I went babysitting tonight and William came with me. I tried to explain how I felt, but we started fighting and before I knew it he was banging on about Yannick again and we broke up. Unbelievably, Madonna's 'Like a FUCKING Prayer' came on... AGAIN! That bloody song! He was totally devastated and kept telling me we were soulmates and I was making a mistake. We were both crying when he left. I feel so horrible. I wasn't even sure I did want to end it, but it's done now and I can never go back.

4TH MAY 2001
LISTENING TO 'BED OF LIES' BY MATCHBOX 20

I sent William loads of texts telling him how much I miss him as a friend and I begged him to be friends cos we got on so well. Can't we be soulMATES?

Text from William: Yes ok but you have to
know that I still love you.

ELEVEN
SPRING 2001

6TH MAY 2001
LISTENING TO 'THE KIDS AREN'T ALRIGHT'
BY THE OFFSPRING

Next Door Andy and I have become pretty good friends over the last few months. He just lives with his dad now cos his mum died when he was younger. He pretends he's a massive player, but he's sweet really. He has these 'parties' every Friday night in his basement before heading into town. Some of his friends are really hot. He always invites me and then pretends I'm stalking him when I turn up. He's all like, 'Urgghhh, Claire again! She won't leave me alone… You might as well come in and join us now you're here.' I don't mind. I find it quite funny and his friends know what he's like. They seem quite happy to have me there, even though it's supposed to be boys only.

We've just spent the whole day together, chatting up on his roof. Next Door Andy is proving to be a very restorative tonic. He says I'm the first friend he's ever had that's a girl. It's so nice to just chill out with someone who doesn't give a shit about 'Doug Guy' or William. When I told him, his reaction was mainly, 'aaand…? I don't get it. So fucking what, Claire? So you drunkenly snogged this "Doug Guy" forever ago and have since broken up with Big Willy (his name not mine!) anyway. My God, you love drama! It's so boring.' I love him for not caring. But I do not love drama!

17TH MAY 2001
LISTENING TO 'IT WASN'T ME' BY SHAGGY

I spent the day with Maggie in Costa today. It was wonderful having her to myself without Gretchen for a change. She told me that she's moving to St Felix's after the summer too! I'm so excited that we'll be at school together. I can't wait to leave the St Catherine's snake pit. Plus William will be there for one year before he goes to uni. YAAAY!

18TH MAY 2001
LISTENING TO 'ALL THE SMALL THINGS' BY BLINK-182

NOOOOOOOOOOOOOOOO!!!! I feel like my life has just imploded. GRETCHEN is coming to St Felix's too!!! I thought she couldn't possibly make my life worse, but now we're going to be at school together? Shit. In the whole of Edinburgh she's moving schools to go to the same fucking school as I'm moving to. I can't believe it. I'm basically upgrading Sofia for Gretchen Bully 2.0. Fuck fuck fuck fuck fuck.

20TH MAY 2001
LISTENING TO 'ARMATAGE SHANKS'
BY GREEN DAY

I got really jealous today when I found out William went to the football with Gretchen. I know I have no right but I just HATE her so much.

22ND MAY 2001
LISTENING TO 'CHASING RAINBOWS'
BY NO USE FOR A NAME

I had a day off in between exams today. It was a really hot day and I invited William round for lunch. We were initially just messing about in my room, but things escalated pretty quick... It had started off as him jokingly trying to find my diary, but then I was straddling him... and then kissing him... and he was so hard... and we ended up having sex. Goddamnit, Claire, keep it in your pants! But it was incredible. It just felt so illicit and passionate. I spent the rest of the day lazing in the sun and doing chemistry revision. I know I'm sending him the wrong message. I hope he doesn't think that we're going to get back together. I just have such strong feelings for him; I'm so confused. I've dumped him twice now, I couldn't possibly do it again. I should really learn my bloody lesson and leave him alone!

26TH MAY 2001
LISTENING TO 'A LITTLE RESPECT' BY WHEATUS

Arrgghhh! Slept with William again. I was revising at home and William came round for lunch. It almost seemed to start off like a dare and then we were both, like, 'fuck it'.

30TH MAY 2001
LISTENING TO 'SOMETIMES' BY NINE DAYS

I was chilling at Psycho Jane's tonight with Dan Jeffries and his friends. Jane and Dan were getting really stoned, which is 'their thing' now apparently. Whatever. I hope my thing isn't ever drugs. I had a bit, which was fun, but then I got a message from William which ruined everything and sent me into a complete tailspin.

> Text from William: Claire I'm so sorry. I can't be friends with you anymore. It just hurts too much.

I was so upset I got three buses from Jane's house to his in the pouring rain. I worked myself up into a complete frenzy the whole way there that by the time he opened the door I was so distraught, I just screamed, 'Well, goodbye then!' and then stormed off.

Daaaarrrraaaaammmma! (Fetches popcorn)

He chased after me and said that he just loved me too much and although he did still want to be friends, he needed some time to try and get over me. He also said Psycho Jane told him I definitely had pulled 'Doug Guy' so he didn't know if he could still believe me about that. Oh, do piss off, Jane, you maniac. She really is the world's worst friend.

5TH JUNE 2001
LISTENING TO 'DND' BY SEMISONIC

I asked William round tonight to try and make peace and prove we are good friends and there doesn't always need to be high drama between us. Obviously the opposite happened. It was the most disastrous outcome and karma took a great big shit on my head. We were just hanging out in my room listening to music when I went to the toilet. When I got back he was just sat there with a face I have never seen before and he was visibly shaking. It was quite frightening actually and I nearly laughed, I felt so uncomfortable. He was just silently staring at me with the angriest expression when I saw the open diary next to him on the bed. Ohhhhh fuck. William read my diary. He found out that I definitely had pulled 'Doug Guy' and God knows what else. It all dawned on me and he whispered the most menacing 'I hate you so much'. I don't blame him. There was nothing I could say to him and he left.

13TH JUNE 2001
LISTENING TO 'TEENAGE DIRTBAG' BY WHEATUS

I've just spent the last week bombarding William with apologies. I really really really am so sorry. I am a bit relieved that it's all out in the open now though. He's obviously mostly annoyed that I lied and he fell out with his friends for me rather than the actual snog itself, especially as we're not even together anymore. The thing is I am miserable when he's not in my life. He is my best friend and I need him. I went round to his last night and told him I would do anything to get him back as a friend. He eventually let me through the door and we spent hours talking it through. I had to do some serious begging and grovelling, but William and I are friends again! He told me it wasn't fair on him though, cos he still loved me and he found it too hard to cut me out of his life, which is what he should do.

He's here now and we're singing Wheatus' 'Teenage Dirtbag' together. I'm so lucky to have him in my life.

I was so selfish. William needed to not be with me. We were toxic together and if we could have seen the future we would have cut ties before things just got uglier and uglier.

18TH JUNE 2001
LISTENING TO 'NOT YOUR SAVIOUR' BY NO USE FOR A NAME

William is driving me completely mad. We were all out last night at Siglo's and the second William arrived he told Angus and me that he'd just pulled and got a BJ off of a FORTY-year-old that used to be a stripper!

Ha. Well, that's clearly a complete fabrication!

I was so upset and angry at him for being so disgusting. I wanted to cause him pain and I wanted to watch him suffer. I literally just walked onto the dancefloor, looked around and grabbed a random guy and started pulling him in front of William. It made him cry, but I don't care. He stared at me with tears rolling down his cheeks and I just laughed at him.

Wow. What a horrible, HORRIBLE person I was (am?!). I have absolutely no recollection whatsoever of this night and in a way, I wish it had remained that way. I don't want to think of myself like this. THAT CAN'T BE ME! These are the words of a cold and heartless sociopath.

We both left, arguing like crazy, but he still walked me home. I think we both just keep going thinking things will eventually resolve themselves and we'll live happily ever after. This is our love story, I guess. But we just end up hating each other even more with every minute we're together. He kept banging on about what a bitch I had been for cheating on him and compulsively lying and how I basically treated him like one big pile of shit. God knows what I was saying, but it was probably more indecisive I love you/I don't love you bollocks.

I feel like I cause all of our arguments. I get so jealous whenever he is with anyone but me. I want to spend all my time with him, but I don't think I want to be *with* him. I want him all to myself, but know that's not possible if I'm not willing to be his girlfriend. I know I'm being a selfish bitch, but I don't know what to do. He turns me into a crazy person and I can't control it. I just Hulk out. The obvious solution would be to stop seeing him, but then I can't stand to be without him. Arrrrghhhhhh. When we finally got to mine he sighed and took my hand. He looked so sad and so tired. Oh God, I've done this to him. I made the happy man sad.

'I think the problem is, Claire, that we both still love each other.'

'Maybe. But it doesn't work and so I think we both just need to get used to not belonging to each other anymore. I do love you, but I'm not sure it's in that way.'

'Friends then still, I guess?'

I nodded and smiled and gave him a huge hug. What I wouldn't give to love him like *that*. I know that I should let him go, but I can't.

21ST JUNE 2001
LISTENING TO 'BAT OUT OF HELL' BY MEATLOAF

4am: I went to The Globe with Next Door Andy and his friends tonight. It was so nice to be out without William for a change.

Psycho Jane came too. She basically spent the whole evening slagging me off 'in a jokey way' and showing off in front of all the guys. One of Andy's friends, Mike, is soooo hot... Hot Mike, I might call him. I told Jane I'd always quite liked him and she walked straight up to him and started pulling him. Unbelievable! What's her feckin' problem? I decided then and there that that was Psycho Jane's final friendship straw. She is an absolutely terrible friend to me and I just haven't got time for it anymore. Fuck her.

Hot Mike then offered to walk *me* home. Screw you, Jane, you fucking psycho! We chatted all the way home and then I said goodnight when we were standing outside mine. I turned to walk away when he grabbed my hand and said, 'Wait...' He was staring into my eyes so intently and said he'd always liked me and would I go out with him? I had to pick my shocked jaw off the pavement. Hot Mike likes me? I was totally elated and we pulled. I felt like he'd just swept me off my feet. I told him I'd always quite liked him too, but I wasn't sure about going out yet as he had only just pulled Psycho Jane. Plus, I was still reeling from William, and going straight into a boyfriend/girlfriend situation with Hot Mike felt a bit much. He said he understood and that he'd wait for me and 'prove himself' to me. It felt really full on, but I loved it so I invited him in to watch a film. We were on the sofa pulling loads and before I knew it, I gave him a BJ! I can't believe I did that! WHAT A SLUT! He left saying he'd call first thing and that he hoped I would say yes to being his girlfriend. I'm in bed now all giddy and excited. Shouldn't have blown him though; that was totally unnecessary. I texted him after he left.

Text to Hot Mike: Goodnight Mike. Thanks for walking me home. Speak tomoz x

21ST JUNE 2001
LISTENING TO 'BORN TO RUN'
BY BRUCE SPRINGSTEEN

4pm: Hot Mike still hasn't replied. I waited all day for him to call and nothing. My God he's hot and he's got such a calming presence, which I feel I probably need. Next Door Andy told me he was the 1st 15 rugby captain at his school and he can never normally 'be arsed with girls'. He said that I was kidding myself that anything could happen. Urgh, he's so right. Someone like Hot Mike would never be interested in me, but what about the whole 'I'll wait for you… I'll prove myself to you…'? Hmmm, writing it now makes it somehow seem totally ridiculous and implausible.

22ND JUNE 2001
LISTENING TO 'BLINDED BY THE LIGHT'
BY MANFRED MANN'S EARTH BAND

First Day at St Felix's!
So long, Jane, you fucking psychopath! Ciao, Sofia, you mega-bitch. Although, hello, Gretchen…

I was shitting bricks about today, but it was totally fine. Everyone was really friendly and welcoming. It was awesome to be able to hang out with Maggie and William on a school day.

```
Hot Mike eventually texted back: Sorry
for being a wanker. I hate myself.
```

Bit weird, but fuck him, he's not worth it. Hot Mike (more like Dickhead Mike) had clearly just spouted all that crap, got himself a BJ and then cut his losses. Well, I hate you too, Dickhead Mike. I can't believe I just lapped it up... and him... ewwwwwwww!

(Ouff, thank fuck no one's ever going to read this.)

25TH JUNE 2001
LISTENING TO 'SWEAT (A LA LA LA LA LONG)' BY INNER CIRCLE

I love my new school so so much. It feels like I can breathe and relax for the first time in years. Gretchen and I have pretty much kept ourselves to ourselves so no issues there (so far). I'm making new friends and it's pretty cool to be able to chill with Mish and Charlie again too. Mish wants to be a doctor too, so we're going to be in a lot of the same classes. I can't believe I wasted so much of my life being miserable at St Catherine's. I laugh in the face of anyone who says, 'The best days of your life are at school.' I bloody well hope mine aren't.

They absolutely weren't.

27TH JUNE 2001
LISTENING TO 'BROWN EYED GIRL' BY VAN MORRISON

Lucy had a surprise leaving party for me at her house with all the popular St Catherine's girls who hate me. Even fucking Sofia was there. Although she'll probably celebrate more than most that I'm leaving, so I suppose in a way, it makes sense that she'd be there to raise a glass to my departure. We went into town afterwards, but it was so shit I went home at 9.30pm and spent the rest of the night on the phone to William. These girls don't like me and I really don't like them. God knows why they threw me a leaving party.

Now I think about it, I suspect Lucy's mum may have played a part in this.

29TH JUNE 2001
LISTENING TO 'PIANO MAN' BY BILLY JOEL

I went to William's tonight and we spent the whole night chatting and watching films. I feel really weird about going to France and not seeing him for so long. I'm mostly worried that I'll be out of sight, out of mind and he'll get a new girlfriend and forget all about me. There's no way we'll be able to be this close if he's with someone else. I don't think we've been more than a few days without seeing each other for the last six months, and most days I probably wouldn't go a couple of hours without speaking to him. He's more than just a friend to me. He's (almost!) everything to me. I spent the night at his and we just cuddled in his bed. I'm pretty sure he whispered an 'I love you' when he thought I was asleep. Do I love him too? Definitely a bit.

TWELVE
SEXY LAURENT

9TH JULY 2001
LISTENING TO 'AS COLD AS ICE' BY M.O.P.

Well, here I am again, stuck in my French goldfish bowl. I spent most of the day sunbathing and reading. Chloe and I invented a game in the pool called Aquagolo and played that for the rest of the day. It was kinda fun, but I miss William. I feel so exposed without him, and the thought of not seeing him for nearly six weeks makes me well up. Everything's going to change and he won't be mine anymore. I can't bear it.

```
Letter to William:

Hey Will!
    It's my first day here and it feels like
I'm dying cos I'm not with you. It's only
```

now we're apart, that I realise how much time we actually spent together. My life totally revolved around you and whatever happens that's never going to change. I was crying last night listening to Brick and Evaporated cos all they do is remind me so much of you. All I wish for is that you were here with me, stroking my hair and kissing me and holding me. Oh god this is so horrible I just want to hear your voice so badly. I don't think this is going to be a long letter cos the thought of being apart from you is tearing me apart. I had a dream last night that I was back in Edinburgh with you and all we did was hug. It was so nice and comforting that I felt so hopelessly alone when I woke up.

Don't forget that whatever happens in France you'll always be my number one guy!

I'll probably still be thinking of you the day of my wedding. I'll be walking down the aisle thinking I care more about you than I do my future hubby!

Missing you beyond belief.

Love you so much,

Claire

Oh sweet Jesus. NO ONE should ever have to read a love letter they wrote when they were fifteen. Thank you to William for keeping these papery torture weapons... all thirty-nine of them.

11TH JULY 2001
LISTENING TO 'NEW WAY HOME'
BY FOO FIGHTERS

William is the only thing on my mind. I miss him so fucking much. I just want to hug him forever. I spoke to him last night and he admitted that he still loved me. I love him too (but obviously didn't say anything). He told me that he pulled a girl called Fiona and the thought makes me want to be physically sick. I always want to be 'his girl'. Why do I care so much? I dumped him. TWICE. Ahhhhhh, I just keep having images of him stroking her hair and kissing her head like he did to me. I'm going to cry.

```
Text from William: I am missing you so
much. You're so special to me. I love you
so much it drives me mad. I keep having
images of you coming back and me holding
you and never letting go. Don't change or
forget me. I think of you before I go to
sleep and when I wake up. I can't help
thinking about what things would be like
if we went out again. Please don't change
your feelings for me. Everything you do,
I can't help but love.
```

14TH JULY 2001

```
Letter to William:

William (My Thin Jabba!)
    It's been a week without you already
and it has been unbearable. I miss you so
```

much and my life seems so boring without you. I've been thinking a lot about our friendship since I've been away. I know that it isn't an ordinary 'best friends' thing but I never want that to change. I feel closer to you now than I ever did. Can you believe it's been 7 months since that first night at Jane's?! I have to admit that they have been the best 7 months of my entire life! I feel more comfortable and at ease with you than anyone I've ever met! I would spend every second of the day with you if I could.

I love you so much and I think I've realised what kind of love it is. It's the strangest kind of love and there is no possible way I could love you more than I do but I don't FANCY you. But the love is stronger than it was when we went out although I realise how strange that may sound.

I think about you all the time and I will never in a zillion years forget you.

I can't wait to see you again.

Love you loads 'n' loads,

Claire x

17TH JULY 2001
LISTENING TO 'ANGEL' BY SHAGGY FT. RAYVON

I wrote William a letter telling him I still loved him, but was confused by the kind of love. I want him, but I don't *want* him.

Lilly, my cousin, and I walked to the village so I could have a cigarette and post my letter. After I sent it, I realised that all William is going to see is 'I love you'. I shouldn't have sent it. Shit.

We stopped at the café and met three guys and a girl called Marie. We sat with them for a bit and Marie invited us to a party she was having tonight. I can't believe I've made friends! I'm so happy! There were loads of people at the party including a guy called Laurent who is super sexy and majorly cute.

Good God, I hate me. Selfish, fickle, shameless teenage me. I love William. I fancy Hot Mike. No no, definitely William. Ooooohhh Sexy Laurent…

18TH JULY 2001
LISTENING TO 'RENDEZ-VU' BY BASEMENT JAXX

It's raining and I hate this shithole. I went to Marie's flat and watched films with the group today. Laurent is so unbelievably sexy – I can't stop looking at him. I don't think he's interested though and he only stayed a little bit and then just left without even saying bye. I think he might be quite shy as he hasn't spoken to me directly yet.

20TH JULY 2001
LISTENING TO 'HELP!' BY THE BEATLES

I went down to Nice with Marie, Sexy Laurent and two of their friends tonight. We bought some rum punch and drank it on the beach. It should have been awesome… drinking on the beach with my new friends in the South of France, but I was sooooo bored. We have NOTHING in common. I'd decided that I was

117

going to try and pull Sexy Laurent tonight. I'm desperate to try and end this William-related pain and I reckon a Sexy Laurent pull is just the ticket! At the end of the night we went back to Marie's and watched a film. I was relieved that we didn't need to chat anymore... what a boring lot! Oh man, I feel so bitchie writing that down. Friendless beggars can't be choosers and all that. Thank goodness I could stare at Sexy Laurent when I got bored (which is all the time). I was desperate to get him on his own so I asked him to walk me home at the end of the night. He flashed me the best smile, stood up, took my hand and said, 'Avec plaisir, mademoiselle l'Écossaise!' It was cute, but the walk home was hell. It was excruciating trying to get him to talk – total opposite of William who never shuts up, and it made me realise how much I'd rather be with William. I wished he was walking me home... I miss that stupid buttface. Sexy Laurent definitely seemed interested though and there was an expectant pause when we got to mine. He just lingered after 'bonne nuit'. I did think about pulling him, but weirdly went off the idea and just said bye.

Aha! I knew I wasn't always a total scumbag!

I'm lying in bed now and my chest hurts, I miss William so much. Wouldn't life be wonderful if I'd never met him? I wouldn't feel so sick when apart from him. Every song wouldn't be tainted with painful memories of when things were good. I would just happily live my life, never knowing what I was missing.

21ST JULY 2001
LISTENING TO 'PORCELAIN' BY MOBY

Sexy Laurent rang early this morning and asked if I wanted to go out with him for the day. I was beyond excited. We cruised round the hills on his scooter and he pulled me when we were having a picnic. It was so unbelievably romantic!

Oh, the danger! THE DANGER. On the back of a seventeen-year-old boy's scooter round the hairpin bends and narrow cliff-top roads of the South of France. The thought makes me shudder. Health and safety hadn't worked its way up to these remote, vertiginous villages yet (where it arguably should have started) and there was nothing stopping you from coming round a bend and driving off the side of the road, straight into the abyss.

23RD JULY 2001
LISTENING TO 'MAXWELL'S SILVER HAMMER' BY THE BEATLES

Last night was so cool. Sexy Laurent picked me up on his 'scoot' and we rode down to Nice and then all the way round to Villefranche. We sat on the beach, listened to the waves and looked up at the stars. He never once tried anything more than a kiss. It's probably better that way though cos any more and I would probably feel like I was betraying William. I know it's stupid as we're supposed to just be friends and he would never know, but I find it so hard being with someone else. Tomorrow's my last day with Sexy Laurent before I go to Brittany anyway. Sexy Laurent is probably not going to be one of my life's great loves. He's bloody lovely to look at though.

Text from William: Have you realised what you want now? I got your letter. We could make it work. We've both learnt more about each other now. If I met you in 10 years time you would be the one I would marry. You would be happy with me. As much as you think we wouldn't work — we could. I've decided never to give up on you. I love you and I can see us being so happy together. You will never find anyone who loves you as much as I do.

THIRTEEN

GAEL

25TH JULY 2001
LISTENING TO 'CALIFORNICATION'
BY RED HOT CHILI PEPPERS

As soon as I got to Brittany I went to meet up with 'Les Marseillais' (Ben and Seb), Marc, François and the twins. I was so happy to see them all again! We had a quick catch up, Pastis, fag and then bed. I can't wait until tomorrow when I see everyone on the beach!

26TH JULY 2001
LISTENING TO 'UP IN ARMS' BY FOO FIGHTERS

I couldn't sleep all night I was so excited about seeing the gang. Here I come, summer, brace yourself! I went straight to the beach and there they all were. There's a new girl called Yasmine and she's going out with Yannick now (who is still so stupidly hot!). She's half French/half Mexican and she is just the life and bloody soul of every party. I don't like her. I played volleyball all day – my wrists are so bruised.

I spent the evening drinking rum with François on the beach. We talked about everything and I spoke to him about my mixed feelings about William. He told me I was being a wanker and I should let William go.

Drinking rum with François is still one of my favourite things to do.

When I got home I called William and I told him we weren't ever going to get back together. He shouted at me, saying I'd been leading him on and I've just ruined the last six months of his life. Urgh, he's right. All I could say was, 'I'm sorry', and now I'm lying in bed feeling awful. I really am sorry. I just feel like we're going through *Groundhog Day*, breaking up over and over again. It's so painful.

27TH JULY 2001
LISTENING TO 'PARALLEL UNIVERSE' BY RED HOT CHILI PEPPERS

About forty of us went camping on the island last night and it was mental! I got a bit drunk and stoned and then literally fell over this guy in the dark who was half in and out of his tent. He's called Gael and he's childhood friends with Yannick, Marc and François. He's got crazy blonde, curly hair and works at L'école de Voile in Saint-Lunaire. He's sooo gorgeous. I spent the whole rest of the night chatting and drinking with him until the sun came up when he kissed me. It felt new and exciting and I forgot all about William.

Gael spent so much time on the water, his nose was a brown-y, pinkish colour and the rest of his face was a constant battle between the fair man's freckle and the seaman's tan. He wore wrap-around Oakley sunglasses and his hair was a mass of ringlets, bleached white from months of sun and sea. I don't think he ever cared much about how he dressed and he was usually sporting an old regatta or sailing club T-shirt. He was so unlike Edinburgh's posh, image-obsessed urbanites that I succumbed to his outdoorsy, coastal charm immediately. Gael was Brittany through and through. He listened to weird French Celtic folk music, loved a drink, hated the Parisians and tasted of salt. Gael was only ever truly happy when at sea. He had an excitable (and sometimes exhausting) energy about him, but the second he got on a boat, you'd watch him take a big gulp of briny air as a peacefulness washed over him. It felt like such a privilege to witness this intimate moment between Gael and the ocean.

What happened with Gael marked the point in my life when I realised that I may actually be loveable. William could have been a fluke, but TWO people loved me. Everything in me changed after Gael.

28TH JULY 2001
LISTENING TO 'DUMPWEED' BY BLINK-182

I spent the whole day on the beach with Gael. He asked if I wanted to be his girlfriend. Ummm... Yes I do! Everyone said we were cute together.

31ST JULY 2001
LISTENING TO 'OTHERSIDE'
BY RED HOT CHILI PEPPERS

I spent the day on the beach playing volleyball with Yannick, Marc, François and Les Marseillais. I convinced my mum to let me go out clubbing with no curfew tonight. I explained to her that I wouldn't be able to go at all if I had a curfew cos no one was going to leave early to drive me home, so she agreed! WOOP! It was Gael's eighteenth and we went to this amazing club that we needed to get a boat to. It was a huge wooden chalet-type building on a beach, lit only by millions of fairy lights. I danced all night with Gael; I'm really beginning to like him a lot. I wish I didn't have to keep pretending I was sixteen though. It's getting a bit complicated when talking about driving tests and exams. A lot of things are 'different *en Ecosse*'.

1ST AUGUST 2001
LISTENING TO 'A WOMAN'S WORTH'
BY ALICIA KEYS

I feel like I'm falling in love. Actual LOVE. Real, heart-shattering, world-rocking, skin-tingling, mind-bending love.

Here we go...

4TH AUGUST 2001
LISTENING TO 'TEARDROP' BY MASSIVE ATTACK

It's been about a week since I met Gael and I have never been more in love. Last night we all went to Mattie's house for a party.

Mattie is Marc's new girlfriend and she seems really sweet, but like all of Marc's girlfriends, a bit loopy. I'm half expecting her to snap and start gnawing on a chair leg whilst singing 'La Marseillaise'. *Crazy* crazy as opposed to Psycho Jane or Gretchen crazy. Her parents are away for ten days and they just left her... so lucky! They have this INSANE beachside property near Saint-Briac. She had about twelve of us over and we had a BBQ and got totally trollied. After dinner, she was just wandering around clutching a bottle of vodka in one hand and a spliff in the other with her tits out. Everyone just carried on enjoying the night and pretending like we hadn't noticed. Very strange...

Gael and I were playing drinking games with Marc and there was a moment when Gael laughed, put his arm around me and kissed the top of my head that I realised that I'd totally fallen in love with him. I wanted to stop it. I'd only just stopped hurting from William and I was infatuated all over again. Gael and I went to bed and left Yannick plaiting Ben's hair down in the kitchen as they sang Chilis hits over a bottle of rum. I reckon the thought of them like that will always make me smile. A beautiful memory. Click. I'm going to need these memories when I'm back in Edinburgh and everything and everyone is grey and bitchie.

Gael and I had a room to ourselves and we were fooling around when he asked if I was ready. It absolutely felt right and we slept together. It was sooo different to William. Totally incomparable. I was having a fag out the window later when Gael suddenly said, '*Je t'aime*.' I was so happy I smiled at him and got back into bed, but weirdly didn't say it back. What is my beef with saying, 'I love you'? I willed myself to take another mental snapshot of the moment and hopefully remember it forever... how the warm sea air smelt through the open window... how the night sky looked... the moon's reflection on the sea... how Gael looked in bed half covered with a white bed sheet. Click.

THE DIARY OF A TEENAGE DIRTBAG

I spoke to William today and he kept asking, 'Have you met someone? Have you slept with them?' I didn't want to lie so I told him.

'Wow, Claire. One week. That's what everyone would expect you to do after only one week. It's like sex doesn't mean anything to you.'

I'm so upset and I feel so cheap and insulted.

5TH AUGUST 2001
LISTENING TO 'FEBRUARY STARS' BY FOO FIGHTERS

I feel really tired and William has really gotten into my head. I'm constantly on the brink of tears. He sent me texts all night and they were so mean. It's exhausting. I feel like such a slut, but I'd never have slept with Gael if I didn't love him. It didn't mean nothing at all. It meant a lot. Who says you can't fall in love in a week? There's no rule! I'm pretty sure I fell in love with William after a week! William Shakespeare and all that...

- Romeo and Juliet – one night
- Aurora and Prince Phillip – 'Once Upon a Dream', *technically* before they'd even met
- Antony and Cleopatra – first sight
- Ariel and Prince Eric – first sight
- 'Baby' and Swayze (*RIP*) in *Dirty Dancing* – a week-ish.

There you have it. Concrete evidence from all the great love stories.

```
Text from William: You're not the person
I thought you were. You made me believe
I had a chance and that we were something
```

special. You're nothing but a manipulative
liar. You never loved me. You've used me.
You've broken me. How you can just have
sex with a random just shows how little
it means to you. You're a cheap whore and
I wish I'd never wasted my love on you.

7TH AUGUST 2001
LISTENING TO 'ROAD TRIPPIN''
BY RED HOT CHILI PEPPERS

Terrible weather. Spent the day playing pool with Gael, Marc,
Les Marseillais and François. It was so nice just to chill out with
everyone.
    I love Gael. I can't stop kissing him.

8TH AUGUST 2001
LISTENING TO 'CASTAWAY' BY GREEN DAY

I got up so early cos Gael rang before he went to work. I then went
and played volleyball all morning – very well if I may say so myself.
My mum was amazing this afternoon and took me to Saint-
Lunaire to surprise Gael. We walked along the beach and had a
coffee. I told him I loved him too, but felt so guilty about William.

9TH AUGUST 2001
LISTENING TO 'ARMS WIDE OPEN' BY CREED

Well, I'm lying in bed crying at the thought of leaving Gael.
It just doesn't feel fair that everything now has a ticking time

clock attached. Whenever I'm with him now, my emotions are heightened and everything feels more urgent and passionate. The second I let myself think about it though, it's all tarnished by the impending, timetabled end. I'm so in love with him and I know that it's not been long and I'm being a massive love-struck, clichéd teenager, but the fact that we're being torn apart against our will makes it seem so much worse! I spent the whole day on the beach playing volleyball again – very badly today, but it was fun. François, Marc and I were in a three, but they just spent the day shouting at me and telling me that Gael has shagged the volleyball out of me... whatever that means! I was pretty distracted to be fair.

We all went to the Potinière tonight. It was super crap and expensive, but I didn't care because I spent the night dancing with Gael. We couldn't keep our hands off each other and he told me he didn't think he'll ever love anyone more than he loves me. Fuck, I'm going to die when I leave.

11TH AUGUST 2001
LISTENING TO 'MISERY' BY GREEN DAY

We went back to camp on the island for a second time. We set off mid-afternoon while the tide was out again. It was a much smaller group this time and the drug boys came too (Jules, Nico, Viking Max etc). The drug boys sat round the fire doing their drug thing while Yannick, Marc, François, les Marseillais and the twins were putting up their tents. Gael was bringing our tent later on the boat after he finished work so I had a few hours to kill.

Viking Max was making up a bong for the drug boys. He's really hot and I've always thought he looks like a Viking. I don't fancy him or anything, but there's no harm in looking. There's just such a lot of muscle and hair that it would be rude not to look. That's all.

I'd never tried a bong and thought it wouldn't be any different to a bit of weed. I asked Max if I could try some and he was, like:

'Yeah, if you're sure, Claire? It's a bit different to spliff...'

'Yeah. Cool. Whatever, it's fine! I'm totally used to it!'

Pah! Used to it my arse!

The second I inhaled, my lungs turned into two heaving fireballs. I couldn't breathe and nearly hacked up all my insides. I started to feel a bit dizzy and they were like, 'Wow, she's having a trip!' WHAT THE FUCK? I NEVER SIGNED UP TO A TRIP! I felt really unwell so I tried to go for a walk, but the sand was moving too much under my feet. It felt like it was crawling up my legs. I finally managed to extricate myself from all the drug boys and sat behind a rock. All the movement was making me feel so sick and I'd somehow convinced myself there was quicksand everywhere. The rocks were all blue and the sky was brilliant yellow with flashing multi-coloured clouds. I lay there for hours (I think) wondering how long these things took to wear off. I think François and Marc came to check on me and I think I was sick. When it finally passed I made my way back to the fire like nothing had happened. Lesson learnt. No bongs and no showing off in front of Vikings.

I was so relieved when Gael finally arrived on the boat. We spent the night drinking round the fire with everyone and then nipping back and forth to his tent to have sex. The whole night is a bit of a blur, but a good blur.

13TH AUGUST 2001
LISTENING TO 'LES NAINS DE JARDIN' BY MERZHIN

We all went to Mattie's again for Seb's surprise birthday, and I realise that I often write things in my diary like 'best night ever' or 'worst night ever!' and it may seem that I live only in extremes, but last night REALLY WAS one of the best nights of my life! Yannick, Gael and Ben headbanged to the Red Hot Chili Peppers with their pants on their heads while François was performing his one-man comedy show – he's so funny. They all make me so happy. Why can't I have friends like this at home?

I made love to Gael five times! I stayed up all night with him and we both cried at the thought of me leaving him. When Gael and I went to bed the Merzhin album was left playing on loop downstairs so Gael and I listened to it throughout the night until breakfast. I never thought I'd say this, but I actually grew to love it by the millionth listen – I might actually have to buy it so I can remember this amazing night forever.

Marc ended up getting completely fucked and came sleepwalking into our room in the middle of the night, opened the wardrobe door, took a piss and then got in and went to sleep. Weird.

14TH AUGUST 2001
LISTENING TO '1979' BY SMASHING PUMPKINS

I had such a lovely morning eating breakfast with everyone on Mattie's terrace in the sunshine and mum rang with my Standard Grade results – straight 1s! So happy but also relieved that all that time obsessing about William didn't trash my future. Gael was supposed to be working and because we only had a few days left together Marc said he would drive me to spend the day on the beach in Saint Lunaire so Gael could see me between his lessons. Seb, François and Yannick came too for a change of scenery. It was so sweet of Marc – I owe him. We spent most of the day sleeping on the beach though – so tired.

GAEL

15TH AUGUST 2001
LISTENING TO 'MY HERO' BY FOO FIGHTERS

Today was my last day with Gael and we spent it lounging about on the beach and bobbing about, kissing in the sea. I was so happy with him, but I couldn't stop crying. I've never felt so depressed at the thought of... anything. Everyone came for drinks at the house and then we went out clubbing and danced all night. It was so bitter sweet.

At the end of the night I gave him the letter I wrote to tell him (in terribly written French) that I'd fallen in love with him and it was going to be the hardest breakup in the world. Gael told me he'd completely fallen in love with me too and he wanted to stay together! Yaaaaaaayyyy! I want this to work so badly! I am 100% going to make this work! We'll be apart for a year, but I'll be busy with my Highers, I won't see the time go by and I'll be back in his arms before I know it. I was desperate to have sex with him one last time that we went and asked Marc if we could use his car. I was a bit embarrassed, but Marc doesn't care – he just winked at me as he tossed me the keys. It felt frantic and emotional and I had to stop myself from crying mid-shag. How very high class of me...

Ah, that Fiat Punto. Almost a member of the group in its own right. No adventure felt complete without it.

When the club closed, Marc said it was time to leave. I couldn't believe I only had five minutes left with Gael. I was in a complete daze. I didn't know what to do with myself. It was a weird, shaky, laughing, crying stunned mix. Gael just held me. I nuzzled my head into his neck and breathed him in for the last time. He kissed me on my head and I jumped into the car as Marc drove off. I couldn't bear to look up and see him disappearing into the night. I sobbed so dramatically and cried myself to sleep. Life is so unfair!

FOURTEEN

ST FELIX'S

20TH AUGUST 2001
217 DAYS UNTIL I SEE GAEL
LISTENING TO 'BASKET CASE' BY GREEN DAY

I met up with Maggie and Hannah in Princess Street Gardens. It's become a bit of a post-holiday ritual for me. We sat and smoked and they spent most of the afternoon making fun of the fact that I was wearing white to show off my tan. Busted. I was totally wearing white to show off my tan. I was so relieved Gretchen wasn't there. It's been amazing not having to deal with her all summer.

I spoke to Gael on MSN Messenger for ages – I miss him so much, although I'm pretty busy with the Opera. It's the opening night tonight – I'm quite nervous.

Our school 'Opera' had been selected to be part of the Edinburgh Festival's line-up. It's laughable that I had anything to do with this really. I'm whatever the opposite of a triple threat is. But what I lacked in acting, singing or dancing talent, I made up for with lorryloads of enthusiasm. I'd chosen to give a very loud and energetic rendition of 'Memory' from Cats for my audition and this eagerness had (rather disastrously) led to me being given one speaking line. This was bad enough when it was still just a school play, but most unfortunate for everyone involved, once we realised we'd be 'in' the Festival. For my part, I was expected to wail about unrequited love and the father of my child or something like that. Ha! Who am I trying to kid here? As if I don't remember the most memorable line of my life!

'NO! (Extra-long theatrical pause) I GAVE HIM ALL! MY VIRTUE AND MY HEART WITH THAT!'

I delivered it with more and more gusto every night, that by the last night I was throwing myself down onto my knees (babe in arms) and screaming to the heavens in THE most melodramatic way imaginable. My dad still visibly shudders when reminded of this. The 'Opera' was an abomination to start with, but I single-handedly cancelled out any promise that it may have had. Whoever had pitifully offered me that line should have had to do time for crimes against the stage.

23RD AUGUST 2001
214 DAYS UNTIL I SEE GAEL
LISTENING TO 'DROPS OF JUPITER' BY TRAIN

I went to the cinema with William today. Things are still a bit weird between us and I'm not allowed to mention Gael. But it just felt so wonderful to be around him again. Like the smell of home. I almost had to stop myself nuzzling into him.

Got my photos back from Brittany today – they are soooo good! Oh, to be with Gael again. Sweet, salty Gael. I miss his smile, his giggle, the feel of his skin, his unruly hair and his flip-flop walk. I miss everything about him. This is torture.

24TH AUGUST 2001
LISTENING TO 'CASTLES IN THE SKY' BY IAN VAN DAHL

After the Opera tonight, I went out with Lucy and the St Catherine's girls. Polly Duff introduced me to a family friend of hers called Finn Ellwyn-Cox.

> *Finn Ellwyn-Cox is magnificently posh. He went to Eton and would be quite at home somewhere between The Riot Club and Made in Chelsea. He was a bad boy in a way that only the most upper-class boys can be. He had dazzling charm, wit and the unparalleled confidence that only the most prestigious education can offer. I'd never met anyone like Finn, and I was really quite taken by his cheek and extensive vocabulary. A cocky little fucker, but instantly likeable despite the annoying feeling that the world really was his oyster before the other 99.9% of the population even got a look in.*
>
> *I was initially struggling with Finn's description so messaged him and asked, 'How would you describe yourself aged sixteen?' He replied, 'Insecure and blustering. I was still really hurting about being horribly bullied until I was about fourteen.' It just goes to show. You never can tell.*

We went out to Frankenstein's, danced all night and did test tube shots. He's very funny, but super posh and ENGLISH.

The horror... English? ENGLISH?!

He walked me home and he promised he'd call me the next day.
I couldn't resist a little peck. Love life!

```
Text  from  Finn:  I  just  couldn't  wait.
Thanx  for  an  incredible  evening.  I  do
object  to  being  called  a  'sleazy  slut'
though and you could have told me it was a
10 mile hike back! Will call you tomorrow.
Promise.  Sleep  well  ma  petite  choufleur!
Finn x
```

Ummm, Gael? What just happened?

25TH AUGUST 2001
212 DAYS TILL GAEL
(OH, SO I DO STILL CARE, DO I?)
LISTENING TO 'THE SPACE BETWEEN'
BY DAVE MATTHEWS BAND

It was the Opera's last night and Finn AND William came to
watch. William had brought some flowers and we bumped into
Finn after the show. He was all like, 'And who the fuck is this,
Claire?!' We had a HUGE fight right outside the school as all the
cast and crew were leaving. I was so embarrassed. Annoyingly,
Finn kept jumping in and winding William up saying stuff like,
'What's your problem, mate? She's not your girlfriend! We're
only having a bit of fun... it was only a kiss.'
STOP FUCKING TALKING, FINN!!!!
The second Finn said 'kiss', William stopped dead and stared
at me then at Finn. I thought he was going to punch Finn, but

instead it looked like he might cry. He threw the flowers down, kicked them and marched off. I'm trying not to think about it cos it'll probably make me cry too. He looked so hurt and he's right; I shouldn't have pulled Finn, but realistically Gael and I aren't going to see each other forever. I went home early after taking Finn to Bertie's and leaving him with Polly and Lucy and co. I didn't kiss him tonight. I called Gael when I got home and we talked for hours. I feel really guilty. I love him.

```
Text from Finn: Well Bertie's is like a
cattle market! I miss you already. It's
been amazing getting to know you. Mind if
I give you a bell sometime soon? Bye bye
Cutie Pie xxx
```

Bertie's really was like a cattle market; a disgusting assault on all the senses. The calibre of girls in Bertie's often left a lot to be desired and little to the imagination. I was not immune to this compulsion to show as much flesh as possible when frequenting this slut-o-sphere. I reserved my most inappropriate outfits for Bertie's and wince when I think back to a particular beaded boob tube that graced this establishment on many an occasion. Even on the bleakest of winter nights, Bertie's would welcome us out of the blizzard, dressed for a night out in Magaluf. We were bare-legged (albeit the obligatory coating of body glitter), coatless and effortlessly skating through frozen snow in strappy, vertiginous stilettos.

I remember Bertie's as clearly as if I was there, just last week. I can still remember teetering through the doors and up the corridor to be greeted by the paint-stripping stench of stale fags, sambuca and Tommy Girl. You had to float without touching anything for every surface was contaminated with an inexplicable lubricant. Bertie's was an utterly revolting place and every night, almost exactly on the stroke of midnight, the ceiling would reach peak condensation and it would start to rain down sweat. The challenge was to make sure you were either out by then or so hammered that you wouldn't notice. Fortunately getting hammered was easy for, on Wednesday nights, all the drinks were 50p. Bertie's was the hottest place in town, hosting Edinburgh's coolest teenagers and its perviest students.

29TH AUGUST 2001
206 DAYS UNTIL I SEE GAEL
LISTENING TO 'ABSOLUTELY
(STORY OF A GIRL)' BY NINE DAYS

5pm: I'm feeling really stressed and down. I started back at St Felix's and although I love it, I've had a shite day and I just feel off.

- Maggie's in my form class, which is great, but this is the only positive thing I can think of right now and she still manages to spend all her time with Gretchen.
- For reasons I don't think even he knows, William is now doing art and is in my flipping class. ARGHH. Why is he doing art?! He's never shown the slightest interest and he's pretty shit. I bet he thought it would be 'easy'. The fucker. Anyway, it's really awkward as we're not talking since Finn and he just keeps glaring at me.
- On the way home I felt so distracted that I left my bag and blazer on the bus. So stressed.

30TH AUGUST 2001
LISTENING TO 'EVERYTHING' BY DUMDUMS

11pm: I spent the whole night chatting to Gael. I tried to do some maths, but I'm in such a bad mood I just want to cry and throw stuff. I tried to just chill out and smoke out my window after everyone went to bed, but I still feel like crap. Likely reasons for mood:

- I miss Gael, which is making me feel low.
- I have this horrible, weird background guilt about William ALL THE TIME. I'm just listening to all his tapes on loop and they're making me feel so depressed. I wish we could be right for each other. Now all my favourite music just reminds me of him.
- Feeling super guilty about pulling Finn.
- Starting to massively stress about work now too.

Arrgrrgrghrhrhrgrhrggh fuuuuuuuuuuuuuuuuuuuuuuuuuuuck. Hate life.

31ST AUGUST 2001
LISTENING TO 'BUCK ROGERS' BY FEEDER

1am: William rang me last night after my entry and we talked for ages. I apologised about being such a slut psycho and we kind of made up. I am so tired though. He tires me out and I don't feel like I have any energy to deal with him anymore. It's so exhausting.

I went out with William and Angus tonight, but I just ended up getting drunk and having another massive argument with William. He basically says he wished he didn't love me because he hates me. Angus (who usually doesn't get involved) said I was a 'headfuck'. I walked home crying. Angus is absolutely right. I am a headfuck, but I don't want to be. I really don't want to be *that* girl.

2ND SEPTEMBER 2001
LISTENING TO 'FATHER OF MINE' BY EVERCLEAR

I met Maggie for lunch at Pizza Hut and then went home and did loads of work. I spent the night on the phone with William, Finn and Gael. If only a man existed that combined the three of them. Obviously I love Gael the most (now), but the emotional extremes I have (eeep, I mean *had!)* for William are unparalleled. Gael is going to try and visit at some point this autumn. Oh God, I hope that's true. I need to see him. If anything so I can stop thinking about other boys!

4TH SEPTEMBER 2001
202 DAYS
LISTENING TO 'THUNDER ROAD'
BY BRUCE SPRINGSTEEN

I'm so busy at the moment, I'm feeling a bit overwhelmed with it all. Work has massively ramped up and I've lost control a bit. Choir every morning for an hour before school rips me from my much needed slumber and Cadets is a bit of a nightmare as I'm now in charge of teaching the rude-ass first years. Thirteen-year-old boys are THE WORST. Fortunately William has volunteered to help me and all the boys love him so, by association, tolerate me. They only like him cos William essentially IS a thirteen-year-old boy! It's really nice to see him with the younger boys though. He'll make an amazing dad one day. NOT WITH ME, JEEEEZ, but with someone. God, it's weird. I really don't like the idea of him marrying and having children with someone else. Will I always be jealous? Maybe we will end up together and this just isn't our time yet.

I found out that Maggie and William are both coming on the New York art trip. It's going to be amazing!

6TH SEPTEMBER 2001
199 DAYS
LISTENING TO 'HERE COMES THE SUN'
BY THE BEATLES

I miss Gael so much. I speak to him every night, but I'm finding it so so difficult. I'm forgetting him and more importantly, how I felt with him.

8TH SEPTEMBER 2001
LISTENING TO 'I WILL BUY YOU A NEW LIFE'
BY EVERCLEAR

Well, last night was a fucking car crash. I went out with Hannah, Maggie, Gretchen and their old gang from Margaret Campbell's. One of the guys, Leo (who I thought I always got on ok with), kept humming the tune to 'Who Let the Dogs Out' then a few of the boys and Gretchen would sing 'neigh neigh neigh neigh' in place of the 'woof'. This has been a running 'joke' for months. Everyone was pissing themselves laughing, so at one point I sang along and everyone literally fell to the floor they were laughing so hard. Gretchen was actually on her hands and knees, slapping the floor with tears streaming down her face. I felt my face flush and a lump form in my throat as the reality of what was going on came crashing down around me. Oh, I see, I thought, this is a joke about me. I must look like a horse now? What is it with me and animals?! I wasn't sure I even knew what 'this' was, but it felt so cruel and I suddenly thought of the list from St Catherine's... *thinks she's cool, smelly, hairy, thinks she's funny...* Maybe this whole time, everyone thinks that, but it's all going on behind my back now. I asked Hannah and Maggie later and they were like, 'Nah, Claire, it's nothing. Don't worry about it. Leo's just a bit of a prick.' I pushed them a bit more and eventually they told me that when I first met them all, Leo and Gretchen thought I looked like a horse and would often sing, 'Who let the horse out, neigh neigh neigh neigh', and giggle about it together.

Leo was a scrawny little EMO boy with an eyebrow piercing and some eyeliner, but trust me, it triggered something in our teenage brains and Leo was HOT. Sadly for Leo, being sixteen was as good as life got as there wasn't a lot going on behind that Blink-182 exterior. His 'looks' were on a steep downward trajectory from this point onwards and a few months later he left school with zilcho education 'because it was a waste of time'. He then landed himself a job in a Z-list motorway burger joint and he looks like Mr Bean in a Slipknot T-shirt. Karma really can be a bitch.

I felt so upset. It took everything I had not to cry. I couldn't believe Hannah and Maggie had never defended me. I'm sure I can remember them singing along in the past. Do I look like a horse? I've never heard that before. Urrgh, it hurts so much just thinking about it. I told Gretchen to go fuck herself and left to go and meet William and Angus in Siglo's. Then we went to Gaia where I think I got my drink spiked. I only had one and it all went very wrong, very quickly. It was the worst thing EVER. My legs wouldn't work and I couldn't make words with my mouth.

I just remember little flashes after William and Angus carried me out. My cheek resting on a cold and damp stone step in the Old Town. A gap. William and Angus arguing about me. Then another gap. Then the smell of vomit mixed with Hugo by Hugo Boss (William's 'scent'). The feeling of my head on his lap as he talked to me, stroking my vomit-soaked hair.

William and Angus stayed with me until I felt better and got me home around 5am. My mum went MENTAL. A bit of a disaster night all round.

9TH SEPTEMBER 2001
LISTENING TO 'SHE'S ON FIRE' BY TRAIN

Worked all day. Grounded, depressed and very tired.

10TH SEPTEMBER 2001
51 DAYS!
LISTENING TO 'I THINK WE'RE ALONE NOW' BY TIFFANY

I'm so excited my mum said I could visit Gael during half term!

Had a really shit day in school. I'm still feeling really weird after the drink spiking. I went for a fag with Tom Southall after school and he was actually being really decent and apologised for how he'd behaved at my birthday last year and for the drug text, as he found out it wasn't me that grassed him up. He asked if I wanted to go out with him and his new friends and take some pills. Errr, no thanks.

11TH SEPTEMBER 2001

Attack on New York, and Twin Towers bombed. I was at the gym when it came on the news. It feels completely surreal. So weird as we had our New York art trip meeting about an hour before the first plane hit. It'll probably be cancelled now. Obviously that's not important, but still.

13TH SEPTEMBER 2001
LISTENING TO 'SUGAR IN YOUR GAS TANK' BY LESS THAN JAKE

So apparently a rumour has spread that I fancy William's friend Chris. I have never fancied Chris, but everyone is talking about it today saying how 'uncool it is to go for Chris given that he's one of Will's besties and Will clearly still loves me'. Oh God, here we go again…

Then Chris, the most ARROGANT, SELFISH, HEARTLESS, COLD-BLOODED SHITTY CUNTING BASTARD I have ever met, sent me this text:

> How come wherever I walk, someone says your name. What have you been saying cos I'm sick of it?! Stop broadcasting to the whole school that you fancy me. Just leave me alone. I thought you had some french boyfriend anyway? I haven't got time for this and there's more important things in life than your petty school girl crush.

Excuuuuuuse me?

Text to Chris: You rude wanker! What a text! Not that it matters but yes I do have a French boyfriend and no I don't have any kind of crush on you, petty school girl or otherwise. Get your facts straight before shooting your mouth off like that next time. Why I would 'broadcast' to the school that I fancy you is completely ludicrous.

Text from William: You know I love you Claire, why do you keep doing this to me? I can ignore french people I've never met and randoms but Chris is one of my best friends, how could you? I think i need some time without having to see you all the time. It's too hard.

Text to William: It's not true! I've never fancied Chris. Even if I did I would never do this to you. Please don't believe these rumours and throw our friendship away over something that isn't true. I promise it's not true!

From William: Whatever. You would say that.

F U U U U U U U C C C C C C C C C C CCCCCKKKKKKKKKKKKKKK

THEN text from Gretchen: Ha! It's so like you to fancy William's friend you massive whore. Word just seems to spread like wildfire at this school… wouldn't want you to get a bad rep now would we? If only we knew where these 'rumours' were coming from...

THE FUCKING BITCH! SHE DID THIS AND NO ONE IS GOING TO BELIEVE ME!! I SWEAR TO GOD I COULD KILL HER.

14TH SEPTEMBER 2001
LISTENING TO 'CRAZY' BY NINE DAYS

I spent most of the day crying. I feel so unbearably lonely. I feel like I'm surrounded by 'friends', but no one I can really talk to. I'm really isolated at school after the whole Chris thing. Everyone just loves William and that fucking witch Gretchen. She's managed to convince everyone that she's super 'chill' and hates conflict and drama. They don't know her like I know her. If you cut her, she would bleed pure evil bitch blood. She'll never pull the wool over my eyes. I see you, Gretchen, you manipulative sociopath. If I ever suggest that her motives are anything other than altruistic perfection, everyone's like, 'Oh no, not Gretchen, she's such a sweetie. She loves everyone. Why are you so mean about her?' Well played, Gretchen. Well played. She's got her claws back into William too. I can see them sniggering and looking at me all the time. Boy do I hate her.

15TH SEPTEMBER 2001
LISTENING TO 'BITTER' BY NINE DAYS

Oh God, I've done it again. William had a massive party and invited me 'to be civil'. I wasn't sure whether to go or not, but figured it might give me a chance to cheer up and make up with William again. I wish I hadn't gone. It's actually made me feel so much worse.

I arrived at William's feeling really low, and everyone there was ignoring me and whispering behind my back. Gretchen was chatting shit, with everyone sat around her looking like slack-jawed morons.

I should have just gone home, but I ended up getting slaughtered and went and hid upstairs with a bottle of vodka. Gael called and said he knew I was about to turn sixteen and not seventeen and they all knew and why did I keep lying? Apparently they've been waiting for a year for me to 'confess' and they're always trying to catch me out. How long was I going to keep this up? FUUUUUUCCCK. I came clean and apologised, but Gael (understandably) wasn't going to forgive me that easily. I can't believe they all knew! It was such a ridiculous lie and I'm so embarrassed.

Gael clearly ran out of phone credit as it cut off and it left me feeling even worse, drunk and sat on the floor in William's sister's room. William came and found me and sat down next to me, taking the vodka off me. He told me he still loved me and that we were made for each other. It was everything I wanted to hear and I believed it. How could I possibly be so obsessed with someone if I didn't love them? We started kissing on the floor and we were getting more and more carried away. I knew we should stop the whole time and I kept trying to make myself think of Gael, but I couldn't stop. I ended up staying the night and had sex with William (three times). HUGE MISTAKE(S?), but he makes me feel so safe and secure and happy. I just wish things could be right between us.

Un.be.fucking.lievable. 'I went and "hid" upstairs...' Honestly. My game play was not only shameful but entirely transparent. Gretchen and I were just as devious as each other.

FIFTEEN
THE 'ICK'

I need to shake off this bad mood. I have been feeling so depressed for the last few weeks, but I have NOTHING to complain about. I have an amazing life. I have friends (some). I have family. I have health. I have freedom. I have opportunities. I have a home. I have food. I don't appreciate how unbelievably lucky I am. I have no right to get 'depressed' when there are billions of people around the world with actual problems. As Chris said: I am nothing but a stupid schoolgirl with stupid schoolgirl problems. I need to buck the fuck up.

22ND SEPTEMBER 2001
26 DAYS UNTIL I SEE GAEL
LISTENING TO 'FAST CAR' BY TRACY CHAPMAN

Arghhh, I still feel so low. What's wrong with me? William has had his knee operation so he has been off school. I normally spend all my time with him so I don't know what to do with myself anymore and I've felt a bit aimless. Maggie is great, but does hang out with Gretchen A LOT and so I try to keep my distance. I overheard them say something about me being a 'short-term friend' (or something like that). I don't really know what that means exactly, but clearly no one wants to be a short-term friend.

I went to visit William a few times and it was all I needed to cheer up a bit. He always gives me the biggest hug when he sees me and when he has his arms wrapped around me, I feel all the hatred, anger and sadness just disappear. We don't talk about Gael or what happened the other night. God, I feel terrible about it.

With William off school, I have spent more time with the boys in my year and tried to get to know them a bit better. I've started hanging out with Mish a bit more and I went out with him and all the rugby boys tonight (Toby Sinclair, Andy 'Lads Lads Lads' Burns, Jamie etc). We went out to Rush, which was good fun, but I still don't feel like I can truly relax with them. I think that a lot of them know me through reputation (what I did to Dan Jeffries and to William) rather than the real me (although I guess that was me really). So they were being a bit cagey with me tonight. Mish clearly doesn't want to commit to being good friends in public yet. It's almost like he's waiting to see what everyone else thinks of me before showing his cards. Andy 'Lads Lads Lads' Burns and I were the only two drinking so we did a couple of shots of tequila and had a quick dance, but it was a pretty tame night, especially with Mish and Grumpy Toby sucking all the fun out of the evening.

Toby Sinclair gave off a 'strong silent type' vibe, but in reality he was just a massive piece of shit. That being said, he was quite a good-looking piece of shit; so I was willing to repeatedly overlook his horrific personality. He almost never went out, didn't smile and hated all things good. He was the anti-fun. I think in the three years that I knew him, I only heard him laugh once. The way in which I bonded with people at this stage was still pretty primitive and usually involved sharing a fag and shots of something disgusting. This (maybe rightly) did not appeal to Toby and his only conversation remit was sport (cricket and golf in particular), which, as far as I was concerned, deserved its very own circle of hell. This meant we had absolutely NOTHING in common once we had exhausted my limited knowledge of Scottish rugby. It's amazing, really, that I should then end up married to a cricketer and relish staying up all night watching the Masters or travelling the length and breadth of the country for a T20 finals day. People do change. I hope (for his sake) that Toby did.

He eventually played rugby professionally and probably turned out ok, but he was not a nice guy when we were at school. I still feel my top lip curl in disgust when I think of Grumpy Toby 'Fun Sponge' Sinclair. I have always been slightly mistrustful of anyone that doesn't drink, and I attribute this gross misunderstanding of people's right to abstain to Grumpy Toby. What are they hiding? What part of them do they not want the world to see? Thanks to this arseface, I now believe that abstinence should really only be reserved for the pregnant, the drivers and the alcoholics. But we'll get to his arseface-ness later.

25TH SEPTEMBER 2001
LISTENING TO 'STORY OF A LONELY GUY'
BY BLINK-182

I wish I could see Gael. I'm finding it so hard. I'm forgetting what it feels like to be with him and I'm weirdly getting insanely jealous whenever I see William with other girls. Do I still like him or am I just being a SELFISH BITCH? I'm dreading the day he gets a girlfriend cos he'll forget about me and replace me with her. I haven't had my period yet and I'm starting to get super worried. I think I'm going to start the pill.

I spent the day praying for my period and thank God it came. Went babysitting down the road and Next Door Andy came to keep me company. We chatted, drank tea and watched *Tommy*. He spoke to me about his mum who died when he was four – MAJOR empathy. It felt like such a privilege being let in to this side of Andy. I think he tries to keep it pretty well hidden most of the time. I suppose I'd do the same if I didn't want to have to think about something like that all the time. I wouldn't want it to define me. I guess that's why he paints himself as this 'Fun Party Guy'.

When I got home I felt like I had clarity. I knew what was important and what wasn't. Boys are not important. Having living, breathing parents growing up is. What the hell was I doing messing about with William and letting it affect me so much? Far worse things happen. People lose their mothers as young children and manage to power through life while I wallow about cos I love two people? Fucking hell.

Text to William: Why do we keep doing this
to ourselves? I love Gael. I'm obviously
still confused about my feelings for you
but that's not fair on you. Everything

gets harder and more complicated when we see each other that we should move on and you should just forget about me.

Text from William: You know as well as I do that forgetting you would be like forgetting a family member. I couldn't and wouldn't let you go. I would love to call you mine. I still love you more and more each day but I can't wait forever to be with you. It's me or Gael? I see he makes you happy and I used to be that person but I hate you with other guys and you hate me with other girls. Doesn't that prove it?

29TH SEPTEMBER 2001
LISTENING TO 'OCTOBER SWIMMER' BY JJ72

Spent the day with William and we were both miserable. What are we doing? I don't know what I want and I'm clearly making him unhappy. We went out and met up with Angus and the other new girls at school (Maggie, Gretchen, Holly and Maria) in Bar Oz. Holly and Maria seem really cool and they're so pretty. I feel a little left out though because Maggie and Gretchen were at Margaret Campbell's together before moving; Holly and Maria were at Robertson's so they're already really close; and then there's me, a solo mover from St Catherine's (although thank God really). We went to Iguana and a new place called Igloo. Got v. drunk and William took me home. We had a fight on the way home about how jealous he is about Gael. So tired... need to sleep.

6TH OCTOBER 2001
LISTENING TO 'UNDERCOVER ANGEL' BY JJ72

Thirteen days until I see Gael! I am so excited it's insane. I can't think about it too much cos the excitement could very well cause me to burst into flames. Keep a lid on it, Claire...

I had such a good night with Maria and Holly tonight. We did a few shots then danced all night. I was totally relieved to discover that they don't both seem obsessed with Gretchen (like everyone else at St Felix's is). They're so stunning though – I feel pretty invisible next to them.

I spoke to William when I got home and he was annoyed that I went out without him! I don't have to justify my life to him! I bet he was just annoyed he couldn't show off in front of the hot girls!

8TH OCTOBER 2001
LISTENING TO '3AM' BY MATCHBOX 20

I just don't know why William and I keep hanging out together. ALL we do is argue. We're so different now and something between us has changed. I think I've finally stopped loving him. I'm trying to work harder this year, which is only making how little he works more obvious. This is his last year at school! I don't get it. His work ethic (or lack of) is so annoying! It's so frustrating to watch him fail cos he's bumming around like an aimless loser.

I had the house to myself tonight. Smoked loads, spoke to Gael, had dinner, and Next Door Andy came round and we watched *Dirty Dancing*. He's hilarious. He spent at least an hour dancing round my living room. Those hips! He's pretty camp is old Next Door Andy...

12TH OCTOBER 2001
6 DAYS UNTIL GAEL
LISTENING TO 'SATURDAY NIGHT'S ALRIGHT
FOR FIGHTING' BY ELTON JOHN

William is annoying me so much. He won't just let me be. I went round to Next Door Andy's after school and we had some beers and watched *Reservoir Dogs*. William texted towards the end of the night saying he was at that fucking bitch Psycho Jane's house getting stoned and drunk. Fucking Psycho Jane…

```
Text to William: I'm sure you two will be
very happy stoners together.

Text from William: Having a great time
actually. It's nice to be with someone who
knows what you're like…
```

Great.

13TH OCTOBER 2001
LISTENING TO 'GIRL LIKE THAT' BY MATCHBOX 20

I've finally saved enough money to buy some trousers from Cult. They're Bench and soooo cool. They're really baggy, khaki coloured and they have full-length black zips down the side of each leg.

I LOVED these trousers and wore them well into my third year at university. They were so ripped and torn, from scuffing under my (equally emo) Acupuncture trainers, that I had resewn and repaired them dozens of times in red and electric blue zigzag stitching (very cool). The zips down either side had loosened to such an extent that they required safety pins to secure them onto the tops of the trousers. These safety pins kept the trousers from literally unpeeling me like a banana. For about a year, I felt like I was in an episode of The Crystal Maze, fighting the complex network of safety pins, every time I went to the toilet. I loved you, epic Bench trousers. RIP (literally).

15TH OCTOBER 2001
3 DAYS UNTIL GAELRAMA!
LISTENING TO 'THERE MUST BE AN ANGEL' BY EURYTHMICS

WOOOOO! I can't sleep. I'm so excited about seeing Gael. I'm at Mamie and Papie's in Paris for a few days then catching a train to Brittany. I'm pretty worried he might not like me anymore when he sees me. It's the most hideous thought to think that I'm going to get off the train on Thursday and Gael will be met by this fat, pale, spotty creature, when his last memory was of thin, tanned, bright-eyed 'Summer Claire'. I hope we're not disappointed having idealised our relationship over the last few months. Hopefully he might not be able to tell the difference and I'll jump into his arms, we'll drive off happily and park in some deserted place, overlooking the ocean, and make sweet sweet love in the back seat of his car.

Gahhhhh! Easy now. Don't make future you curl up and cringe too much.

Oh God! I can't wait! I love him so much! I just hope we can prove the whole world wrong.

18TH OCTOBER 2001
0 DAYS!
LISTENING TO 'TALKIN' 'BOUT A REVOLUTION' BY TRACY CHAPMAN

Gael met me off the train and it was initially kinda weird as I really didn't find him that attractive straight away. He looked... different. But it's ok. I got over it. I'm clearly not the only person who looks better in summer. Now, I'm happily lying here on Gael's bed and my heart has been beating twice as quickly since I got here. He's working right now and he looks so serious. It's insanely sexy.

I watched his fencing training this evening and then had dinner with his parents. I'm REALLY scared of his parents. I'm not even allowed to sleep on the same floor as him. So excited though. *La vie est belle!*

20TH OCTOBER 2001
LISTENING TO 'CIGARETTES AND COFFEE' BY OTIS REDDING

I said goodbye to Gael today.

Well... life WAS so beautiful, but last night something beyond my control happened. I was sitting with Gael and I suddenly couldn't feel 'it' anymore. Poof! My feelings suddenly vanished... like they'd just dropped out of me. I lost the love and I knew it was gone forever. I was looking at him and felt nothing. I didn't fancy him, I didn't love him. Nothing. The thought of leaving him made me feel... well, nothing. I had total apathy towards him. It was over. My summer romance was dead. My gorgeous, blonde, tanned sailing instructor was no more. I knew I would never be able to love him again. It felt completely different to when I didn't want to be with William anymore. Suddenly, comparing Gael to

William made me think that maybe all this emotional headfucking was cos I do love William and maybe I do want to be with him. I've never stopped loving him… I've definitely never felt nothing.

After my depressing epiphany we went out with Yannick and Marc, and although we had a right laugh I was feeling like I was having to fake it with Gael. I genuinely didn't know what to do or how to act. When we left I thought I should probably check it was over before prematurely kicking my love into the gutter, so Gael and I ended up having sex in his car… briefly. I mean really briefly. It was the speediest ever. I just had to be sure… I couldn't bear to accidentally break up with someone again. I know that the sex shouldn't matter that much, but the love is gone and so, it appears, has the oomph. Arrghhhh fuck fuck fuck. I don't know what to do. This is the most horrible feeling in the world.

What makes everything even worse is that he's just spunked a whole load of money on coming to Edinburgh next week and I really wish he hadn't. I now think we'll have to break up AFTER he spends a week in Edinburgh. I wish I could break up with him now, but I don't think I can now he's flying to see me. I can't exactly ask, 'So, umm, are your flights refundable? No reason…' ARGGGHH.

25TH OCTOBER 2001
LISTENING TO 'EVERY TIME I LOOK FOR YOU' BY BLINK-182

I spent the day with Maggie, which was cool. I love her so much when she's not with fucking Gretchen. I'm not really seeing William anymore. I don't think he can stomach the whole 'Gael' thing and he knows he's about to visit so he's keeping his distance. I'm keeping my distance cos I'm in total denial about maybe still having feelings, and not seeing him means I don't have to address it. He's been spending loads of time with that crackpot, Psycho Jane, though. God, I'm glad I'm not a fly on the wall when they're chatting.

27TH OCTOBER 2001
LISTENING TO 'VERTIGO' BY AMERICAN HI-FI

I've just come back from the best Saturday night ever up town. I met Lucy and the old girls in town for lunch and Lucy got her bellybutton pierced! She came back to mine and we went for a drink at Next Door Andy's. He clearly didn't realise I had 'cool' friends like Lucy Murphy and kept saying things like, 'I can't believe you guys are friends… Claire's such a fucking loser!' He'd say it with a nudge and a wink, but still. Truth hurts, mate. Stop showing off just cos I brought cool friends round to your house!

Lucy and I then went and met Mish for a drink. Lucy was hammered so she went home, and Mish and I went to the Blind Poet where there were tonnes of people from St Felix's – it was amazing. Grumpy Toby Sinclair was there and he just sat there all brooding and mysterious. Wow, he's a little hottie. Bit tricky to have bants with him though. He doesn't seem that comfortable talking to girls in general though; so it's not just me. Come to think of it, I'm not sure he looks that comfortable talking full stop. So I was quite drunk (and still am as is evidenced by my handwriting) and had some good banter with Mish.

It appears that 'banter' has now well and truly entered my lexicon. The above is an abridged version of me simply listing everyone that was there and that I had 'good banter with them'. I use the word a total of eight times.

I rather embarrassingly told Grumpy Toby that he was 'the cutest guy in the whole world' because… well, because I wanted to.

157

Text to Grumpy Toby: Oops — I'm sorry I shouldn't have said that you were the cutest guy in the world. I have a boyfriend. Hope you have a good night. Love ya, Claire.

5TH NOVEMBER 2001
LISTENING TO 'ALWAYS GETTING OVER YOU' BY ANGELA AMMONS

So Gael finally left Edinburgh yesterday after spending a week here and it was the longest, most painful week of my life. I knew I still didn't love him the second I met him at the airport. I wonder what happened? He's obviously not changed so how can I suddenly go from an all-consuming infatuation to utter revulsion at the sight of him. His beachy, carefree clothes suddenly looked so out of place in Edinburgh's winter, city streets. I didn't want him to mix with my Edinburgh life and I was really ashamed of anyone seeing him. I know I sound like the world's biggest bitch, but I can't help it! Everything about him that made me melt now makes me want to curl up and die. I fake laughed and squirmed my way through the whole week. How did I ever love him? I'm devastated it's over. He came to meet me after school each day and I would usually squirrel him away before anyone saw him.

Made in Chelsea (the fountain of my psychology knowledge) first named this feeling for me. It's called getting 'the ick'. It's an inexplicable feeling of disgust born out of initial love or lust. 'Getting' the ick is as sudden as it is incurable.

I eventually had to take him out for one night with everyone cos they all were like, 'Why are you hiding him? When are we going to meet this sexy Frenchman then?' Gretchen even planted the seed that he was an elaborate lie as no one had ever seen him, and there was no way I was having that. We went to Bertie's and he actually got on quite well with Andy 'Lads Lads Lads' Burns and Maggie etc. Holly said she thought he was super sweet and she could see why I liked him, which just made me feel horrible about all my anticipated embarrassment.

The night was going quite well when William arrived. Noooooooooooo! I don't know if curiosity got the better of him or if he genuinely didn't know we were there, but he was clearly pretty shocked to see us. Gael (totally clueless) was all like, 'Oh, 'ello, Weeleeam. Eye am Gael. Doo yoo want ah bee-er?' William looked like he might explode, but just politely excused himself and left. That could definitely have gone worse.

We didn't have sex all week cos I couldn't bear to. He was clearly finding it a bit odd, but I managed to make up (kinda) plausible excuses. On his last night he asked if I wanted to sleep downstairs with him. My mum had said I was allowed to, but I pretended I wasn't. He looked so hurt and I think he knew then that it was over, but I smiled and kissed him *bonne nuit* before hurrying upstairs. Man alive, I'm such a bitch.

When I finally waved him off at the airport, I felt so relieved. I could breathe again, but felt awful as I could see Gael's head and shoulders were more droopy than they had been when he arrived. My mum just sighed and said, '*Pauvre* Gael.' Yeah alright, Mum, I get it. This isn't exactly my idea of a perfect ending either, you know?! When we got home, she helped me write a breakup email because my written French is too shit to carefully construct something like that by myself. How has it come to this?! My mother spell-checking (and essentially writing for me) my breakup email to the ex-love of my life (well, one of them). She made me feel soooo awful about it.

And that was that. Bye, Gael.
Sorry.

SIXTEEN

BACKSLIDING

I have a bit of a crush on Grumpy Toby Sinclair. I just can't work him out… that sexy wee enigma. Last night we were all at Maggie's house and we decided to play strip UNO. I ended up in just my pants, with Jamie totally starkers. I was so aware of how I was sitting with Toby sat opposite me. Obviously I was hiding all the important stuff, but still. Gretchen didn't like it though as her and Jamie have just started hooking up. She stormed off and Jamie quickly got dressed and ran after her. Chill out, Gretchen! It's only a bit of fun! Ha! It's nice to trigger a smidge of jealousy in her for a change.

Jamie had rugged good looks and oozed bad boy charm, but he was a kind, sensitive soul. I had a real soft spot for him. He was your standard issue millennial boy. He liked the simple things in life: his mates, girls, beer and

160

rugby. Sadly for him, Gretchen had her evil eye on him and he was helpless to her powers. She sniffed out his sweet, impressionable virgin soul and systematically, over the next few years, sucked all the light out of him.

There were loads of rumours flying around at school today about Grumpy Toby and me. He had apparently told Mish that he thought I had a 'good body' and that he 'rated me'. I was so chuffed. I was pretending to be embarrassed by the gossip, but secretly quite liked it. Gretchen clearly hated it and said, 'I don't know what the big deal is. It's not like anything's going to happen between you two. I just don't think you're his type.'

She was absolutely spot on, but at the time my self-inflated confidence was impenetrable. 'We'll see,' I said with a little sashay of my hips and a flick of my hair. There are times when it is all too clear why Gretchen hated me. Luckily for her, my cockiness didn't last long.

In the afternoon, we had a year group meeting to discuss exams. The 'Toby and Claire' whisperings were ongoing and I kept trying to make eye contact with him and give him a sexy little smile, when out of the blue he stood up and shouted, 'I DO NOT FANCY CLAIRE LE DAY, ALRIGHT?!! I DON'T EVEN LIKE HER!' It was so mortifying. I was sat right there! I just wanted to die. I sank down deep in my chair as everyone turned round and stared at me.

Later in the day, William and I had a massive screaming match outside one of the classrooms. He'd heard about the Grumpy Toby thing and said I was a 'massive slapper'. I was so angry I kicked his post-op, bad knee and he screamed before whacking me hard across my back with one of his crutches. I stormed off and said I never wanted to see him, speak to him or be friends with him ever again.

He rang me later and we kinda made up. We were chatting about how we're both eventually going to get with someone else (in Edinburgh) and we'll probably both find it difficult, when out of the blue he told me he fancied Holly! In that instant, a part of me died. I didn't mean *him*! I thought I would always be the one for him. Part of me even thought we might get back together. That small glimmer evaporated. He likes someone else?! I am absolutely brimming with jealousy. Fucking Holly? This is the same idiot who asked what time the one o'clock gun was. Not only is she a ditzy airhead but she's so ugly. Ah fuck. No she's not. I wish she was. She is an airhead though, just a smoking hot one. I'm really hoping he was just trying to get a rise out of me.

YOU GOT MY ATTENTION, WILLIAM!

NOW WHAT?!

7TH NOVEMBER 2001
LISTENING TO 'OXYGEN' BY JJ72

I'm still annoyed about the whole Grumpy Toby thing and William seemed to spend the whole day flirting with Holly. I was just glaring at them play-fighting as I felt my blood boil. I actually felt like I was breaking inside. By the end of the day, William and I were talking and the jealousy got the better of me cos I told him I'd never loved him. I wish that were true.

10TH NOVEMBER 2001
LISTENING TO 'SMOOTH CRIMINAL'
BY ALIEN ANT FARM

Mish said the reason Grumpy Toby wasn't interested was cos I'm not 'cool enough'.

Of course he did.

William and I are just about on speaking terms, but I'm so ridiculously envious of him and Holly, even though I don't think anything has happened.

Yet.

It's weird but I do actually feel 'green'. I feel bitter and angry and hurt and… well… green. It's like someone has tied a knot in my throat and it's just sitting there, slowly choking me to death. My heart stops whenever I think of them together.

I went out with Mish tonight and found out that William, Gretchen and Holly were all getting drunk at Psycho Jane's. Oh, for fuck's sake. That sounds like a lovely wee get together. Why not invite Sofia and they could do some target practice with my yearbook photo? Just bring your weapon of choice.

14TH NOVEMBER 2001
LISTENING TO 'SMOKESCREEN' BY FLYING BLIND

Everyone at school was talking about William and Holly. I was such a wreck at the thought of him with that witch! Apparently, at the end of the day Holly told William she wanted to go out with him, but he said no cos he didn't want to upset me. Thank God for that. The tiny remaining human part of me felt a little guilty, but the overriding selfish cunt part felt totally relieved.

16TH NOVEMBER 2001
LISTENING TO 'CHEATING' BY JETTINGHAM

Sixteenth Birthday Night
I had such an amazing night out. Lucy, Maggie, Charlie and

Mish came round for a drink at mine before we walked into town. William, Angus and Andy 'Lads Lads Lads' Burns met us at the Mexican restaurant and then Jamie, Gretchen and Holly arrived ridiculously late and totally fucked. After a lot of silly Mexican jokes, Mexican accents and twenty gallons of tequila, we went to The Globe, Igloo, Bertie's and Bar Oz.

Everyone was absolutely fucked and we were having such a laugh dancing and drinking until Gretchen and Holly ruined everything by doing this weird dirty dancing with William – I did not like it one bit! Holly was wiggling her arse into William's crotch and he had such a stupid, gormless expression on his face. He almost definitely had a hard-on. I was furious. I hate that I had to invite them just to keep the peace. Why they even came is beyond me. We clearly all hate each other. Maybe one year I could celebrate my birthday without a bunch of girls that hate me! Sigh… who am I kidding? Gretchen's ALWAYS going to be there. I'll probably end up having to have her as one of my bridesmaids or something.

William walked me home and we watched *Monty Python and the Holy Grail*. We must have watched it a thousand times together, but every time we watch it, it feels like we get to reset and start again. I had my head tucked in under his chin and he was stroking my hair. It felt so warm and familiar and he told me he still loved me. *I LOVE YOU TOO!* I thought, but I didn't say it. I've been messing him about and leading him on enough as it is. I need to be sure this time. Not now, I thought; not drunk. But then before I knew it, I kissed him and then, arrrrrrgghhhhhhh, he was going down on me. I definitely wanted it to happen at the time and I'll always love him, but did I let this happen/make this happen cos I was so jealous of Holly and I wanted to try and keep him to myself?

Yes.

I know I really love him though. There's obviously a reason I keep going back there. Maybe we should give it another go? Maybe it would work this time? I'm going to give it the weekend and think about it and if I still feel the same on Sunday – I'm going to tell him I want to get back together. AHHHHH, what if he said no? That would be the worst.

Text from Lucy: Hey Claire — how ya doing? Last night was such a laugh! I didn't get home till 3am and then had to play hockey this morning — but totally worth it! I'll give you a call tomorrow. X

Text from Angus: Well done on a fabby night out sweetie! Call you l8r in the week. Luv u and hapi bday you separator! (William & Holly!) say ta 2 ur mum 4me xxx

Text from Mish: Happy Birthday Sexy Claire. Cheers for a fun night! Captain Spunky x

Text from Maggie: BEST. NIGHT. EVER. Happy Birthday my sexy beast. Feeling a little fragile today. Did you leave with William? Ay aye? Your Maggilicious x

Text from William: I love u so much. Not being with u drives me insane but I need to move on if we aren't going to be together. I still care about you and want to make you happy. The day I stop caring about you is the day I die.

18TH NOVEMBER 2001
LISTENING TO 'PHOEBE CATES' BY FENIX TX

4pm: I've decided I'm going to ask William if he wants to get back together. I'm so nervous that he might say no. I know he tells me he loves me all the time and all he wants is to get back together, but he might not actually want to. I feel dizzy with excitement and love the idea that this might be it. This is finally our time.

4.30pm: I just rang Maggie to tell her what I was going to do and see what she thought, when she told me William and Holly pulled last night at the play rehearsals. Just ONE day after we got together again. If it's true, it's ruined everything. Hopefully it's bollocks. Please be bollocks. Please just be something Gretchen made up to fuck with me.

4.45pm: I rang him to see if it was true, praying with every cell in my body that it was just a rumour.

'So I was calling cos I heard about you and Holly pulling last night…'

'Look, you should probably know we're going out now. It's not like I was going to wait forever for you.'

I nearly vomited there and then. I am so sick with jealousy. It's the most horrible feeling and it's completely floored me. It's like someone's had me in a giant hole punch and… 'chop' the second he uttered those words. Everyone says you get over heartbreak with time, but I don't believe it. There is no way this feeling will ever pass. I'm fucked forever. I may find someone else and fall in love, but even in fifty years, when I think back to this day, I will still be able to feel this pain and anguish. Fuck him. Fuck Holly. Fuck love. FUUUUUUUCCCCCCKKKKKKKKKKKKK!

19TH NOVEMBER 2001
LISTENING TO 'LEARN TO FLY' BY FOO FIGHTERS

I am so miserable and I've been crying all day. I hate Holly so much I wish she'd just die. Well, maybe not die but at least disappear. William finally replaced me. Every time I close my eyes I see him looking at her like he used to look at me... laughing at her jokes... stroking her hair... coming up behind her and grabbing her perfect, peachy arse. I know I should be happy that he's moved on, but this is the worst pain I have ever felt. I feel like someone died (just sadly not Holly)... Ahhh, stop joking about Holly dying. FYI Detective that reads my diary if Holly dies of suspicious circumstances – I realise I am a good suspect right now, but I did not kill her! I know I'm being so selfish, but I want him all to myself more than anything in the world. I need it to be just the two of us again, but it's over. Arrrgghhhhhhhhhhhhhhhhhhhhhhhhhhhhhhh!!!!!

> Text from Finn: Claire baby cheer up. You deserve way better than William anyway... u deserve me! Ur a fab gorgeous lovely girl who I adore. Keep smiling and forget him! xxx

20TH NOVEMBER 2001
LISTENING TO 'FALLIN'' BY ALICIA KEYS

Well, Happy Fucking Sixteenth Birthday to me. It's been utter shite. I'm still devastated about Holly and William. I keep waking up feeling normal and then I remember and my heart aches. Not just my heart actually. EVERYTHING aches. I can't believe I've lost him. He waited for me for six months and then got with someone else twenty-four hours before I was going to get back with him. I feel hollow and sick. So sick…

Why didn't I tell him I loved him too on my birthday night? None of this would have happened if I'd just fucking said it! I saw him in school today and just about managed to say, 'Hi', when he launched into a huge rant cos Maggie told him I couldn't stop bitching about Holly, saying, 'She's got a fat arse.' Well, she does. Just (annoyingly) in a very sexy way. FUCKING BITCH!!! I have pure hate and anger pumping through my veins. I've turned into such a monster. This is how all the baddies start in films. I'll be plotting the end of the world before we know it.

Shit chat, Claire. Ahhh, just stop writing bollocks and go to bed.

Oh God, this is awful. I'm such a mess.

23/11/2001 5am
Letter to William:

Will,

I can't sleep and I am totally fucked off. I am completely in love with you where I want to be with you every second of the day and I feel empty when you're not around. It drives me insane — literally — to think of you with anyone but me.

But I am happy for you that you have finally found yourself a girlfriend — that is what you wanted, right?

I love you, William — I actually do. I would do anything for you.

I've just realised that everything you said was bollocks. You kept going on about how much you loved me and that you would

do anything to make me happy. You told me
that you loved me more than I ever did or
ever could. Well, that's clearly not true.
You have hurt me so much you couldn't even
begin to imagine. I have been crying myself
to sleep for the past week at the thought
of being replaced. What happened with the
other girls was hard, but Holly is right
under my nose so it makes it so much worse.
I love you William. Why can't you fucking
see that?! I don't know what stopped me
wanting to go out with you cos you are
clearly the love of my life. You mean too
much to me and my heart is in constant
pain. I feel sick all the time. Why can't
you be with me? I didn't want you but I
always loved you. I need you by my side.
    Claire x

It's too much! I can't read any more!

23RD NOVEMBER 2001
LISTENING TO 'RAINING IN BALTIMORE'
BY COUNTING CROWS

11.40pm: I found out William broke up with Holly today. Thank
Christ. I feel I can breathe again. I went to his and we watched
Hercules and then a porn film. I just started kissing him and
then he played with me for hours. It was amazing. He told me
he wanted to see what my eyes did when I came, but it turns
out it's very difficult to keep your eyes open during an orgasm.
It's a bit like when you sneeze and your eyes shut or when your

mouth automatically opens when you're applying mascara. Weird William fetish aside, I'm completely in love with him. Life without William would not be life at all. I wanted to tell him I wanted to get back together, but I was so scared he'd say no and ruin an amazing night. I thought it would seem like I was just wanting to because of Holly (even though I'd made the decision in my head ages before that slut got involved). Instead, I waited for him to say something (cos he normally does). I thought he'd say, 'I love you', at some point and then I could finally say it back. But he didn't. So I went home feeling nervous about what that meant. Maybe he didn't break up with her for me? Maybe he doesn't really like either of us and I'm just his plaything.

25TH NOVEMBER 2001
LISTENING TO 'SEVEN DAY MILE' BY THE FRAMES

After Friday at William's, I spent the weekend starting to imagine what it would be like to get back with him. Maybe it would work this time… BUT I've just found out (from fucking – *you should probably know* – Gretchen, thank you very much) that Holly and William spent the whole party on Saturday together getting their frickin' rocks off. I can't believe it. What is this? Friday night with me and then Saturday night with Holly? I feel so betrayed. I really love(d?) him and I feel so heartbroken. I will NEVER get back with him now. It's over. Whatever he says or whatever I end up doing with him, I won't let him back into my heart. I'll never be his girlfriend ever again. I will simply refuse to love him anymore. I can't go through this 'will they?/won't they?' again. I have to close that metaphorical door, lock it and vaporise the key.

Holy cow, I'm so miserable. This emotional rollercoaster is reeking havoc with me. I'm finding it so hard to get to sleep and I've even lost my appetite (not the worst thing in the world!).

It's almost too much to bear and I feel like I can't even cope with the little things in life. My dad made some comment about me stinking of fags yesterday (not new) and I just about disintergrated… I screamed at him for ten minutes then stormed up to my room and spent the whole evening listening to music, painting and smoking out my window.

> *It's almost like I was trying to portray as many clichés associated with the emotional turmoil of adolescence.*
>
> *'Yeah I just smoke and cry and paint, listening to punk rock…'*
>
> *Eat some fruit, Claire, go to bed and get some sleep.*
>
> *This was around the same time that I used to put my hair up with a paintbrush, wear oversized paint-splattered shirts and A LOT of black kohl eyeliner.*

30TH NOVEMBER 2001
LISTENING TO 'BECAUSE I GOT HIGH'
BY AFROMAN

I've just had a really annoying day at school. I didn't do well in my English oral and my screen print in art was awful. I just can't concentrate on anything. Oh fuck. I need to seriously get my head down or I'm about to screw up my life.

William came back to mine after school and he got his head down and did well on his oral… nudge nudge wink wink.

> *Ewwwwwwweeeeeeeeeeeee!*

Maggie and Gretchen are inseparable again. It's so annoying. It makes me feel so petty not hanging out with Maggie, but I can't abide Gretchen and they sadly seem to come as a pair now.

Why don't I get to have a best friend? Am I not made of the right stuff? Lucy dumped me for the popular life (even though we are kinda friends again). Psycho Jane turned into a nutcase/ was always a nutcase. Hannah fucked off back to Australia. Mish likes to pretend he's not my friend when there's anyone else around. William and I fell in love. Life is so much harder without a special someone alongside you through thick and thin. I just want a best friend who loves me *because* of my weird peculiarities. I want someone to chuckle knowingly when they see me eat my burger with a knife and fork. It's probably too late now. Everyone's coupled up. I can't just get a school best friend now. They're all taken. When people get married there's always a bridesmaid 'that's been my best friend since school' alongside the obligatory uni friends and sister. I won't have that. Humph. Oh God, what if I don't make uni friends? Although at this rate, I won't even be going to uni or getting married. Or ever be happy ever again.

A nod to the great bridesmaids... my sister, Tron and Mad Dog. There was indeed no one from school and it was just perfect.

9TH DECEMBER 2001
LISTENING TO 'DON'T STOP ME NOW' BY QUEEN

William and I have basically spent the last month in bed together. I know I should stop. It's ridiculous. What the hell am I doing?

We went to a party last night and it was almost like we were *together*, but neither of us said anything about it. I went outside for a fag with Tom Southall and he said he liked me and tried to kiss me! I let him for about half a second before pulling away. Argh! BLOODY TYPICAL! I told him I liked him too, but couldn't do anything at the moment until I knew what was going on with William. William then found out that Tom had made a move (I think Tom told him) and had kittens. What the fuck?! I turned Tom down, you buttface! I turned down someone who I have fancied for years to protect YOU. We're not even together. Much.

```
Text to Tom (night of party): Sorry tonight
was so awkward. I don't really know what
I want. I was probably flirting and giving
you the wrong impression. Or maybe not. Ah
sorry I'm a bit drunk.. you probably were
too and maybe you didn't even want to kiss
me. I fancied you for ages but I guess the
timing is not right now. X
```

```
Text from Tom (night after party): I was
fairly drunk but that's not an excuse. I
just wouldn't have had the guts if I wasn't.
I just feel a bit annoyed that I missed
my chance with u. It's a shame we can't
have met 2night and discussed things — I
actually left a voicemail on that number u
gave me suggesting we meet up.
```

14TH DECEMBER 2001
LISTENING TO 'BREAKOUT' BY FOO FIGHTERS

MUST. STOP. SHAGGING. BLOODY. WILLIAM.

William had a party last night, and Angus and the rest of William's friends (who have always hated me since 'Doug Guy' gate) told me I was ruining his life. Urgh, they're probably right. I'm so embarrassed by the person I turn into when I'm around him. I've behaved so badly. I know I get horribly possessive and controlling, but I just can't stop it. I told William our relationship was really unhealthy and it can't carry on like this. We then spent the whole night chatting and having sex. Not quite what I meant...

> Text from William: I cant hack this
> anymore. I love u and u love me isn't that
> the best reason to go out? Every night
> could be like last night if we went out.
> The words I Love You aren't good enough
> anymore.

22ND DECEMBER 2001
LISTENING TO 'IF I HAD $1,000,000'
BY BARENAKED LADIES

Just got back from Medlink in Nottingham and it was (surprisingly) quite a lot of fun. I was staying in halls and pretty much got to pretend to be a student. I met a really nice group, especially a guy called Chris who's got this super cool skater look. He's got a girlfriend, but he's still nice to look at. He didn't seem particularly interested in any of it and he just wanted to *hang*. I definitely want to do medicine now. I'm going to have to knuckle down.

I thought Skater Chris was very cool indeed. He dressed in a way that was only acceptable if you were sixteen years old in the early noughties. It was a strict uniform that included wide-legged, floor-length jeans and a FUBU or Weird Fish hoodie with hair gelled into twisted spikes. He wore a wooden beaded necklace (with an obligatory shark

tooth on it) and a mix of leather and rubber wristbands.
He had a tatty, pleather skull and crossbones wallet on a
chunky chain and a small bar pierced through his eyebrow.

Daddy Skater was a surgeon and Chris grew up feeling
that it was his destiny to follow in his father's footsteps.
As far as he was concerned he was pretty much already a
doctor. He was extremely arrogant, but that just added to
his appeal at the time.

According to Facebook, Skater Chris has persisted
with this noughties skater boy look with the addition of a
multitude of piercings, a receded hairline and the distinct
lack of a medical degree. He's probably still singing along to
'Heaven is a Halfpipe' in his parents' garage and applying
skating branded stickers to a board that has never really
been skated. He deserved a proper introduction as he
crops up again in a bit...

23RD DECEMBER 2001
LISTENING TO 'CALIFORNIA'
BY RUFUS WAINWRIGHT

William and I have become inseparable again. We're hooking up
every day, but it's in a weird secret sex way rather than an open
proper going out way. It's totally silly. We had sex in the bath last
night. It was just awkward and made a huge mess. I can't go on
like this. My life needs to change and we both need to move on.

SEVENTEEN
AUSSIE JASON

Oh, Claire… be careful what you wish for.

27TH DECEMBER 2001
LISTENING TO 'GOTTA GET THRU THIS'
BY DANIEL BEDINGFIELD

I spent the morning trying to do maths, but had to stop for fear that it might kill me. I am going to be in serious trouble come exam time.

I went out with William and Angus to Siglo's, and then William and I went to drunkenly sing karaoke at ABBAR. Some random Australian guy called Jason started chatting to me at the bar when William was in the toilets. He was pretty cute, but I couldn't be bothered with the hassle of dealing with William's jealousy so I was quite off with him. Just before we left, though, I thought, *Fuck it*, secretly slipped him my number and gave him a wink. William and I went back to mine and I had a million orgasms.

Ouft, I feel very uneasy reading about these ugly levels of confidence and promiscuity. I have two daughters and pray they take after their dad.

28TH DECEMBER 2001
LISTENING TO 'UNDERGROUND'
BY BEN FOLDS FIVE

I was so surprised to find a voicemail from the Aussie guy first thing.

'Hey, it's Jason, from ABBAR, it was really nice to meet you and wondered if you fancy meeting for coffee later?'

OOOOOOOh, how exciting! This is my way out. New boyfriend. New friends. New life. This is my chance to start again and be a better me. He doesn't need to know about William, 'Doug Guy', Gael and all the lying and the cheating… I could end this mess with William and fall in love with someone new. My Jason life wouldn't even need to have a Gretchen in it…

I rang him back and we arranged to meet. I told him straight away that I was sixteen cos I didn't want a repeat of the whole French boys fiasco.

Aussie Jason was cocky, 99% brawn and reached the highest possible levels of unsophistication. Jason and his Aussie mates were all pierced, waxed and oiled with a ubiquitous 'O' at the end of their names: Rick-o, Sam-o, Sean-o, Shane-o… etc. They were so offensive, but I didn't really care because Jason wasn't William. He was just what (I thought) I needed.

Aussie Jason and I met at Native State and before I knew it, we were getting drunk on 241 pitchers and getting on like a house on fire. I really liked him and I wasn't going to hold back.

What does that mean? It's hardly like I'd been demonstrating nun-like restraint up until this point.

William (obviously) wasn't too pleased that I was on a date with a random Australian and kept asking, 'When did you even meet this guy?' It was awkward cos it was last night when I was out with him. Obviously I couldn't say that so I made up some crap about meeting him when I was out with 'people he didn't know'. It was a stupid answer. I can't even remember the last time I was out without William, and he knew everyone I knew. He sniffed out my lie and said he never wanted to speak to me again. Fine!

Aussie Jason and I then went to Henry J Beans where he introduced me to all his friends. We danced and pulled before he walked me home and properly asked me out. I had that little skip in my heart…

Text from William: I love you and I know this is going to ruin everything but either way it's ruined. I'm sorry you don't want me. I bring you down. You're better than me. I'm useless.

This text breaks my heart. How could I have been so cruel as to let him believe that? We had (unknowingly) spent months chipping away at each other's self-esteem and it culminated in me dating Australia's biggest meathead and this text, which I did not reply to.

1ST JANUARY 2002
LISTENING TO 'FRIDAY I'M IN LOVE' BY THE CURE

Hogmanay 2002

I've spent every day and night with Aussie Jason since we met. He's good fun, I like him and I don't feel as emotionally dependent as I did with William and Gael. Thank God.

I went to meet Aussie Jason and his mates last night at the Southern Cross on Cockburn Street. They'd hired the whole downstairs for the evening before going to the street party. We did loads of shots and Aussie Jason kept grabbing my arse under my dress… I realllllllly wanted him, but I was also a little embarrassed that he kept accidentally exposing my butt to all his friends. I can tell that the girls think it's weird that I'm with him and so young. I guess it is when I think about it, but when I'm with him, I really don't feel the age gap.

We spent the evening playing drinking games and then walked to the street party as a big group. Aussie Jason and his mates kept flashing randoms under their kilts cos they were 'real Scotsmen' for the night. It was so embarrassing. They may be in their twenties, but they're definitely not very mature.

William was calling me non-stop all night. He left about a million texts and voicemails laying the guilt on thick, but I've had enough of his bullshit. I feel bad but I completely ignored him.

The stroke of midnight was magic. It felt like I was in a film. Aussie Jason was kissing me and the fireworks were going off and it felt like the thousands of people around us disappeared. I had my whole body pressed into him and it was almost too much to bear. He is SUCH A GOOD KISSER!

We were all pretty drunk and we walked back to their flat. Every time I looked at my phone there was a new missed call or text from William, which I kept ignoring. I feel bad about it now, but at the time I was just getting more and more annoyed by him 'ruining' my night. His messages basically alternated between calling me 'a massive cheap skank who never cared about him' and 'the love of his life and his soulmate'. In the last voicemail he was clearly crying, but I just used everything I had to block it out. I do hate myself a bit now. I didn't want to hurt him. I don't want William to feel pain, but I don't want him in my life anymore. Nothing good comes of it.

Last text from William 1/1/02 3am: I can't do this anymore. Why are you treating me like this? You keep telling me we're soulmates and that you love me but you can't even pick up the phone or reply to any of my texts?! I don't deserve this and I never deserved a bitch like you. Fuck you! Please don't come crawling back to me when you sober up and you realise this Aussie fuck is just going to fuck you over. I loved you so much but I just don't know why anymore. I don't even know who you are anymore. Don't worry I won't ever call you again.

There was such an amazing atmosphere when we got back to their flat and Aussie Jason was wandering about in his boxers cos his clothes were soaked in beer. I hadn't realised what an amazing body he has! His skin was like rippled silk... like the guy from the Diet Coke advert. Then, yep, I'm ashamed to say it but we had sex. Morals aside, it was amazing and I loved every minute. Morals not aside... not great. I feel so bad about William. Part of me wonders if I went for it as one big 'FUCK YOU!' to William. I obviously wanted to, but I think I also thought that if Aussie Jason and I had sex, I would definitely get over William. I'm not sure it really worked... I feel really guilty. Again.

Nooooooooooooo! The initial title for this book was going to be 'SLUT!'. I suggested it to my husband and he said it was 'a hard no'. I wonder now if it would have been a more apt title. My memory of Aussie Jason was that we'd been dating for months before we had sex. Not days... yeesh.

4TH JANUARY 2002
LISTENING TO 'JUST A DAY' BY FEEDER

William's turned up at mine after Hogmanay and wanted to go for a walk and a chat. I felt flooded with emotions the second I saw him. Oh God, and the guilt. Why do I feel so guilty? It's not like I've cheated on anyone! I bit the bullet and told him about Aussie Jason or 'That Aussie Fuck' as William likes to refer to him. I might as well have stabbed him in the chest with a rusty blade and pushed him off the side of the bridge. He looked devastated, but maybe we'll be able to move on now. Then we bumped into Mish down the road from mine and William was like, 'Oh, so what do you think, Mish? Do you think it's ok for a sixteen-year-old to have sex with a twenty-year-old Aussie Fuck after only a few days?!' Mish clearly didn't want to be involved, but muttered a 'No, it's probably not ok but it's Claire, you know...' Errrr, say what now? Thanks a fucking bunch, Mish! God, he's such an arsehole sometimes.

14TH JANUARY 2002
LISTENING TO 'SMILE' BY THE SUPERNATURALS

I went out with Lucy at the weekend and bumped into William in Frankie's. I felt like I'd been punched in the stomach when I saw him. I miss him so much. I'm really trying to invest my feelings in Aussie Jason, but it's so hard. William and I went and sat upstairs for a chat and a drink and we kissed. It was so soft and familiar and I realised how much I still loved him and I wanted to cry.

STOP CHEATING ON EVERYONE, CLAIRE!

But then I realised what a fucking disaster we are. Arghhh. The kiss was only for about a minute and I managed to tear myself away and say, 'Sorry. This really needs to end.' He told me that was the last straw and I'll never get another chance. I left hurt and upset and feeling bloody guilty (AGAIN!) that I've cheated (AGAIN!).

I've been going out with Aussie Jason for three weeks now and it's mostly good, but he can be a massive twat at times. I was round at his on Saturday and I'd invited Lucy to come with me to meet him and his mates. We left just after Jason passed out on the floor drunk. I was so embarrassed as Lucy and I were literally stepping over him to get out the door when she asked, 'Does he do this a lot?' What a loser. Not a proud girlfriend moment.

Just before that (and before I realised how pissed he was) we were sat on his bed and he told me he thought he could fall in love with me. It seriously freaked me out! Maggie and Gretchen have done nothing but bang on about how it's blatant that a twenty-year-old would only be up for a relationship with me for sex. Maybe they're right, but then why bother with the whole love thing if that's true? Mind you, he hasn't *actually* said anything.

Text from Aussie Jason: There are three words I wanna say babe. X

Urgh. Babe?!

Text from William: I can't stop thinking about you. I'll always love you no matter what I say. If u ever change your mind about me, I'll be waiting but for now I need us not to be us anymore.

Text from Finn: Will you marry me please because I want good looking kids. Oh and you're quite nice 2. I hope this is ok. Many Thanks. Urs sincerely, Finn xxx ps you're so sexy and lovely baby!

20TH JANUARY 2002
LISTENING TO 'BOYS DON'T CRY' BY THE CURE

I am a sad sad person. I ruin people's lives just for a moment's happiness. It's pathetic. I started going out with Aussie Jason partly for a bit of fun but also probably to try and get over William. It has totally backfired! I'm not over William and Aussie Jason has taken the whole thing really seriously. I don't know how to end it now. Ah, for fuck's sake. I just love trampling over everyone! Like with William: if I hadn't begged William to be friends and then clearly slept with him at the slightest hint of him losing interest, he would never have ended up so... how he is now... mean and broken. His heart is so hard and icy now. If I'd just let him go he could have got over me about six months earlier, lived his life and probably been way happier.

But noooooo, Claire wanted all the attention. Claire wanted all the cakes with all the frosting and all the sprinkles and all the candles. But would Claire eat the cakes? Noooooo. She'd just smoosh them up so no one else could have them. God, I was so selfish. I AM so selfish. I need to dump stupid Aussie Jason…

28TH JANUARY 2002
LISTENING TO 'NARCOLEPSY' BY BEN FOLDS FIVE

I just got back from the New York art trip and I'm exhausted. I wrote a separate diary while I was there so I've just stuck it in:

22/1/02: Wow, New York is cold but amazing. I'm feeling pretty lonely though. It's not quite what I'd expected. Maggie and I aren't really that close anymore cos of Gretchen. It turned into a bit of a 'her or me' situation before we left and she chose her. I said something bitchie about Gretchen, and Maggie got really defensive and said that if I couldn't be friends with Gretchen then she couldn't be friends with me.

```
Email from Gretchen 21/1/02: Maggie told
me you thought I was two-faced huh? Seems
a bit hypocritical not saying it to my face
don't you think? So I guess I'm finally free
from you and can keep all 'our' friends (not
that they were ever your friends anyway).
What did you think was going to happen?
We've all been friends for years and you
think you can come in with your shit chat
and people are going to want to be friends
with you more than me? You did this and for
once, you can't blame anyone but yourself.
It was only a matter of time until everyone
```

saw your true colours and stopped being
friends with you. Good Riddance. G x

So Maggie and I have not really been hanging out much. William
has been quite distant with me since our kiss in Frankie's and he
is clearly keen to spend as little time as possible with me too.
So this is great! No one to hang out with in one of the coolest
cities in the world. Is Gretchen right? Did I really bring this on
myself? Probably a bit. I still fucking hate her though.

23/1/02: I feel so lonely. I can't believe what a loser I am. I
have NO friends. I am sharing a room with Anna, a girl who I
don't know very well who doesn't seem that fussed about getting
to know me. We bonded (a bit) last night by spending an hour
killing cockroaches in our shithole room, but otherwise we like
different things. Namely not each other.

*This girl turned out to be a famous, Bafta Award-winning
actress. Whenever she's on TV I shout, 'We were friends at
school and shared a room on our New York art trip!' Well.
Friends-ish.*

24/1/02: I should have made a better attempt at keeping track
of where we've been – what a twat. What I can remember: the
Whitney, the MET, the Guggenheim, the Museum of Modern
Art and tonnes of galleries I've lost count of. Damn! When I
realised I was simply a big loner, I decided to use the trip and
just immerse myself in the art. It's actually quite enjoyable. I
can just sit quietly in galleries doing sketches. When will I ever
get another opportunity to do this? William seems to be doing
the absolute opposite; he doesn't take anything seriously. It's so
annoying. Wherever I am, I just hear his fucking laugh. ALL THE
FUCKING TIME! Whatever I'm doing, his laugh seems to be the
soundtrack to my life, constantly mocking me. It's like everything

is a big joke to him. He is SHIT at art – why is he even here? He's just larking about doing the odd crap sketch for the hell of it then back to prancing about like a big clowny man-child.

26/1/02: Bugger. William and I have naturally found ourselves hanging out more and more. It's so frustrating. Why am I so drawn to this imbecile?! He irritates the hell out of me, but I just want to be around him all the time. We both bought the new Ben Folds Five album – *The Unauthorized Biography of Reinhold Messner*. It's utterly beautiful and heart-wrenching. Last night, we sat together on the deck of the Staten Island ferry listening to it during the sunset. I was looking at him thinking he looked really handsome. I've not thought of him as handsome for ages, but there he was looking out over the water, the wind rustling his stupid cow's lick, looking damn handsome. I shuffled in right next to him and leant my head on his shoulder. We sat like that for about a minute without moving and staring at some fixed point in the distance. My heart was racing just being close to him again. He then imperceptibly turned his head in like he was going to kiss my head, like he has done a million times, but stopped himself, knuckle-rubbed my hair and stood up. Cock. How is this happening again?

There is no doubt that I had subconsciously been triggered by the sun setting over the Manhattan skyline. There were complex and deep-seated powers of suggestion at work. I spent my youth watching nineties romantic comedies where beautiful people fall in love in New York. Meg Ryan had unknowingly been grooming me to believe in a world where if you are in a certain environment at a certain time of day, you would almost definitely fall in love. See also: the top of the Empire State Building, ice skating at the Rockefeller Center, painting a room together or baking a cake together. I mean, what doesn't say true love like throwing a handful of flour at someone?

27/1/02: I kissed William last night. I'm breaking up with Aussie Jason anyway. I don't know what it means or what I was thinking. Shit.

We went to Ground Zero, which was so weird. The air felt thicker and stiller and no one dared to say a word. It was still just mounds of cordoned-off rubble and hundreds of billboards with letters, photos and a harrowing amount of teddy bears. It was so easy, when at home, to disconnect from it all. It didn't feel real cos it was so far away. Well, it sure as hell felt real today.

On the flight home, William and I sat together. I was relieved to be sitting with him and quite looking forward to maybe having a little kip on his shoulder like old times. Well, THINK AGAIN, Claire! We spent THE WHOLE FLIGHT fighting and then eventually we were both crying. It was hell.

We were listening to *Reinhold Messner* on loop and this only heightened the emotions. I'm not even sure either of us really knew what we were fighting about by the end. It was mostly the usual: he can't stand to be friends with me if I'm seeing other people cos he's still in love with me. I desperately still want him in my life and am in part totally in love with him, but I don't think I want a relationship with him anymore since getting stung with Holly. I feel like that boat has sailed for us, but then part of me still wonders if I'm just being stubborn. We went round and round in circles.

13TH FEBRUARY 2002
LISTENING TO 'LOVE HAS PASSED AWAY'
BY THE SUPERNATURALS

I finally broke up with Aussie Jason. It was his twenty-first and he'd hired the downstairs of Frankenstein's. I was thinking I'd probably wait to break up with him later on in the week (no one wants to be dumped on their birthday), but he made it impossible for me to resist. So we were all having a good night, although he was behaving like a bit of a drunken dick… I mean how many times can you just shout 'Let's get plowed!'? God he's a twat. He came over to me early on, grabbed my arse really hard and shouted 'I'm so blasted babe!'. Good for you! What did I ever see in him!??! I managed to remove my buttocks from his sleazy paws and went back to chatting with one of his old friends when Jason stood up on the central bar, dropped his trousers and set his pubes alight. My jaw literally dropped. What the fuck was he doing? What. A. Massive. Bellend. All the Aussie boys were pissing themselves laughing and told me this was a 'twenty-first Aussie tradition'. Well, this 'tradition' got us thrown out and got him dumped. He may have been twenty-one, but he was without a doubt the most immature guy I've ever met.

EIGHTEEN
DICKHEAD MIKE

27TH FEBRUARY 2002
LISTENING TO 'ADDICTED TO BASS' BY PURETONE

New Diary. New Me.
From now on I will not be so pathetic and dependent on others.
I will be strong and live my life the way I want to. Until now I
couldn't imagine living my life without William, but he said he
didn't need me anymore, so fuck him.

I am free now. I was sad at first, but I am growing stronger and
stronger without him. Things are really going to start going my
way. The problem is that if I have a quiet moment or close my eyes
and let my mind wander I can still hear William shouting at me.

*'You're the worst person I've ever met and you've ruined
my life. I'll never forget what you've done to me and how
you've made me feel. You're an evil bitch who cares about*

nothing and no one but herself. I don't love you anymore and I'll never love you again. I wish I'd never met you. This is goodbye.'

Mustn't dwell… anyway, it's a good thing! I'm free! I'll admit that he pretty much had me on my knees. Every word out of his mouth felt like a new blow and when he finally finished I felt like all the air had been punched out of me. I know it's dramatic, but in that moment, I felt like my world had ended. He wanted to hurt me. For the past year I've always felt that no matter what, William loved me and wanted to protect me. Not anymore. My God, it was awful, but like ripping off a plaster, it had to happen at some point. I've come to realise that although we had our good times, neither of us could be genuinely happy together.

No more tears. No more heartache. Done.

28TH FEBRUARY 2002
LISTENING TO 'TOMORROW' BY JAMES

A poem to celebrate 'New Me':
I woke on this rainy, February day,
Expecting it to be dismal.
And rotting with heartache.
But I rose from my warm suffocating tomb.
And I was alive. A different person.
A happy person.
Better. Healing.
The rain drove on.
But I felt a blissful ray of happiness
escape its prison.
A year has passed with ups and downs,
I was sick and festering.

Oblivious until the shattering of this depressive shell.
A new life was born.
I licked my wounds and emerged.

And the award for self-indulgent cunt of the year goes to…

1ST MARCH 2002
LISTENING TO 'ALWAYS ON TIME'
BY JA RULE FT. ASHANTI

11am: So William is going out with a fourteen-year-old! The fucking pedo. It's so disgusting. What is he playing at? Plus he looks so happy. Urg. I'm reallllly trying to keep smiling, but I'm sat in art and he's in the other room. All I can hear is his booming laugh. I can't believe he's so happy. He's so louuuuddddd. He's all I can hear over my headphones. SHUT UP SHUT UP SHUUUUTTTT UPPPPPP!

1am (2/3/02): I pulled Dickhead Mike again. Every time I go out with Next Door Andy I end up kissing that beautiful dickhead. Fucking hell, my life would be so different if I could just show a smidge of self-restraint.

3RD MARCH 2002
LISTENING TO 'LUCKY DENVER MINT'
BY JIMMY EAT WORLD

The new me was coming along nicely until William called yesterday morning in tears because his uncle died. He said as soon as it happened he only wanted to speak to me. I spent hours on the phone with him comforting him. Then he started to apologise for everything that he's said in the past and that he still wanted to be friends. I felt torn. Old me was flooded with relief, but new me felt annoyed and didn't want to get dragged back down. New me went 'poof' and I agreed to meet up with him. I have missed him. Then he says, 'Maybe it's not such a good idea being friends with you after all. I'd just have to sacrifice my life for you again.' What the fuck?! I feel so stupid for having even picked up my phone. I was all 'new me new me' and he clicked his fingers and I came running. I am so angry. I saw red, told him to fuck himself and die and hung up.

4TH MARCH 2002
LISTENING TO 'LULLABYE' BY BEN FOLDS FIVE

I called William back tonight. I've had some time to calm down and I just wanted some friendly civilised closure. He's obviously having a tough time at the moment and all we had can't just end with such a bitter taste in my mouth. I started by saying that it was clear that we couldn't be friends, but surely we could try and part kindly? He told me that as far as he was concerned he's had to sacrifice his life for me for the last six months and he couldn't believe I'd asked him to put me before his uncle dying. I NEVER DID THAT! He said he could never be friends with me cos I will always resort to putting myself first and treating him like shit. God, I hate him so much. I am soooo angry!

8TH MARCH 2002
LISTENING TO 'WALK AWAY' BY BEN HARPER

Who was I trying to kid? My life is no different. I'm no different. I thought if I believed it enough it would be true.

Turning over a new leaf? Being free and liberated? Fuck off am I. My life is exactly the same except my best friend and soulmate is now missing. I have no one to turn to. I isolated myself from everyone when I was with William and now I'm on my own.

14TH MARCH 2002
LISTENING TO 'TRUE LOVE NEVER DIES' BY FLIP & FILL

I saw William's girlfriend today. 'The Toddler'. She was dressed like a five-year-old with her high-waisted cargo pants and visible tennis socks. Bleurgh. Her hair was greasy and mousy. She was disgusting, BUT she was his. Just looking at her made me feel like I couldn't breathe.

18TH MARCH 2002
LISTENING TO 'THE MIDDLE' BY JIMMY EAT WORLD

For the last month I have spent every Friday night at Next Door Andy's with his friends. Dickhead Mike's been there and we usually end up pulling at the end of the night after he's walked me home. He is BEAUTIFUL, but I'm just a little reluctant to get too close to him after the whole 'I'll wait for you', whoopsie BJ then 'I hate myself' business. Plus I'm still feeling pretty vulnerable after William. Anyway, this little, no strings Friday night snogging is lovely and quite therapeutic.

25TH MARCH 2002
LISTENING TO 'HEY BABY' BY NO DOUBT

I went into school this morning with my head held high, ready to face the world and pretend that William wasn't in it. But he is in it. He's in it, on it and all-bloody-over it. Even if I manage to catch my breath away from him, Gretchen and Holly always find a way to shoehorn him into the conversation. I will literally never get away from him.

4TH APRIL 2002
LISTENING TO 'WAITING ON AN ANGEL' BY BEN HARPER

I'm back in Brittany and it feels like I can breathe again. I've spent most of the past week hanging out with Yannick and Marc, although they're both working and not around loads. I am sooooo bored during the day trying to revise.

Last night Marc invited me to his friend Ewen's house for dinner, round the corner from his flat in Rennes. We had some drinks at Marc's flat first with his super cool housemates.

This may have been France in the early 00s, but most of Brittany was stuck in a time warp where they thought it was still 1974. Young women seemed particularly susceptible to this historic sentimentality and Marc's flatmates were no exception. I'd usually feel instantly intimidated in my modern, city mouse clothes and heels when faced with these bohemian goddesses. They were dreadlocked, pierced all over, utterly stunning and stoned off their tits. They lounged about in their hareem pants and vegan sandals, swearing in their husky smoker voices.

Their meals consisted of fags and black coffee, and I spent most of my adolescence trying to emanate these beautiful deadbeats.

When I got to Marc's flat, the incense was burning, the girls were rolling spliffs and everyone sat around listening to Pink Floyd on embroidered leather poufs that some wanker had brought back from Morocco.

I was really taken aback to see Gael was there. I hadn't spoken to him since his less than perfect departure from Edinburgh, and seeing him brought all the emotions crashing back. He had never replied to my breakup email and DID NOT seem pleased to see me walk through the door. He seemed different too… older and angrier, and he was smoking a spliff! Gael hated smoking. We had a slightly awkward '*bise*' hello and I sheepishly got stuck into a bottle of Pastis.

I was well and truly trashed by the time we went to their friend Ewen's house. When we got there, 'dinner' was simply saucisson and weed. Before I knew it I'd turned on the 'flirting machine' with Ewen (HAHAHA, I'm so glad no one will ever read about my 'flirting machine'!). I suppose he was a bit like the brunette version of Gael: handsome in a watersports kinda way with long curly brown hair and a smile that would knock the cast of *Brokeback* off their mountain. Hahaha, I am talking a lot of shit. That makes no sense! Knock *Brokeback*, what now? I'm an idiot and I dread to think of all the crap I was talking. Anyway. Before I knew it, it was suddenly 4am and Marc said we had to go.

The walk back to Marc's flat was so funny, but also a total nightmare. Gael was soooo fucked and yet he wouldn't stop drinking. He was running around the street and in front of cars shouting total bollocks and clutching a bottle of Pastis that he was drinking neat. Marc and I were chasing him trying to get the bottle off him when we gave up, realising that Gael drunkenly running away from us was ultimately more dangerous than a few more gulps.

When we got back to Marc's flat, we put Gael to bed and Marc and I sat down for a nightcap, a fag and a chat. I was giggling away saying how I don't know why Gael gets so drunk and Marc went all serious and stared at me.

'Ummm, he got *sooo* drunk because he still loves you, you broke his heart and you've just spent the night flirting with his friend in front of him.'

Well, that sobered me up pretty sharpish and I went to bed on the sofa. I'm feeling pretty shitty and booze bluesy now.

12TH APRIL 2002
LISTENING TO 'BREAKIN' DOWN' BY BEN HARPER

Bloody smooth-talking beautiful Dickhead Mike. I knew I shouldn't have fallen for his charm. AGAIN. People do not change. Me included it seems. So anyway, Dickhead Mike and I have been having little kisses after nights out for the last few months now. I haven't been expecting much and it's been quite nice.

Last Wednesday, we were chilling at Next Door Andy's before they all went out. I wasn't going out cos my mum is being a total bitch at the moment saying I need to revise more and I'm going out too much. Dickhead Mike said he'd stay with me while the others went out and we ended up with Next Door Andy's house to ourselves. We pulled a bit and then he asked me out. PROPERLY.

'Will you be my girlfriend?'

I raised an eyebrow and said, 'Well, this chat seems familiar...'

'No, I mean it. I was a dick last time. I really like you and I think we'd be great together.'

Fuck yeah! I was so excited! He then asked if I would give him a BJ. Ballsy beautiful dickhead! I think he said it as a joke, but I wasn't sure. Either way, not tonight. I kissed him goodnight and went home ecstatically happy to do some work.

Oh, good girl, Claire! No no, no oral sex for me, I'm off to learn about the Krebs cycle! Toodle pip.

I spent the whole of yesterday telling EVERYONE that Dickhead Mike and I were going out. I was daydreaming about him all day and went round to Next Door Andy's after school who kept saying he was 'surprised', but not a lot else.

Then after dinner, I got a text from that beautiful dickhead:

```
Sorry Claire but I can't commit.
```

Arrgghhhh. I. AM. SUCH. A. TIT.

NINETEEN

MAN SHOES

19TH APRIL 2002
LISTENING TO 'ALL MY BEST FRIENDS ARE
METALHEADS' BY LESS THAN JAKE

Well, I don't want to speak too soon, but I am pretty content at the moment. This isn't one of my usual hyper, excited and falsely happy times, but I'm just at ease and comfortable. Work is going ok. I've got a good, normal group of friends. I'm hanging out with Maggie and Gretchen a lot more. Maybe Gretchen and I could even be friends one day? At the moment it's a weird pretend niceness and both of us know this fragile friendship could shatter any moment, but it is far more civilised and pleasant than our usual all-out war.

William has turned into the most immature cockhead since he got dumped by The Toddler (which is utterly hilarious!) and I don't think we'll ever be able to be friends. We just seem to have endless bitchie MSN chats after trying to be friends...YET AGAIN.

21ST APRIL 2002
LISTENING TO 'THE BLOWER'S DAUGHTER' BY DAMIEN RICE

I am such a drunken knob jockey. I went out last night with Lucy and the old girls and had a really good night until I got completely wrecked and had the most uncontrollable, off-my-face urge to go to William's cos I knew he had a free house. I have no idea what I was thinking! I guess for a second I'd forgotten what a dick he'd become and I missed him. As soon as I arrived, I realised how fucked I really was. I don't really remember how the conversation went, but we were both crying and shouting at each other before I knew it. I just can't handle him bringing up all the shitty things I'd ever done ALL THE TIME. If I hear about 'Doug Guy' or Yannick or 'That Aussie Fuck' ONE MORE TIME... but then he told me he still loved me. I don't think that's what I had planned. Although I'm pretty sure there wasn't 'a plan' at all. I wanted to hear it though. I'm an awful person. I wanted to know that it wasn't all over yet; that there was still something special between us. It's like I just need to get a rise out of him to know he still cares. My God, I'm a wanker.

22ND APRIL 2002
LISTENING TO 'FAKE PLASTIC TREES' BY RADIOHEAD

Wow, I'm a jerk. I wish I'd never gone to William's yesterday. I just had to stir things up again.

28TH APRIL 2002
LISTENING TO 'HOW YOU REMIND ME' BY NICKELBACK

I'm feeling seriously lonely, crap and ugly. I spent most of the weekend at school doing art and saw practically no one. Then finally went to meet Mish and the rugby boys in the pub, but didn't get in cos the bouncer recognised me as having ID'd me in the past. I didn't have enough money for a taxi so I had to walk all the way home. I had no fags and it pissed it down with rain. What a shite weekend.

Also William has a new girlfriend. I think she's a normal age, but wears man shoes.

4TH MAY 2002
LISTENING TO 'ZOMBIE' BY THE CRANBERRIES

I'm so pissed off. The prefect announcement is coming up and it's really bringing out the worst in people. Out of the girls, Maggie probably deserves to be made a prefect and I think I do too, but I'm a bit worried that there's going to be some kind of reverse nepotism because of my mum. Mish told me that everyone is pissed off with me (Maggie, Gretchen, Grumpy Toby, Charlie, Jamie etc) cos I have the 'unfair advantage' of my mum being a teacher. Mish just loves to have a dig at me. What could he possibly hope to achieve by telling me that? How is this my fault?! That's not how it works! I've got the exact same chance as anyone. Apart from maybe the likes of Gretchen who clearly won't be a prefect. Although apparently she's been complaining to the headmaster about my 'unfair advantage'. The headmaster and my mum hate each other, so he'd have loved that chat and taken her concerns sooooo seriously. Now, if I do get it, people will think it's cos my mum pulled strings (which she can't do). I really think I deserve it. It doesn't feel very fair.

```
MSN chat with William:

From William: Do you not think it's petty
calling Maggie a traitor for being friends
with me?

To W: Oh fuck off will you and get your own
friends. You can't go getting all high and
mighty cos u got a new gf.

From William: I'm not getting all high
and mighty but u don't need to slag off my
girlfriend all the time which is what I've
heard. Ps Angus is here and says he never
liked you.

To W: Ah well these things happen. I'm not
going to let how you're behaving turn me
into a cold hard bitch which is more than
I can say 4u.

From William: Yeah seems that way by
slagging me off behind my back. I dont get
angry at my friends 4 speaking 2u. Don't
even think about trying 2b the strong one
here.

To W: Well I am. You're so fucking
insecure. U slag me off too remember — ull
always be weak.
```

From William: I ain't said jack shit so
don't try that on me although maybe I
should cos you're the world's biggest
bitch. You cheat. You lie. You broke my
heart and you don't care about anything or
anyone. Just fuck off and leave me alone.

Ouch.

9TH MAY 2002
LISTENING TO 'FLOWERS IN THE WINDOW' BY TRAVIS

Mish and I are hanging out all the time, revising and walking his
dog together. It's cool, but the other day he told me I behaved
differently in school and I was much cooler 'in real life'. Really?
I wasn't aware I behaved any differently. I mean, it's a little 'pot
calling the kettle black'. Mish is such a people-pleasing wanker
at school compared to his normal self the rest of the time. How
dare he say that *I* behave differently. It's actually really upsetting
that he thinks that, especially as I don't even know what I'm
doing differently, other than probably responding normally to
his split personality. How does he always manage to make me
feel so small?

14TH MAY 2002
LISTENING TO 'MAMA'S GOT A GIRLFRIEND NOW' BY BEN HARPER

I feel giddy with excitement. Today was the last day of classes for
the year. The prospect of never having a maths class again makes

me want to burst into song and kiss a stranger in the street. Even more excitingly though, I realised I never have to see William again. School is over and he's off to college. I can finally live my life! I can say bye bye and... that's it! I can't believe it – I'M FREEEEE! Admittedly we had something at one point, but that ended ages ago. Seeing him every day at school has been hell.

Byyyyyeeeeeeeee Asssssssshole!

21ST MAY 2002
LISTENING TO 'UNDERNEATH IT ALL'
BY NO DOUBT

I was in Costa with Maggie and Gretchen today when I turned round and in walked William with his new girlfriend (Man Shoes). I tried not to look, but I could not unsee her T-shirt, which was HORRENDO with purple glittery butterflies! Her man shoes require no further comment. Are they actually men's shoes? I felt terrible. I thought I was going to have a panic attack just seeing him. How does he still have this effect on me?! He pretended like he hadn't seen me and was all over her – it was disgusting. Urrrgghhh, I thought he might catch something, or she might. Either way it was a health crime and it made me feel physically sick.

23RD MAY 2002
LISTENING TO 'YOU HELD THE WORLD
IN YOUR ARMS' BY IDLEWILD

I feel so sad. I just took down the Polaroid photo of William, Angus and me drinking test tube shots in Siglo's. It reminded me how much I loved our little going-out routines and all the millions of nights out we had together and how much we laughed! Probably hundreds and hundreds of hours spent laughing together. I will NEVER let myself become so dependent on anyone ever again. If I can, I will never let myself fall in love again. Oh God, why am I even thinking of him? He's a useless waster who ruined a year of my life. Ahh, but I miss him. I'm nearly in tears. I must remember we tried so many times and it didn't work. I probably spent more hours crying than I did laughing. He hurt me and made me so unhappy. Good fucking riddance.

27TH MAY 2002
LISTENING TO 'JAH WORK' BY BEN HARPER AND THE INNOCENT CRIMINALS

Wooohooo, I've just finished maths forever! The exam actually went ok and I've come home to the most hysterically immature email from William's email account. It's apparently from a 'friend'. I'm pretty sure it couldn't be William as he has not only spelt his own name wrong (and William probably isn't clever enough to double bluff to that extent) but nearly every single word. The spelling is so atrocious it's laughable.

```
Look you silly whore, this isn't Wiliem
but its someone that is fed up of seeing
him take a buse from a slag like you. You
think you're so cool being able to slag
him off... well your not and none realy likes
you as you are a whore... Wiliem is to nice
to right an email like this but im not
because I just hate you because you smell
like fish and you dont shave your back
which you should... and you have a big snail
```

trail. I've met nicer girls in leith than you. Why? Because you are loose / easy / abit of fun is what people regard you as, not someone with feelings but a sad little women that is up herself. Goodbye… and shave.

It was simply too bad to be upsetting. It turned out to be the little brother of one of William's friends and he really wasn't worth fretting about. I did smile when he sold my husband and me a hotdog about fifteen years later. I mean no disrespect to hot dog vendors. My 'smile' was not because I was being a condescending bitch but because he didn't recognise me and he called me 'Madam'. Madam now, huh? Pass the mustard, you little shit.

29TH MAY 2002
LISTENING TO 'HIGH AND DRY' BY RADIOHEAD

I'm a little drunk so the writing must be excused. Tonight was Maggie's birthday night out. It started off well, but the fact that William and Man Shoes were there was really distracting. She was all over him. Gretchen kept saying things like, 'Awww, aren't they cute together. It's so nice to see William happy for once. He deserves it.' She was blatantly just saying it to fuck with me. Fucking BITCH. Jamie was the sweetest person ever though. He gave me a huge hug and said he could tell it upset me but that everything was going to be ok. I'm genuinely contemplating trying to pull Jamie to piss off Gretchen. That'd shut her stupid face up.

TWENTY

POST-EXAM EUPHORIA

4TH JUNE 2002
LISTENING TO 'GOLD TO ME' BY BEN HARPER

Ah… The start of a new month. Summer is on the horizon with the prospective smell of bonfires, sun cream, Pastis and the ocean. I couldn't be happier. I have finished my Highers and I'm completely ecstatic.

> *As natural highs go, I don't think you can beat post-exam euphoria (PEE).*
>
> *Becoming 'a grown-up' comes (for most) with a regrettable level of responsibility. You suddenly have to care about your health, what you're eating and how much exercise you do. You wake up one morning and Bang! You're an adult. Before long, all-night parties are replaced by sleepless nights wondering if you forgot the pomegranate*

off your Waitrose order (and how could you possibly do that Ottolenghi feast without it?!). BUT... I believe that for twenty-four hours after an exam, you are granted a delicious pause on the daily grind and you can behave like an idiot again. You've earned it; all that revision, hard work and stress has to go somewhere, right? No! Not into the exam, you loser! It goes into what happens AFTER the exam. The second that I walk out of an exam, I can mentally put a tick next to the 'work hard' section on my life's to-do list.

To give an example: the final exam to become a GP is a gruelling high-pressure, nowhere to hide, beast of an exam that you have to cough up £1500 for. It is the culmination of everything you have done up until that point and potentially your last ever exam after a minimum slog of five years at medical school – two as a junior doctor and three GP training. It represents the finish line and the stakes are high. Even I, sanguine to the end, felt pretty twitched by this exam.

When it eventually came to an end, the relief was indescribable. Finally. I'm done. No more early nights. No more 'No, I'm not coming out, I'm revising.' No more guilt for watching TV or reading for pleasure. No more exams! It's over. This is literally THE BEST FEELING IN THE WORLD!

So I stepped out, squinting at the daylight, and post-exam euphoria took control. PEE squashed my glimmer of self-doubt and convinced me to blow all the money I may otherwise have used for the resit. I danced out of the building straight into the Euston Tap (the nearest pub) where I did a mini jazz hands and ordered myself 'a pint of your finest ale, my good sir!' before recruiting everyone I knew in London and embarking on an eighteen-hour-long bender.

But every up must, of course, come down, and PEE is usually brought into line, pretty quickly, by a juicy anxiety-

filled hangover. I woke up on the morning after my GP exam on my friend's bedroom floor, crippled with booze blues and genuinely believing that I'd tried to pawn off my engagement ring in exchange for getting into some sticky London cesspool. The bouncers were denying us entry after I regaled them with the fact that I'd just done a tequila shot out of my mate's armpit. I was in the midst of my Newsnight-worthy story when I fell (from stationary) straight down the stairs into the club. I was subsequently bundled into a taxi, shamefully clutching a broken shoe and half a fag that the taxi driver (outrageously) wouldn't let me smoke in his cab in 2012!

I lay on my friend's wooden floorboards for a few minutes sweating and groaning before I nervously checked my ring finger and was genuinely relieved to discover that I hadn't flitted away my future for another cheap shot of sambuca. Whether I'd tried or not is anyone's guess, for PEE was calling the shots (and forcing me to drink them).

Oh, how I miss you, post-exam euphoria.

Everyone was on a massive post-exam high after our Highers finished. I went out with Jamie, Mish, Maggie, Gretchen and Holly to PoNaNa last night. I'm getting along really well with Jamie, which is lovely, but also has the added benefit of pissing Gretchen off.

Ha.

6TH JUNE 2002
LISTENING TO 'DREAMING' BY BLONDIE

God, I hate William. Maggie and Gretchen (who are obviously still friends with him) suggested we all go for a coffee today with William and Man Shoes. I suspect this was Gretchen's idea. I felt like I had to prove that things didn't affect me anymore so said, '*Yes, I'd love to, with fucking pleasure.*' Nawwt! It was such an effort and it took everything I had to sit and smile and make small talk with someone so sad (with the WORST shoes) going out with someone I love. He just sat there smiling smugly at me with his arm around her and kissing her constantly. Bleurgh.

I spoke to him later tonight and stupidly said I missed my best friend. He said he definitely didn't want to be friends with me because I've proved time and time again that I care about only myself. He said all he'd ever wanted was for us to be together, but it's too late now. The red mist descended and I let rip. I can't quite remember what I said, but it was bad. *Real* bad. He hung up, but I'm not sure at what point during my torrent of abuse he stopped listening. God, what's wrong with me?

Text from William: Y do I bother? U say things not even people who hate me would. I really need a friend at the moment and you just proved that I can't count on you. I've loved you and you just want me to be your puppy. All you do is cheat. You don't care about anyone but yourself.

Text to William: Ha! If only you were a puppy! You'd still be a little bitch though. All you have done is hurt me. Please just leave me alone. It doesn't matter anymore but I only ever cheated on you once.

Text from William: And Jason? Gael? All with me. See you in hell bitch!

*Busted! How interesting though that it seems even then
my memory was wiping itself of all the whoopsies I'd done.
Done a bad thing? Don't worry, Claire, let's just wipe the
memory slate nice and clean. Taahhh dah!*

9TH JUNE 2002
LISTENING TO 'BURN ONE DOWN'
BY BEN HARPER

Hmmm, well, that was eventful.

Friday night: I went out to PoNaNa with Mish, Lyla (Mish's
new lovely girlfriend) and Jamie.

> *Lyla was truly lovely but a little 'meh'. She was Mish's trophy
> girlfriend, cookie-cut to suit his golden boy requirements
> perfectly. She was a master of the clarinet, wanted to be a
> paediatrician, captained the hockey team, and was destined
> to be head girl of her school. She was a wholesome, natural
> beauty that Mish's mum (Binky-jolly-bloody-hockey-sticks-
> Allison) approved of. She had a big bosom, sturdy, child-
> bearing hips and a penchant for country casuals.*
>
> *Mrs Binky-jolly-bloody-hockey-sticks-Allison was
> a snooty bitch who supposedly received the best possible
> education at a boarding school with Princess Anne. This
> education was put towards hunting out and marrying
> a rich, big-chinned boffin. Binky was usually dressed in
> a mixture of cashmere and Harris Tweed and spent her
> days attending shooting parties and ladies' lunches whilst
> simultaneously meddling in her children's Oxbridge
> applications. She was part of Edinburgh's old school high
> society and didn't approve of me very much at all. Mish
> would happily tell me what she thought of me.*

'Mummy called you "a floozy" at supper last night.'

No one says 'supper' in Scotland unless it is in the context of 'a fish supper' (battered sausage and all). Certainly not when referring to your evening meal. So anyway, I spent my adolescence holding my breath every time I had to ring his home phone. I could hear the disgust in her voice every time she answered and realised it was me.

'Hamish, it's that Claire [audible eye roll]. Again.'

Jamie is very much on/off with Gretchen at the moment and I have completely lost track of if they're on or off. It's been going on for months and he has spent hours crying down the phone to me about her. Part of me finds it annoying, but misery loves company and all that…

We had an amazing night, and Jamie and I left to catch a bus home. When we got outside, Jamie put his hand in the small of my back and pulled me into him and kissed me. Completely out of nowhere! Tongue and all! I was so shocked and I pulled away saying, 'Gretchen would kill us…' When we got on the bus I thought, *Fuck it, Jamie's a nice guy… What's a little kiss between friends?*

… and it would drive Gretchen bananas?

I told him to close his eyes cos I had a 'surprise' for him. He closed his eyes and I leant in and kissed him, but this time *he* pulled away! He said it was wrong and he still loved Gretchen and it wasn't worth her wrath. Oh God, the wrath of Gretchen. What were we thinking?!? I'm probably going to have to emigrate to Australia tomorrow. No point in staying here. I'll be dead by Sunday. Gretchen and I are almost friends at the moment and it's over if she finds out. My life won't be worth living. Keeping the peace with her has been a full-time job for the last few months and I thought kissing her on/off boyfriend would help? Stupid, thoughtless Claire.

We decided it would be our secret, but by the next day I was bursting and had to tell Mish.

Yup. Good. Excellent idea.

He promised he'd keep it to himself, but later told me Jamie had told Gretchen anyway. Jamie's version was of course that *I* kissed him outside PoNaNa and *he* pulled away. He then fairly accurately recounted the bus 'I have a surprise' thing (which feels so cringey now I think about it). I can't believe it!! Fucking arsehole! We're both as good as dead (but mainly me!). Stupid 'bus thing', which, it appears, he has now kindly thrown me under.

Then on Saturday: Mish, Lovely Lyla and I went out to PoNaNa again and met up with Jamie and co. Jamie was ignoring me so eventually I was like, 'What?! Why are you ignoring me?' He just told me to 'fuck off'. What right did he have to be in a mood with me? He pulled me first! And *he* told Gretchen! I'm so hurt. I thought he was a friend, but he's just a lying, self-preserving little shit like the rest of them.

Maybe if I stopped kissing everyone...

```
Text to Jamie: I'm sorry u think I came on
to u and u neva did me but more importantly
im sorry that u would say nething to please
G even if it means lying and hurting ur
friends. Sorry to get in the way.
```

```
From Jamie: Thanx for that! I shouldn't
have to explain what happens btween G and
I — you'll never understand.
```

```
To Jamie: I dont want an explanation and
I certainly don't ever think I could
understand! I just dont want to be the
bad guy. Friday was stupid — can we please
just forget about it?

From Jamie: As I explained to G, i still
value ur friendship. Don't worry. Night x
```

10TH JUNE 2002
LISTENING TO 'VEGETABLE' BY RADIOHEAD

Apparently Gretchen isn't annoyed about 'bus snog' and still thinks of us as friends. Really? She must be! I have to admit I'm half relieved, but the other (slightly mischievous) half is a little bummed that I couldn't get to her. Just this once. But phew. Mainly phew.

18TH JUNE 2002
LISTENING TO 'MESS' BY BEN FOLDS FIVE

Well, the bloody impossible happened today. The prefects have been announced. Amazingly Charlie is head boy over Mish. Mish is just a lowly prefect – ha! I wasn't chosen to be a prefect at all, which I'm a bit disappointed about but not that surprised. Maggie's a prefect, which was fairly predictable, BUT I would never have guessed the other girl. I assumed if there was another girl chosen it would be me, but thought they'd probably just have one. But nooooooo, I couldn't have been more wrong. IT'S FUCKING GRETCHEN. Fucking-'I'm going to throw babies out of windows to see if they'll fly'-Gretchen. I still can't believe it. WHAT THE

FUCK?! She is an utter psycho with ZERO attributes. I get why sixteen-year-old boys like her, but a prefect? She does no extracurricular stuff, no sport, she's not academic, not arty, not musical… NOTHING. She's useless. She prances around talking crap thinking she's your schoolgirl answer to Nietzsche. I don't mind not being made prefect, but I do mind her getting it over me.

The flying babies comment probably needs some explanation. Teenage Gretchen wanted to paint herself as this profound, all-knowing goddess with her fake spiritual and philosophical spraff. I knew her game though. She would have been in her element on her gap year, flouncing around in beaded friendship bracelets with her 'expanded mind'.

Gap Year Gretchen would have been just as irritating as Julia Roberts' sanctimonious character in Eat, Pray, Love (the most sickening film of the millennium). The book was fine; I purely have beef with the film. You can tell a lot from a person who lists it as one of their favourite books. See also: fucking Shantaram. Now, you reeeeally can tell a lot about the person that says that fucking Shantaram is their favourite book. It is 933 pages of teeny tiny-fonted bullshit. Lin-The Liar-baba is a hugely dislikeable and self-involved character who deserves absolutely no praise for this abomination of a cult classic. I trudged through it convinced that I would somehow get to the end, hold it against my chest with a tear in my eye and feel enlightened. I hoped I'd finally read the last page and it would all make sense. All the meandering around India with endless characters and more and more ridiculous and implausible stories would suddenly have meaning – if I could just get to the mother flippin' end. Well, it bloody well didn't. Shantaram stole a part of my life. Rantaram over.

Rantaram: verb; to enjoy ranting over Shantaram, everyone involved in it or anyone who likes it.

So, I digress; the flying babies. I remember listening to Gretchen monologue at a party where she had a captive audience of impressionable young men hanging on her every word. I picked up part of what she was saying.

'I mean, we just don't know what we're capable of. Our brains are totally amazing yeah and we know we don't access them properly. Our abilities as humans could be limitless. We just get told stuff as babies and take it as gospel. We should question everything! Like how do we know we can't fly? Maybe if we encouraged babies to fly, they could... I'll never tell my children that they can't do anything. If they think they can fly, then fly, my babies.'

Barf.

20TH JUNE 2002
LISTENING TO 'BEER' BY REEL BIG FISH

Argh, Gretchen is such a huge Jobbie! She has been scowling at me all day. It's amazing how she can make my skin crawl with nothing but a sideways glance. I knew something was up today. Although she didn't *actually* say or do anything she may as well have started smearing her shit all over me and screaming, 'I hate you!' I was clearly in her bad books... again.

```
Text to G: R U in a mood with me? You have
no right cos I haven't done anything. I
thought we were friends now?
```

```
Text from G: I've heard what uv been saying
about me and that's really bitching.
```

Hmmm, does she actually know what I've been saying about her? I was definitely not impressed by the prefect thing, but I'm pretty sure I only voiced that to my parents and Mish who totally agreed with me and called it 'a disgrace'. Had he said something? Prefect code?

J'accuse! Sabotage! How am I not seeing Mish as the conniving wee Judas he so clearly was? He's just there in the background, stirring up some shit with his giant wooden spoon. It was always him! The puppeteer... my wizard of oz.

I decided to try and call her bluff.

```
Text to G: I think ull find I haven't said
anything. I was surprised (and possibly a
little disappointed) not to get prefect
but thats all. Why r u so desperate to find
anything wrong with me?
```

```
Text from G: Its not exactly hard. Im
not going to let this go. Its completely
unfair — I wont be bullied.
```

Bullied?! Gretchen? Ha! Excuse me while I choke on every single slice of Gretchen's bully-bitch pie she has been ramming down my throat for the last two years!

There is a small part of me that wonders if Gretchen's diaries were released, I would understand it all. Would it reveal a vulnerable and damaged young girl who viewed me as I viewed her? Did we bully each other? Only a small part... The rest of me thinks there would just be hundreds of defaced pictures of me with creepy cartoon dead eyes.

Text to G: I cant be bothered with this petty rivalry. I'm not bullying you! If anything its been the other way round! I thought we were mates and past this?

Text from G: Grow up and stop feeling sorry for urself. Im forever wiping up ur crocodile tears. Maybe if u treated ur mates better, ud have a few more.

Text to G: I dont feel sorry for myself. The only thing I feel is stupid for thinking for a second that you weren't the two faced person Ive always known u 2b.

Text from G: Youve got it wrong. I stood up 4u in front of everyone! *(Subtle dig)* Im not two faced anymore. Im the one whos under attack here, not u so stop this.

To G: Iv not got it wrong. You started the bitchie messages.

From G: Dont u fucking dare. U started the texts! Stop txting me, I can't be arsed!

27TH JUNE 2002
LISTENING TO 'ANYONE CAN PLAY GUITAR' BY RADIOHEAD

6pm Text from William: Hey Claire, I'm just wondering if you'll sign my yearbook. Hope ur well love William.

6.30pm Text from William: Ok — u dont have to text me then. It's ok — don't mind me. Listen if you're never going to talk to me again then I want my CDs and videos back ok?

I still have all the CDs. Ha.

To W: I didnt txt back because I thought this was finished. Iv had a crap day and u randomly txting doesnt help. I have nothing to say to u.

From W: So not being rude but will you write in my yearbook?

To W: Please leave me alone. I dont want to be reminded of u. Its clear y ur bk out the blue — u must be alone again. Im sorry but I dont want to know about u. I want to 4get about u.

From W: Listen. Your signature is worth points and the winner gets a shot in Jamie's car. Thats all. I only wanted 2 get your signature. Dont flatter urself. I'm with tonnes of people right now all laughing at your texts.

To W: I don't care who ur with. My point is leave me alone and stay the fuck out of

my life. You've hurt me and it still hurts
when you pop back into my life.

11.45pm From W: Claire, u wouldnt believe
how much I would die to be back with u.
I love you beyond belief. I still care
about u. As much as I did last year. Can
we please hang out as friends before I go
to college? I miss you. Youre still my
everything. Take care. x

29TH JUNE 2002
LISTENING TO 'AMERICAN GIRLS'
BY COUNTING CROWS

I called William after his text last night. I initially just wanted to
emphasise the fuckoffness that clearly wasn't getting through via
text, but instead we ended up talking for hours and not arguing.
This power he has over me is astonishing. He then asked me to
go to the leavers' ball with him. It was just going to be for old
times' sake before he leaves. A drink and a dance and pretend
like nothing had ever happened. I couldn't really resist. I'm so
pathetic. It just sounded idyllic and such a perfect end for us.

I was so giddy getting ready tonight. I came down in my
dress and my parents were like:

'Err, you look nice. Where are you going?'

'William's asked me to go to the leavers' ball with him. Just
as friends...'

My mum rolled her eyes and mumbled something that I didn't
hear. I was going to get all defensive, but decided not to. I know
what they're thinking and they're probably right. They are so over
the whole William thing. WHAT THE FUCK AM I DOING?

So he picked me up and I felt really emotional when I saw him standing at the door in his kilt. It felt like we'd come full circle. We hadn't even got to the ball before having a blazing row in the street and I turned around and went home. WHY DO I KEEP DOING THIS?! WHY CAN'T I LEARN FROM MY MISTAKES?!

TWENTY-ONE
SUMMER 2002

3RD JULY 2002
LISTENING TO 'NO SURPRISES' BY RADIOHEAD

This is absolute hell. Happy summer holidays my hairy arse! I'm five days into sitting in a soaking wet tent at RAF camp. I am cold and drenched and tired.

9TH JULY 2002
LISTENING TO 'WHY DON'T YOU GET A JOB?'
BY THE OFFSPRING

I'm back in the South of France, tanning, reading and eating. It is glorious.

Sexy Laurent from last summer rang and asked if he could take me out (he's got a car now!). He is still sexy as hell and we went out last night, which was incredible. We went on a mini bar crawl through Nice and the chat was definitely better than last year. We were sat in a bar behind the Cours Salaya when he smiled at me and took my hand. He told me he really wanted to pick things up where we left off last year but that he was actually going out with Marie now. Whaaatt? I said no way if he had a girlfriend, so he then said he was breaking up with her anyway. Hmmm. Not sure if that was true five minutes ago. Do I really want him to end it with her for me? We were walking back to the car when he suddenly stopped, spun me around and pulled me. Woah there, that was hot! Alright then, dump her ass! I'm only here for two weeks though, so I'm not going to get too attached to him and have a repeat of the Gael debacle.

15TH JULY 2002
LISTENING TO 'NANCY BOY' BY PLACEBO

Shit shit shit and triple fuckety fucking bollocks. Life is sooo unfair. Obviously I've totally fallen for Sexy Laurent. Goddamnit, Claire! Why do I only like people I can't have? It's sooooooo unfair.

Life with Sexy Laurent is dreamlike. I spend my days being driven around the Côte d'Azur, from beach to beach, without a care in the world, bobbing about in the turquoise sea with my legs wrapped around the hunkiest guy in France. He picks me up again after dinner and takes me to another amazing spot with an amazing view and we chat and drink and smoke and kiss.

I'd really like for things to move up a notch, but he's too sweet. I'd never get a guy like him in Edinburgh. Firstly, they don't exist, but more importantly if they did, they would not be into me. They'd get snapped up by the Sofias and the Hollys of the world. Fortunately for me, Sexy Laurent lives in a tiny village in the South of France with the odd feral dog and ancient goat herder, but CRUCIALLY – no hot girls. In fact, no girls at all (except for Marie, but that ship has sailed). Plus I'm practically exotic here as a blonde. So yeah, I fare pretty well in this remote village with no competition and get to bag guys like Sexy Laurent. It's funny though... he is without a doubt the best-looking guy I have ever seen, but I don't have the same feelings for him as I did for William and Gael. AHA! Personality obviously *is* important to me. Not that Sexy Laurent hasn't got a good personality and I definitely really like him, but he doesn't make me laugh like William and Gael did. I find it comforting to know that I'm not a total superficial bitch. Ooft, he is hot though... man, I would LOVE to have sex with him. He is a great big fiery ball of sex appeal. He's working as a gardener ad hoc to earn some extra cash and all it's done is make him EVEN sexier. He's just alllll glistening, tanned muscle. God, he's gorgeous.

16TH JULY 2002
LISTENING TO 'HOT IN HERRE' BY NELLY

I couldn't resist anymore. It was the village fête last night (which was insanely lame). The DJ was playing yet another 70s hit by Claude François when Sexy Laurent and I snuck back to his after having had a fair amount to drink (haha or a fête amount to drink). He was really quite drunk (people in the south really can't handle their booze). So anyway, we were messing about and one thing led to another and we started having sex... It was so crap. I really like him, but that was a bit of a shocker.

21ST JULY 2002
LISTENING TO 'SHE'S GOT A WAY' BY THE SMITHEREENS

Every kiss with Sexy Laurent sends fireworks through my body! Just holding his hand is absolute bliss. How do I only have two nights left with him?! I'm going to miss him and our little dreamy South of France life together. I think I love him. I honestly do. The two of us are so perfect together yet we live so far away! He told me he loved me tonight and, true to form, I didn't say it back. Is this cos I dont really love him or cos I like the upper hand? I hate me sometimes.

31ST JULY 2002
LISTENING TO 'STEAL MY KISSES' BY BEN HARPER AND THE INNOCENT CRIMINALS

I've been in Brittany for the last few days and I'm so happy here. It's unreal. I've been far too busy having fun to write, but it boils down to simply being happier here than I ever could be in Edinburgh. Also: Sexy Laurent who? I feel a bit bad cos he's still messaging quite a lot, but I'm not doing a Gael again. That was a total catastrophe and lesson learnt. Plus I won't see him for a year so... well, sorry, Laurent. I probably didn't love him.

On my first night back I went to *Le Festivalas* with François, Marc, Marc's new girlfriend, Les Marseillais, Gael and Yannick. Marc's new girlfriend seems to be even more mental than Mattie was. She was there for about a minute at the start of the night and then out of nowhere told us all, '*Allez vous faire foutre, bande d'enculés!*' (*Rough translation: Go and fuck yourselves, you bunch of wankers*) and stormed off into the night. We all stared at Marc in a 'what the hell just happened?' way and he just shrugged and said she did this all the time. I sometimes wonder if he's the one sending all these women round the bend. Surely they can't all be this nuts to start with?

It turned out to be the most hilarious night after that. We were all smoking in Marc's car then spent the whole night slipping and sliding around in the mud. I have NEVER laughed so much. All the bands sounded the same to me though... generic druggie French reggae. I slept in a tent with François and Marc and we could not stop giggling. I could burst with love for them. I wish I could bring them all back to Edinburgh with me. They are true friends. I wish I had some true friends in Edinburgh, but I don't.

It's so nice to be friends with Gael again. I do feel quite bad about how it went down in Edinburgh and over Easter though. My mum still talks about how terrible it was for '*pauvre* Gael', but he seems to be over it and has a new girlfriend called Suzanne who I haven't met yet.

4TH AUGUST 2002
LISTENING TO 'WHEREVER YOU WILL GO' BY THE CALLING

Hmmmm. I'm a bit less happy. I was on the beach today and Gael arrived with Suzanne. It was totally different to how William likes to parade girls in front of me. It almost made me feel a bit jealous and remember some old feelings. I know it's a 'grass is greener/ want what you can't get' scenario, but it still hurts a bit. She seems really nice and he definitely seems happier than when I last saw him at Easter, but it still twanged my heart strings a little.

When I got home my mum had a massive go at me cos apparently my grandparents feel like Chloe and I do fuck all. She's made me feel really guilty.

Oh, how we did fuck all. I was at an age when I really didn't care about anything or anyone other than myself. I was never in and if I was, it was to sleep and eat. I spent no time with my family. I feel so sad thinking about it now and glad that I had a few more years with my grandparents in order to try and redeem myself.

There are nearly 100,000 words in this book and only about a fifty of them relate to my family. I had no awareness of how lucky I was to be surrounded by this invisible, protective love, that as such, it went undocumented. My parents are wonderful and my lack of words are simply because there was nothing bad to report. What sixteen year old wrote in their teenage diary about how much they loved their parents? I love my parents. I loved them then and I love them now.

8TH AUGUST 2002
LISTENING TO 'RAIN KING' BY COUNTING CROWS

We went camping on the Island last night. I organised it this year and coordinating the food and booze shop for thirty people was a bit of a headache. Gael and Marc's friend Ewen (who I flirted with at Easter) was there and Gael wasn't. I figured Gael was happy with Suzanne now, so his mate was fair game.

So we were all sat round the fire having a good time and I put my hand on his and looked at him with the best come-to-bed eyes I could muster (not with actual come-to-bed intent though!). He just looked back at me unapologetically and rolled his eyes.

'*Il me reste plus que quelques jours de vacances et avoir une fille ça me fait chier.*'

Well, that was clear. Massive KB. Enough said.

Literal translation: 'I've only got a few days of holiday left and to have a girl makes me shit myself.' The verb 'faire chier' is a tricky one to translate because he obviously wasn't going to shit himself if he had a girlfriend. It can be used in so many different ways, but it's somewhere between being pissed off and being bored. There were absolutely no mixed messages in his statement. He basically couldn't be arsed with any potential girl-related shiz. Or me.

12TH AUGUST 2002
LISTENING TO 'SUZIE BLUE' BY BEN HARPER AND THE INNOCENT CRIMINALS

I woke up to Mum telling me the Highers results were arriving a day early. I almost died falling down the stairs. The first thing I saw was a C in English. I couldn't believe it and burst into tears. Shit.

B in chemistry – was expecting an A

B in maths – fair dos

A in French – I'd bloody well hope so

A in biology – phew!

C in English – thought I'd scraped an A. Disgusted. How did this happen? I had an A for my coursework and a predicted A. Was my exam that bad?

I wonder if it may have had a little something to do with me memorising an essay on Macbeth from those revision notes books and regurgitating it all in the exam? I can't remember the extent of the plagiarism, but I suspect this may have contributed to my downfall. I got busted. Oh well. Look who's writing an entirely original unplagiarised book now!

So basically my entry into medicine at Dundee this year now depends on me getting an A in AS art, which I'll find out in three days. If it doesn't work out, I shouldn't be too down. I think I'm too young to start medicine this year anyway. I can't start medical school at sixteen! Actually, I think I'll do another year at school and smash some A-levels regardless of my art grade.

I spoke to Maggie and there were a few other exam surprises.

William failed English so can't go to his college now – HAHAHA.

Mish got AAABC. Looks like we'll both be squeezing AS and A-levels into one year now.

Text from Finn Ellwyn-Cox: Hey Claire baby, where are you? I will be in Edinburgh from the 22nd. Please be free to meet! It would be so great to see you! Lol. F x

'LOL' was still Loads/lots of love. People didn't feel the need to explain that they weren't laughing quietly to themselves in 2002.

15TH AUGUST 2002
LISTENING TO 'THE ZEPHYR SONG'
BY RED HOT CHILI PEPPERS

Boom! Smashed it! A in art. Phew. Not that it matters now anyway, but it's nice to know I could have done it and I'm not totally delusional.

21ST AUGUST 2002
LISTENING TO 'UNIVERSALLY SPEAKING'
BY RED HOT CHILI PEPPERS

On the plane going back to Edinburgh. I have had THE BEST SUMMER. I'm nearly crying at the thought of it being over.

François and I have been doing these dares/bets all summer. I can't remember how it started, but we got a bit carried away with it all.

Bet Number 1: We took a dingy out into the bay at midnight, took all our clothes off with our backs to each other and the first person allowed to get dressed and to turn around had to have drunk four neat shots of Pastis (bleurgh!). I won. Although, I didn't feel like much of a winner when I had my head over the side of the boat five minutes later.

Bet Number 2: We had an *apéro* on a public bench overlooking the sea at sunset, naked from the waist down. We had to keep our eyes dead straight, hope no one walked past and had a Pastis and some saucisson before getting dressed again.

Bet Number 3: We had to make as many people show us a private body part at the bar as we could (cheeky nipple etc). If they didn't, we had to do a shot of rum. It of course ended up as a giant rum-fuelled game of Cock or Ball?. We called it a draw and went for a celebratory breakfast and *café calva* the next day.

I remember all these bets with François so fondly, but wince at the thought of sharing them without them sounding weird and a bit pervy. They weren't, but they invariably involved us taking our clothes off and drinking in various risky locations. It felt reckless and liberating. I'd completely forgotten about this blatant excuse for exhibitionism, so messaged François and asked if he remembered any more 'dares' that we did over the years. He reminded me that we once had a shower together after a day on the beach. We were blindfolded (because looking was forbidden and this somehow made it less sexy?!), when I slipped trying to get out the shower and banged my face on his semi-erect penis. Oh, how we laughed! We only just decided they were totally out of order the year I met my husband, which makes me realise (only now!) that they were probably never appropriate. But isn't that what being young is all about? Being carefree and then looking back and squirming? Maybe I'd be stripping off now if I hadn't got it out of my system and embarrassed myself back then?

Le café calva was almost definitely created by some high-functioning alcoholic like Ernest Hemingway. Brittany (like the UK) is absolutely full to the brim with closet drunks masquerading as social drinkers. Every country makes up certain 'rules' about when or where drinking is appropriate. In the UK, pre-midday or solo drinking is frowned upon unless it's at the airport, Christmas morning or your wedding day. These rule-breaking occasions allow for champagne, buck's fizz or an airport pint. Pimm's is also ok but entirely seasonal and weather dependent. Definitely no spirits before 5pm, and even then it's probably only gin before 7pm, THEN the gloves are off and anything goes.

The French don't believe in anything so arbitrary or restrictive. My grandparents' ageless old gardener, Monsieur Barralisse, was a prime example of the rules not applying in France. He roamed the hills of the Côte d'Azur, climbing up olive trees and living off a diet of tomatoes, rabbit and rosé. He was a bit like a tortoise, both in the texture of his skin but also if we'd ever found out how old he was, we'd have been shocked to discover he was about 129 years old. He looked like he'd just sprung out of the Bertolli advert. I remember, as a child, having breakfast on the terrace with my grandparents. It was early enough that the cicadas hadn't started singing and everything was still cool and dewy. Monsieur Barralisse would arrive: weathered, pot-bellied and toothless.

'Bonjour à la famille!'

He would have a dead rabbit the size of a sheep over one shoulder and a rake over the other. He'd creakily sit down with us and mutter something entirely incomprehensible as my grandfather would offer, 'Café, Monsieur Barralisse? Non? Croissant? Non, d'accord...' I'd finish my bowl of chocolate Nesquik and he would continue to sit there looking expectant. My grandparents would exhaust the breakfast-appropriate options until he'd eventually agree to a glass of rosé. He'd drink the bottle within the next fifteen minutes before deciding to tackle the forty-foot palm sans harness.

So, anyway, the rules are different in France and morning drinking is absolutely fine if you have coffee with it (hence le café calva). Le café calva was a HUGE glass of calvados for breakfast made perfectly respectable by a strong espresso. Monsieur Barralisse probably decided to forgo the pretence of a coffee when he turned a hundred.

Nothing made me feel more French and edgy than smoking a cigarette and drinking a café calva at 9am. It's what we did and it felt like a completely normal thing to do age sixteen.

23RD AUGUST 2002
LISTENING TO 'HEAVEN'
BY DJ SAMMY FT. YANOU & DO

I met up with Finn Ellwyn-Cox today. We hung out at the flat that he was staying in and had some drinks. He's still pretty awesome and he makes me feel smoking hot. We had a little snog again and it makes me tingle every time… such a good kisser. He invited me to come and stay with him in halls at Exeter Uni. I was thinking about applying so maybe I'll go if I get an interview.

TWENTY-TWO
SKATER CHRIS

TUESDAY 27TH AUGUST 2002
LISTENING TO 'BY THE WAY'
BY RED HOT CHILI PEPPERS

6am: I've just had the most amazing couple of days down south at Skater Chris' house. I'm leaving in a few hours and I feel insanely sad about it.

Skater Chris was the arrogant wannabe doctor I'd met at Nottingham's Medlink. We'd kept in touch and he'd invited me to stay with him and visit the medical school near his home town.

Friday: I arrived just after lunch and after having a look at the uni, I had dinner with his parents, his sisters and his girlfriend, Steph. We then spent the night watching films, listening to music and chatting.

233

Saturday: We had a wander around the town and flirted together quite a bit. We have exactly the same sense of humour, taste in music etc etc. As Skater Chris (rather inappropriately just out of Steph's earshot) said, we were a perfect match.

That night we went clubbing, which felt like a really strange thing to do when there's just two people. I'm glad it was just the two of us though as we had such a laugh! We did some dirty dancing and played I Have Never. His statement was: 'I don't fancy the person sitting next to me', and we both drank! My stomach lurched.

We got back to his about 4ish and lay on his bed chatting. We were so close to each other that our noses occasionally touched. He eventually confessed that he wanted to pull me but kept changing his mind. It was torture just lying there on the precipice of a kiss. I wanted to pull him so badly, but he's got a girlfriend. He eventually gave a great big sigh and held my hand.

'I don't know what you want, Claire, but it would be wrong for me to *initiate* a kiss...'

Hint taken, buddy. I got ya. So I moved in. We kissed for only a few seconds before he pulled away and said he couldn't cos of Steph. Excuuuuussse me?! He said he'd much rather be with me, but he didn't know what to do because I lived so far away (never heard that before!). I just got up and went back to the guest room. WANKER! Did he just want to see if I'd do it? What kind of sick game was this? He'd just been eskimo kissing me and leading me on all night only to say, 'Oh no, sorry... my girlfriend.' I wouldn't have wanted my boyfriend behaving like that. I finally got to sleep, frustrated and angsty about an hour before having to get up. Boys are scum.

Sunday: I spent the day on the beach with Skater Chris and Steph. I felt tired and grumpy and jealous as hell. Steph can tell that I'm bad news and the sooner I'm gone, the better. She was just bitchie enough for me to notice, but not enough for it to be perceptible to the male eye. I don't blame her. That night we were all watching TV and he kept trying to hold my hand under a cushion so she couldn't see. What a pig. I kept pulling my hand away. Not cool, Skater Chris. Not cool.

Finally a smidge of morality.

When I came back from the toilet a bit later, they were having a massive fight and she stormed off and said it was obvious he'd rather be with me! I slowly backed away and went up to my room. I heard the front door slam about ten minutes later and he came upstairs and seemed totally fine.

'Are you ok?'

'Yeah. She can be a bit mental sometimes. Sorry. I've decided I'm going to break up with her anyway. Spending time with you has made me realise that we're right for each other. I've never felt this way about anyone. I want to give us a chance.'

I'm such a sucker. OBVIOUSLY I fell for it. We then stayed up all night listening to music and he was running his fingers up and down my back.

'I can't stop thinking about our kiss, Claire. I think this could work. We could apply to go to the same medical schools? It's only a year and then we could properly be together.'

I'm not going to lie. He was saying all the right things and I was like, heck yes! Let's do this. Let's fall madly in love, study medicine together and get married! We'll spend our weekends on the beach and teach our kids how to surf. Take meeeeeeee. But there was obviously no way I was going to give my psycho game away and say anything like that. I also didn't much fancy humiliating myself again and kissing him so I just mumbled, 'That sounds nice. Maybe it could work...'

He then put his hand on my waist and pushed me round to face him. He started kissing me with his whole body pressed against me. It was amazing! We spent the rest of the morning kissing and dreaming about our imaginary future.

Monday: Skater Chris and I took a picnic to the beach and spent the day kissing and dozing. I tried not to think about how I've once again managed to get myself into this mess. We spent all night kissing again and he just makes me tingle. Yet another sleepless night and here we are. It's all coming to an end.

LISTENING TO 'PLACE SO NEAR' BY ROOTJOOSE

Tuesday, 10am: I'm sat on the train heading back to Edinburgh and I can't stop crying. Not having slept for days is probably not helping. It's almost on the same level as when I had to leave Gael. Why do I get swept up so quickly? I've been with Skater Chris for about a second, but then maybe that's why it's so hard? I don't get to find out what happens. How does it end? Every time I start something exciting and full of passion and promise, the love rug is pulled out from under me. Plus, there's something about public transport that makes me crazy emotional. I do seem to spend a lot of time crying on planes and trains... weird.

Text From Skater Chris: I'm going to miss u so much baby. Hope you're having a good journey. I found it hard to read your note through all the tears! I really wish we could be 2geva. I cant help loving you to bits. Fingers crossed we go to the same Uni. If I didn't know any better I'd think I was falling in love with you. It's crazy huh? They say everyone has one perfect partner. Mine just happens to live in a different country. Wud u prefer it if I split with Steph coz i would for u?

To Skater Chris: I dont know wot 2say. I thought u said u wud… U kno i like u but its not my decision. I cant ask u to do anything like that. I'd do anything to make u mine, i might even eat coconut.

Skater Chris: We'd make a great pair! I think if we want to be 2geva we will even if it means working all next year and neva going out so i can go to uni with u.

TWENTY-THREE

AUTUMN 2002

There is then a massive gap in the writing until the end of September and I only have some texts to try and piece things together.

1/9/02

Text from William: Thank you for not coming to the party cos I seriously was about to snap! I cant believe uv come back from ur summer and have another fake bf. Even if it is a half (still made up) bf? What the fuck does that even mean? If u see me leave me alone. I dont want to see that face of urs or hear ur voice ever again ok?

2/9/02
Text from Skater Chris: I love being in love with u and I love 2 feel loved. We will be 2geva one day! Im thinking of breaking up with S. If I did would the long distance thing work? My sisters think ur my dream girl. I love u to bits. I'll come to Edinburgh somehow xxx

14/9/02
To William: I'm sorry.

From William: What RU sorry for — seems random.

Me: I'm sorry you've turned into such a self absorbed prick. You somehow manage to make everything I do about you.

W: Oh ok. That's polite. I thought u were actually saying sorry. Weird huh? It makes sense now cos ur an evil whore who enjoys hurting people and lying. I just want u to go away FOREVER.

Me: God I hate you. I heard you've been telling people I'm a slut who's slept with 'dozens of guys'.

W: I want u to hate me.

Me: Well congratulations! All I said was that u had a shite sense of humour.

W: Better than having a shite EVERYTHING!

Me: Good one.

W: Youre the weakest piece of shit ever. U need everyone around u to fight ur battles but unfortunately the only friends youve got are the little voices in your head you nut. You need to stop trying so hard to be popular. Your red trousers are mingin, you've small tits, a weird pussy and a hairy ass crack. I don't know why I ever bothered with a mess like you. Oh yeah and I read your diary — you never slept with Yannick you liar!

Me: I shouldn't have to explain myself to you anymore but I had no reason to lie.

W: So you lied in your diary? Whatever.

Busted! I'd forgotten about this. This makes the confession before my wedding even weirder now.

Me: William get a fucking life! How long ago was this? Youre so pathetic! I wish you would just leave me alone. I hate u so much and I have done for months! You're such a fucking loser! What happened years ago means NOTHING to me. You are the least relevant person in my whole life. Why are you still clinging on to this?! You bringing up these things from years ago is so sad. JUST FUCK OFFFFFFF!!!!!

26TH SEPTEMBER 2002
LISTENING TO 'BLACK-EYED' BY PLACEBO

Argh! I haven't written for ages. Right, quick summary:

- William is DEAD to me. He's back with 'The Toddler' too.
- I'm still in love with Skater Chris, but he does have this little pretentious side now and again, which is so off-putting. Unbelievably (despite a near daily 'Would you like me to end it with her?'... 'Fucking yes I would!') he is still with Steph. He's coming up in three weeks though and I'm really excited!
- I had a hilarious night last week with Next Door Andy. I really love him (as a pal)! We had such a fun night out then went back to his and stayed up all night chatting and drinking. We were so pissed and he ate a huge spider! I thought I was going to wet myself.
- I've made a new friend at St Felix's! The amazing Herbert McNash! I'd always thought he was a bit weird, but he's awesome! Admittedly, yes, he's still a bit weird but in the most glorious way possible. He's different to everyone else at school and he's just the kind of friend I need.

Ahhh, Herbie, my extraordinary friend. We shared some classes together, but it took me a while to see past his nonconformity. He is still to this day one the most eccentric characters I've ever had the pleasure of meeting. Even at seventeen, Herbert was an old-fashioned intellectual with the most wonderfully bonkers sense of humour. He would have held his own amongst the great pre-war comedians, but he was born long after his time and struggled to find his place in the superficial world of the millennial teen. We were all smoking, getting pissed and using a limited vocabulary while Herbert grew up without a TV, devouring book after book and writing brilliant screenplays in his exquisite, arsenic-green, Victorian town house.

Mr McNash (who was only ever known as 'The Captain') was probably as old as Monsieur Barralisse, oozed old-school British military charm and took zero shit from anyone. He was utterly terrifying but someone to be revered and respected. Herbie adored his father in a way that I'm not sure exists outside of nineteenth-century literature. Growing up under The Captain's rule meant that Herbert spoke in posh, complex, educated tongues and it always led me to wonder if he was on the spectrum or just soooo intelligent that he existed in a different dimension to the rest of us. Having a chat with Herbie was often like trying to communicate with someone on drugs. We are still good friends, but I'm pretty sure he has always thought of me as 'his thick friend'. Most of what he says simply passes me by as I chuckle stupidly and try and get him drunk to level the playing field.

MSN chat with William:

W: Right, can we sort this whole thing out once and for all. I wont shout or say anything mean ok.

Me: Fuck you

W: No, Im not joking.

Me: Neither am I. Who the hell do you think u are?

W: I dont mean any offence I just think its better that we sort things out.

Me: No its not better. You've been such an arsehole and I don't want to have anything to do with you. The sort of stuff you've been saying about me is so fucked up!

W: Oh yeah. Look I'm sorry. It wasn't all me.

Me: Yeah whatever. What's with the sudden change of heart anyway? Oh look I dont care. Leave me alone.

W: Well when I saw you the other day the look of disgust and hatred you gave me made me think ok I dont want things to be like this.

Me: Well u should have thought about that b4 ur lifetime goal became trying to make my life a living hell.

W: You gave as good as u got ok but im sorry for the way I was treating u.

Me: Bullshit

W: Ive been a twat to so many people for the last 6m, you included.

Me: I left you alone and you wouldnt just let me be.

W: I dont want to be friends or call or text I just dont want to be hated.

Me: Well too late. I DO hate you and I always will.

W: Yeah I know and you tell everyone you do when u know its going to come back to me.

Me: Look I despise every breath that comes out of you, whether you know it or not is of no importance to me.

W: Ok fine

Me: You've been the biggest arsehole I've ever met and I never thought I could hate anyone this much, let alone you. You've made my life hell and what exactly did I do to deserve that? I can't believe you think you can sort it out after what a dick you've been. Fuck off forever.

9TH OCTOBER 2002
LISTENING TO 'SLAVE TO WAGE' BY PLACEBO

Urrghhh, I'm feeling so unhappy at the moment. Mish is being a massive arse. He thinks he's so much better than me and that he shouldn't be seen hanging out with me now that I'm not a prefect. Wanker. He's happy to be my bestie out of school and when it suits him, but then seems embarrassed to even say hi to me at school. Why do I settle for these shite friends? Surely I have more self-worth? Well, apparently not.

Fuck. I just feel so lonely.

10TH OCTOBER 2002

Email from Finn Ellwyn-Cox:

Dearest cute-cuddly-french-lady-friend,
How YOU doing?! I am in my room at uni
and I'm waiting for your call (in the non-
XXX hotline way) so do get in touch soon,
especially if you need cheering up or a
good chat. I cannot believe how soppy I
have become. I actually WAS crying on the
phone with you the other day! You mean so
much to me and it rips me apart to hear
you so sad. If I had it my way, I would
surround you with love and comfort and
NICE PEOPLE (!) and you would get what you
deserve. Claire you are a GREAT girl and
I miss you so much.

Stay smiling and just keep your head
down for the last push until the finish.
Then uni will be a blast. You will be such
a success I know it.

Lurve You baby, F xxx

THE DIARY OF A TEENAGE DIRTBAG

16TH OCTOBER 2002
LISTENING TO 'JAMES DEAN (I WANNA KNOW)' BY DANIEL BEDINGFIELD

Skater Chris is coming in two weeks! I'm so excited!

Maggie told me she really fancied Charlie! They get on so well, I think they'd probably make an awesome couple.

4TH NOVEMBER 2002
LISTENING TO 'SPECIAL K' BY PLACEBO

Skater Chris came up last Tuesday. I'm so in love with him, he's the best! I said bye to him today and once again I feel like I've just been repeatedly punched in the stomach. I'm going to miss him so much it makes me want to cry. How is my life just one giant goodbye?! We're going to go to Bristol to visit the med school together soon and I'm wondering about having sex with him. We are kinda together, but then he's still with his pissing girlfriend and he's a real sneaky fucker at times so I think I'll just play it by ear. So, recap from my week with Skater Chris:

Tuesday: Skater Chris arrived. We had dinner with my parents then stayed up all night pulling and watching films. My mum seems to like him and she is unpredictably difficult to please so that's a plus. My dad is impossible to read so I won't even bother trying to decipher his thoughts on Skater Chris.

The only opinion he ever offered on any of my 'boyfriends' was, 'That crocodile [Aussie Jason] is a bit brash, isn't he?' Yes he is, Dad.

Wednesday: We spent the day with Maggie and we walked around Edinburgh showing Skater Chris the sights and then went up Arthur's Seat. I think that sunset up Arthur's Seat is the most romantic place in the world.

Thursday: Deacon Brodies, The Trond, *Miss Saigon* at the theatre then Three Sisters bar – So In Love!

Friday: Dinner at mine with Mish and Lovely Lyla, Maggie and Charlie, Gretchen, Lucy and Herbert. Maggie and Charlie are officially together now – exciting! Mish was really rude to Skater Chris and basically made him seem like a bum who wasn't worthy of having dinner with us. He laughed in his face and spat half his dinner out when Skater Chris said something about this skater video being really 'dope'. It was soooo rude. I wonder why I'm friends with Mish sometimes. After everyone left, Skater Chris and I had a bit of a fight. We'd spent about an hour pulling (and stuff) on my bed and he kept telling me he loved me and wanted to have sex with me. He's still with Steph so I didn't really want to but massively did at the same time. Five seconds later, I went to the toilet and overheard him on the phone to Steph saying he missed her and 'I love you, baby'. Fucking hell. How am I in this mess? He told me it didn't mean anything and he loved me more. Whatever.

> 3/11/02
> Text from Skater Chris: I'm shite at saying this stuff so I'll text it. I love u so much baby and I'm going to miss u when I go. Now you have this text don't mention it cos I'll either get embarrassed or cry. Lol just remember I love you. I can't wait till Bristol and I ain't even left.

Saturday: We went to see *They* at the cinema, Petit Paris for dinner, The Last Drop, Frankie's, Espionnage then home for a snuggle.

Well, that's not a bad A-Z list of pubs and clubs in Edinburgh during 2002.

4/11/02

Text from Skater Chris: My god I miss you. A week isn't long enough. I must look stupid with these tears in my eyes.

6TH NOVEMBER 2002
LISTENING TO 'ON MERCURY' BY RED HOT CHILI PEPPERS

Missing Skater Chris loads, but it seems he doesn't really give a shit about me now he's back home with his girlfriend. Tosser.

8TH NOVEMBER 2002
LISTENING TO 'COMPLICATED' BY AVRIL LAVIGNE

This is barely legible…

Not going to write much cos am really drunk and it's going to make my diary messy. Went to Next Door Andy's and then to his friend's party with that beautiful Dickhead Mike (who's still hot and still a dickhead). Nearly pulled him – phew. He'd make a lovely boyfriend though if he got over his commitment phobia.

Love Skater Chris. Although I think he'd make a shite boyfriend/he is a shite boyfriend.

Next Door Andy looked cute tonight. Weird.

I miss William. A part of me always misses William. Bastard.

18TH NOVEMBER 2002
LISTENING TO 'KARMA POLICE' BY RADIOHEAD

I'm hanging out with Mish so much that it's weirdly making me fancy him a bit. Is there no one I wouldn't fancy?! I wish he liked me the way I like him, although we are so flirty with each other and it seems to be getting worse. I'm not even sure who initiates it. It's harmless (ish) if I pretend I don't know what's going on and that Lovely Lyla doesn't exist. Do I only attract guys with girlfriends?! Mish and I spend our weekends hanging out and we make each other laugh so much that I start to wonder, *What if...*, but then he flips back into Edinburgh's biggest arsehole come Monday morning at school. It's obvious that he doesn't even want people to know we're friends (never mind 'best friends', which he tells me everyday in secret!) and gets embarrassed if I even mention us hanging out outside of school in front of other people. He literally never talks about Lovely Lyla – it's ridiculous and yet he makes me feel like such an idiot if I even mention her.

'So... how are things going with you and Lyla? I feel like I haven't seen her in ages!'

'Oh, they're fine. Do we have to talk about it? It makes you sound jealous.'

My lord! What a massive jerk!

Text from Mish: Hey sexy. Ur such a honey! You really have become my best friend. I thought you looked stunning tonight, love me xxx

TWENTY-FOUR
BRISTOL

22ND NOVEMBER 2002 (AGE SEVENTEEN)
LISTENING TO 'COME HOME' BY PLACEBO

Wooo, new dairy! I feel I have to sum up for the sake of starting a new dairy.

Boys

- I'm kinda going out with Skater Chris when we see each other, and we're in love blah blah blah. Only, he still has his friggin' girlfriend on the go. I'm getting a bit confused about my feelings for him. I'm just not sure why I'm not 100% into him (having a girlfriend actually isn't it!). Most of the time I don't see it (although I'm not really sure what 'it' is), but then sometimes I get the sense that something's off. We're seeing each other in Bristol soon so I'm sure if there's an issue it will surface.

- Got a bit of a crush on Mish, but there are several problems attached to this.
  1. He's a very good friend of mine and I don't want to fuck that up.
  2. He is going out with Lovely Lyla who is perfect for him and need I say... lovely.
  3. I don't think he likes me like that... bit of a bummer.
  4. I spend half my time hating how badly he treats me when we're in school that I don't even want to be friends with him.

Friends

- Gretchen, Maggie and I are all getting on now... for now.
- I am civil with William when I see him, which is loads given that he never left Edinburgh so he is EVERYWHERE.
- Next Door Andy is a rock and some welcome stability in my friendships.

Work

- In summary? I'm fucked. Prelims and revision are a catastrophe.
- I was selected to do a speech at the Speakers' Dinner tomorrow and I am totally shitting myself.
- Medical school interview on 6th December – again shitting myself. BUT I'm staying with the amazing Finn Ellwyn-Cox.

Fun

- Fun is dead right now.
- Delayed my bday night out till December as there's so much going on at the moment.

24TH NOVEMBER 2002
LISTENING TO 'LET DOWN' BY RADIOHEAD

Mish and I went out after the Speakers' Dinner (which was amazing!). We'd been chatting about Skater Chris and how I thought I was falling in love with him when he scoffed, 'Are you not ashamed of yourself to be seeing him knowing that he's still with his girlfriend? Come on, Claire, that can't be love. You're behaving like a fool.'

He caught me a bit off guard and my cheeks blazed with shame. I felt like a scolded toddler and I had the overriding desire to go and hide behind a sofa.

'But I'm just waiting for him to end it with her. He's told me he will before we see each other in Bristol. I thought he was going to ages ago. It's not like I want to be "the other woman"! I'd love to be his girlfriend.'

'But you're not though, Claire, are you?'

I guess not. I felt so embarrassed. I didn't want to be having this conversation and I thought I might cry. Am I really being quite as ridiculously naive as it seems?

26TH NOVEMBER 2002
LISTENING TO 'DILEMMA'
BY NELLY FT. KELLY ROWLAND

Ahhhh, I am so stressed out. I had a migraine last night and I was so sick and got about an hour's sleep. My mum still made me go to school today though. There was no convincing her this morning. So today was hellish and I've been working all night since I got home. I'm nowhere near finishing, but I have to stop. It's almost midnight and I'm just getting flustered now! I am so tired and I'm worrying about a million and one things.

It feels like I'm getting one thing done and in that time I've accumulated three more things to do. It's never ending and I'm drowning.

- French oral on Monday
- Need to send provisional driver's licence away
- Medical school interview prep
- Biology AS practical write-up
- Revise and learn EVERYTHING
- GET A GOOD NIGHT'S SLEEP
- Stop being such a fat arse

30TH NOVEMBER 2002
LISTENING TO 'I SAW A PRAYER' BY JJ72

> Text from William: Do u want to know something really strange? I've thought of you all day. I heard the Feeder song and it still reminds me of the best day of my life with you. I just wish we could go back to when everything was perfect. Do you think that could happen? My mum said if we were older we would have made a perfect couple. It's strange how much I miss you. It's coming up to 2 years since we met.

I cried reading that message and it's taken everything I had not to reply. I want to text back and throw myself back into his arms, but it won't do anyone any good. Maybe his mum's right. We'll never know. I can't go back there.

1ST DECEMBER 2002
LISTENING TO 'JUST' BY RADIOHEAD

Bristol Weekend with Skater Chris
I'm sitting in the departures lounge at Bristol airport and I feel
so annoyed that this weekend was such a big disaster. Skater
Chris and I stayed at his sister's student house for the weekend
while we both had a look round Bristol Med School.

As soon as I arrived I discovered he was still with Steph
despite saying he'd end it and a daily text saying he loves me
more than he ever could her. I told him it was starting to make
me feel really weird that he still had a girlfriend as we were
getting more serious. I then asked him (outright) to end it with
her, which up until this point I haven't actually done. I thought
that was reasonable seeing as he said he would in August! I also
still had the conversation with Mish banging fresh in my ears.

'Aww, Claire, that's really sweet and you know I would for
you, but you don't *need* that to know I love you. You're more
secure than that.'

Well, if he thinks I'm going to fall for his manipulative
psychobabble bullshit, he can think again.

'Err, no, Chris. You apparently love me and you told me you
would end it. Don't twist it.'

He looked at me like a three-year-old, and with a patronising
tilt of the head, he explained to me that he always needs someone
to give him love and attention in person. Don't I understand?
There would be no point in ending it with Steph cos if he wasn't
with her he'd just be with someone else! So what? Any girl will
do? Fucking loser. I'm sorry but who's insecure? I was speechless
and so disgusted, but he didn't even notice.

'So I was thinking, Claire baby… it's probably time for us to
take it to the next level?'

'Excuse me?!'

'I'm surprised that you're not showing more enthusiasm! I just want to make love to you, baby.'

Bleurgh! FUCK THAT! I laughed inside at the thought of me having ever even considered it. No chance. Grow some balls, Skater Chris, and dump your girlfriend, you needy, polyamorous dickhead. I said nothing of course and he didn't get a whiff of my outrage. I tried to pretend the conversation hadn't happened after that cos I didn't want to ruin the weekend completely.

So anyway, last night, we planned to go to this drum and bass night, but went out for some food beforehand in this really nice (and quite pricey) Italian restaurant he'd picked. My God, he was getting on my tits. Has he changed or was I completely blind to his arrogance and compulsive lying beforehand? I was still pissed off about our chat and he then spent the whole of dinner spraffing such a load of crap I wanted to smack him and scream, 'Shut up, SHUT UP, SHUUUTTTTTT UPP!' I was having visions of stabbing him in the eye with my grissini as I laughed politely at the stinking bullshite pouring out of his gob. He then told me he'd met and bought a drink for the Red Hot Chili Peppers. I mean, COME ON! Why the fuck would one of the biggest bands in the world sit and have a drink with a seventeen-year-old boy from Devon? We've listened to countless Chilies songs together and spoken nearly every day for the last three months... and this never came up? If I'd had a drink with the Chilies it would be one of the first things I would tell anyone I met.

'Hi, I'm Claire. What a beautiful day. It's like the sunshine state... or California... Hey! That reminds me of the Red Hot Chili Peppers... I bought them a drink once.'

Jeez. And where exactly was this chance encounter? Oh! In your local countryside pub? And what did they want to drink? Champagne, you say? But you had a glass with them of course?

Of course you did. I would say you couldn't make that up, but it seems you can.

He was already annoying me so much, when all of a sudden it comes to paying and he's forgotten his wallet so I had to foot the bill. I'd babysat every night last week to save enough for my Bristol weekend with Skater Chris and I'm almost blowing the lot on dinner. Come to think of it, I ended up paying for loads when he came to Edinburgh. I bought the theatre tickets, drinks, taxis... HOW DID I NOT NOTICE HE WAS SUCH A STINGY GIT? It makes buying the Chilies champagne even more ludicrous. All I wanted to do was go home, but we went off to the drum and bass night anyway. I obviously had to pay for everything and the drum and bass was shit, but I really wasn't in the mood anyway.

When we got back we were both staying on the sofa bed. I was watching him getting undressed and then WATCHED HIM TAKE HIS WALLET OUT OF HIS BACK POCKET!!!!!! THE LYING FUCKHEAD! I didn't say anything, but mentally decided that it was O.V.E.R! I'm not quite sure how to dump someone who is actually going out with someone else, but Skater Chris is sooooo dumped. He got into bed and tried to kiss me, but I pretended I was asleep. PRICK.

```
Text from Skater Chris after we said
goodbye: Baby u know how shit I am saying
this to your face so I'm writing it in a
text. I love you so much but after this
weekend I have the feeling u no longer
feel the same. Am I right? Please tell
me wots going on in that gorgeous head of
urs. Do u want me to do something?

To Chris: Im sorry but I feel like things
have changed. Im findin the u having a gf
```

thing a bit 2 much now but its not just that. Im sorry but I just dont feel the same nemore. Sorry I really did want it 2 work.

From Chris: That's cool. I don't understand how your feelings changed so quickly though. Love is love surely? So you neva loved me? and it's not crying u heard, only illness!

To Chris: If Im honest, I dont understand how they changed so quickly either. I did love u and I loved loving u but I cant make myself feel it anymore. I really am sorry and feel so sad about it.

From Chris: I know u still love me. You're just saying that. Sorry, I'm just upset still. I don't want to believe you don't feel the same way. I do feel like youve led me on and messed me around a bit. Love Chris.

To Chris: That's not fair. I have been fully honest with you. I can't force feelings if they're not there anymore. I did love you, I just don't anymore.

From Chris: Maybe you don't know what love is. It does seem that you fall in love with everyone. I should have known it wasn't real.

To Chris: Wow that's rich. Why don't you go home and cry some more on your GIRLFRIEND'S shoulder. You cheating fuck x

2ND DECEMBER 2002
LISTENING TO 'THE BALLAD' BY MILLENCOLIN

Oh no. I miss him… Obviously I'm just thinking about how much I loved Skater Chris (I think?!). I'm listening to his bloody stupid mix CD on loop and thinking of all the good times. Damn it. I feel so lonely I want to cry. Why did he change? Fuck! I'm just tired and it's making me emotional. We don't get on anymore – end of story. He's a lying, cheating, up-his-own-arse cheapskate. Remember the Chilies and the wallet… Chilies and wallet… Chilies and wallet.

TWENTY-FIVE

FINN

5TH DECEMBER 2002
LISTENING TO 'NAMELESS' BY JJ72

I've been preparing for my interview on the train to Exeter, but it's so hard to concentrate. I'm so excited about seeing the wonderful Finn Ellwyn-Cox. We've spent so long talking over the last few years that I feel we know each other so well. AHHHH, I can't wait, but I look like shit today. Finn's only seen me in the summer when I just got back from France looking amazing (well, ish). I'm so fat, pale and spotty right now. God, I look a right state. Urrrghh, I hope he still says I look good. Shit, one of the few people who thinks I'm hot is about to be shocked by the cruel, ugly reality of 'Winter Claire'. Great.

'Winter Claire' is very much a thing. For reasons that I don't understand and my heritage doesn't fully explain, I magically go a very dark shade of brown if my skin has

a mere soupçon of sunshine. I get it from my dad whose colouring definitely calls into question what went down while my grandad was at war. But that's an altogether different story (and far less interesting than what happens to my tan throughout the seasons). Sadly my glorious summer skin doesn't last, and by October, the translucent Scottish blue hue has fought its way back up to the surface. It is such a stark contrast from the summer months, that 'Grey Claire' has an almost daily 'Are you feeling ok? Do you need to go home? You don't look very well.'

7TH DECEMBER 2002
LISTENING TO 'THE SCIENTIST' BY COLDPLAY

Claire Ellwyn-Cox... Finn and Claire Ellwyn-Cox. JOKING! Well... ish. I can fantasise if I want! Finn has totally swept me off my feet. After I arrived we went out with his friends and got quite drunk at the union bar. We stayed up and watched *Stick Men* (which was spectacular) with his friends. He kept putting his hand down on my thigh, but *just* on the inside that my heart was racing a bit. He'd offered me his bed and set up some cushions on the floor, but I told him not to be ridiculous. He didn't need much convincing and before I knew it we were cuddled up quite nicely in his bed. He was circling his finger in the small of my back and telling me all the things I wanted to hear.

'You are so hot, Claire. I'd love to be yours. I must have done something right in my life to be lying in a bed with you right now!'

Was Finn a sleazebag? I honestly don't know. If some eighteen-year-old dared utter words, even slightly to that effect, to one of my future seventeen-year-old daughters, then that person is definitely a MASSIVE SLEAZEBAG.

And he kissed me. But it was more than a kiss. The term *embrace* (or the French *embrasse*) feels better. It felt like the kind of kiss that happens at the end of a black and white movie. It was mind-blowing. I'd forgotten just how great some kisses could be. My entire body was surging!

The next day I had my interview and it went quite well.

Et voilà. The story of my life and how I became a doctor.

I met Finn and his friends in the pub after my interview and we stayed there all afternoon before heading back to his halls for the formal dinner and dance. Finn couldn't keep his hands off me while we were getting ready. He's perfect. I had the best time partying with his friends. Uni life certainly seems better than normal life. I was in my element.

When we went to bed, Finn and I were getting a little carried away and I wanted him so badly! I really wanted to have sex with him, but all I could hear was William's voice in the back of my head saying, 'Wow, Claire... after only two nights? You've become more of a slut than I could ever have imagined.' But then I thought: fuck William. It's not really two nights anyway. It's more like two years. I want to do this. No one needs to know. So we had sex and it was absolutely incredible. I feel like I've known Finn my whole life and there was no awkwardness at all. Afterwards, he told me he would do anything for us to be in the same place so he could be my boyfriend. Ahhh, I can only dream. Then he made me orgasm about five times. Wow. This guy is GOD. I mustn't let myself but I could fall for Finn in a big way. He really is perfect, but I suspect he isn't doing too badly with the ladies at uni.

It's weird, after a weekend of drinking, smoking, sex and not sleeping I feel detoxed and cleansed. Ahhhh.

Ewwwwwww.

8TH DECEMBER 2002
LISTENING TO 'FORMULAE' BY JJ72

Bloody typical. Back at Bristol airport feeling all the melancholy in the world. This bloody airport! Why does he have to live at the other end of the fucking country?! It's so so so unfair!!! Humph.

Text from Finn: I miss you so badly. I am
sad now :-(I loved having you here and
making love to you. I am smitten. Come
back to me soon baby, kisses, Finn xxx

To Finn: I can't believe how much I miss you
after only a weekend. We should probably
never spend longer than that together or I
risk really falling for you. I can't wait
to see you again. A bit of my heart will
always be yours. Xxx

From Finn: I'm glad you haven't forgotten
me already. I guess you can have a piece
of my heart too! Thinking of u. I really
love u baby. Kisses all over xxx

To Finn: You can kiss me all over any time
you want...

From Finn: Ohhh naughty. I can do cheeky
texts too u know! But don't get me started.
I wish I could be inside you and touch you
forever until you're begging me to stop.
I want to make you shudder and scream out

my name. I miss your touch and your smile.
I want u.

STOPPPPPPPPPP.

11TH DECEMBER 2002
LISTENING TO 'BLURRY' BY PUDDLE OF MUDD

Christ. I can't stop thinking about Finn. The prospect of him with another girl is driving me mad. He's got every single quality I want in a boyfriend. I want Finn to hug and kiss me and tell me he loves me. I want him to make me laugh and orgasm. I want to have endless chats with him and I want him here. Now.

He's convinced me to visit him again in January – I can't wait!

12TH DECEMBER 2002

Text from William: (*Feeder 'Just a Day' Chorus lyrics*)

Text to William (*Ben Folds Five 'Evaporated' lyrics*): Don't you know I'm numb man? No I can't feel a thing at all. Cos it's all smiles and business and I'm indifferent to the loss. And I've faith that there's a soul somewhere that's leading me around and I wonder if she knows which way is down. Here I stand… sad and free…

14TH DECEMBER 2002
LISTENING TO 'LIKE I LIKE YOU'
BY JUSTIN TIMBERLAKE

I had my birthday dinner at mine last night and it was brilliant! Maggie and I got completely wasted and laughed so much! There were about twelve of us including Lucy, Mish, Maggie, Gretchen, Holly, Jamie, Charlie and Herbert. Next Door Andy came round a bit later with that beautiful Dickhead Mike. I can't believe he had the nerve to come round after twice fake asking me out. It was a bit hazy after that but we went into town and I downed a pint! I was so drunk. We went to Medina's and before I knew it Dickhead Mike and I were pulling for the rest of the night. He walked me home, but 'none shall pass'. Argh, it's so annoying. I keep really liking him, but there's no point. He's proved that. It's just a shame he's so goddamn handsome. That beautiful dickhead... that sounds like a Pogues song. Is it a song?

I stayed in tonight and was very surprised to get a call from Dickhead Mike saying he was at Next Door Andy's and did I want to go round? Errrr, yup! When I got there, they were all really drunk. I was only there a few minutes and Dickhead Mike kissed me, winked and squeezed my hand before they all buggered off into town. Does that mean something? Is it code for something? It felt conspiratorial like he *actually* liked me. Oh, I don't know. Boys are twats.

I sent a long email to Finn saying how I missed him and how I felt about him and then I waited AGES for a reply. I eventually got one back, but it was sent to twenty other billion people saying he was off to Costa Rica to visit his new 'brilliant girlfriend'. He signed off 'lucky me'. And that was it! I can't believe this is how he's told me! I must really mean nothing to him. I sent a gut-wrenching email basically telling him I'm falling in love with him and I just get a shit group email update that he's got a new supermodel girlfriend. No one takes me fucking seriously. Everyone just kisses me and fucks me and asks for blowjobs as if it means nothing! ARRGGHHHGHHHHHHH. I'm devastated.

23RD DECEMBER 2002
LISTENING TO 'SK8R BOI' BY AVRIL LAVIGNE

In Gay Paris for Xmas and although I am sooooo bored, it's nice to spend some time with Mamie and Papie and get away from Edinburgh for a while.

25TH DECEMBER 2002
LISTENING TO 'YOU'RE A SUPERSTAR' BY LOVE INC.

Well, I've sent a few texts to Finn, but he's been in Costa Rica for a week and still no sign of life. I think about him waaaay too much. I know we weren't together, but the ease with which he has deleted me is stuck in my throat. I don't know what to do about visiting him in January now. I can't believe he convinced me to book tickets and then got a girlfriend a few days later!

TWENTY-SIX

GRUMPY ARSEFACE TOBY

1ST JANUARY 2003
LISTENING TO 'HALF THREE' BY JJ72

Happy New Year!

Next Door Andy had the house to himself and was having a daytime NYE party. I spent the afternoon at his and was kissing Dickhead Mike a lot. WHY WHY WHY?! He's just toooooooo hot! That's why. I can't resist. It's weird, but he obviously likes me, and Next Door Andy said he never pulls anyone and he's only ever seen him with me in at least the last year. He kisses me in a boyfriendy way rather than a random pull way... so why not?

I left them all to head to Gretchen's party about 6pm (this was clearly an enormous mistake) where there were about fifty people from St Felix's and Margaret Campbell's.

Leo Le Loser was there. I can't believe I ever cared about what that stupid emo face thought of me.

The party was awesome but uneventful overall. I chatted to Mish for ages in the garden, but I'm pretty sure he left before midnight. And come to think of it, Lovely Lyla wasn't there. Most people had left by 6am and there were only a few of us still up. Gretchen and Jamie went up to her room and Grumpy Toby and I got a blow-up mattress to sleep on. We spent ages pissing about and failing to try and blow it up that we just threw some cushions down to sleep on those. It's the first time I've seen him relax a bit and he was being really funny! Who'd have thought there was a person behind the grouchiness. We'd been flirting like mad all night being all jokey and touchy feely. We were lying next to each other giggling and then started to pull WHEN, the fucking insult of the year (so far, given that we were only a few hours into the new year), the bastard suddenly stood up, chundered on Gretchen's rug then took himself off to sleep on the floor in the other room. I was just lying there thinking, *Did he just vom after kissing me?!* I can't believe he didn't say anything to me. Am I really so revolting that I can make a grown man puke?!

We all felt like shit this morning and I could barely look at Grumpy Toby, never mind talk to him. I feel so embarrassed by what happened. I wish I hadn't pulled him.

Two 1st 15 rugby captains in one night though – nice one, slut.

You said it.

```
Text from Dickhead Mike: Hey gorgeous. Did
you have a nice NY? I missed you. I wish
I could have been with you at midnight.
Things aren't the same when you're not
around x
```

2ND JANUARY 2003
LISTENING TO 'EDDIE WALKER'
BY BEN FOLDS FIVE

Text to Grumpy Toby: Hey. How's it going? Have you recovered? I'm finally fighting fit again. I've read you should use a hair dryer for blow up mattresses. Who knew?

Text from Toby: Do you mind not telling anyone about the other night. It wasn't even a pull, just a kiss. I don't know about you but I was really drunk.

To Toby: Charming. I didn't realise there was such a strong line between a kiss and a pull. Way to make a girl feel special! I only told Mish.

From Toby: Let's just forget about it. It is a fine line and there was a £50 bet involved so please don't get the wrong idea.

To Toby: Oh nice. I feel much better now. Thanks.

Yup. He pulled me for a bet. Mish later told me that some of the guys (but apparently not him) had bet Grumpy Toby to pull me 'for a laugh', but he said he'd only do it for £50. I feel great. How lovely. I'm torn between curling up into a tiny ball and crying myself to sleep or ripping his tiny fucking bollocks off!!!!!
ARSEHOLLLLLE.

4TH JANUARY 2003
LISTENING TO 'I WON'T SPEND ANOTHER NIGHT ALONE' BY THE ATARIS

MSN chat with Grumpy Arseface Toby:

Me: alright? Listen, what happened the other night doesn't really give u the right to ignore me like you did today. I said 'morning' and you completely blanked me in front of everyone. It's making it a little awkward as we've got the same friends. You can't just pretend I don't exist!

T: im fine, bye

Me: jesus. Ok look u were ruder than iv ever been 2u — u publicly humiliated me (again!) and I never did anything to you. There's no need to be even more of a dick. Can we not put it down to a drunken moment that has been blown way out of proportion.

T: okay then… why u call me gay? Cause I turned u down?

Me: oh wow. u wish. U already did that when you announced to the whole year that you didn't like me. That was another high point for me btw. u made me look like such an idiot and I just joked to Mish that 'I'd turned you Gay'. More self

269

deprecating than insulting you (not that it would be an insult anyway!). I really thought u were a decent guy till u said about the bet.

T: I thought I would be honest about the bet. It was also a way of telling you nicely that I didn't fancy you.

Me: There was no need. It would have been much nicer to say u didn't fancy me. Actually the nicest thing to do would have been to say nothing and just leave it. I wasn't expecting anything.

T: I was just saying why I'd done it. That's all. Sounds like you did expect something that's why you text me the next day.

Me: I txt loads of people the next day and I don't fancy any of them.

T: Oh and you text me all the time! You phoned Jamie for my number.

Me: you 'kissed' me! You need to get back down to earth.

T: aaand I'm off.

What an arseface! Oh, how I would love to get my hands on teenage Toby now and take him downnnnnnnn.

TWENTY-SEVEN
BIG SAM

5TH JANUARY 2003
LISTENING TO 'EVERLONG' BY FOO FIGHTERS

Friday night is verging on being one of the worst nights ever. Next Door Andy was having some of the guys round before heading out and asked if I wanted to join. He's off skiing soon for the rest of his gap year so it'll be nice to hang out and say bye. I'm going to miss the bugger. It's going to be weird not being able to just nip next door for a chat whenever I want.

So I went round after dinner, but they were all super drunk already and about to go out. I said I wasn't that up for going to Bertie's and then Next Door Andy went off on one saying:

'It's a lads' night out, Claire. You can't come. Who even invited you?'

'You did, dickhead!'

'Only for a drink. You can't come out with us.'

271

I was quite hurt, but then Dickhead Mike and Big Sam said they wanted me to come and made Next Door Andy apologise. Which he did (reluctantly) and we went out.

Big Sam was different from the others. He was, as his name suggests, quite a big guy. He wasn't much of a looker back in the day, but he made up for it with shedloads of charisma and the kindest eyes in Scotland. His friends were all drunken louts and although he played along you could always tell that he lived on a different moral plane. His thoughts ran a bit deeper than 'Lads, Lash and Pussy' (which Next Door Andy circa 2003 was championing). Big Sam and I had so much in common I was instantly drawn to him. We shared a love of music, booze and films. We have remained friends and his youthful, fresh-faced puppy fat has been replaced by a cut-glass jaw, bulging muscles and the bushiest, most Scottish beard you ever did see. He got hot. Have you ever seen the memes with handsome kilted Scottish men? They're usually topless with one foot suggestively propped up on a rock in the Highlands, their kilt caught in a cheeky breeze with a caption like 'Making knickers drop since the 1600s.' Well, Big Sam looks like that now.

So we all walked to Bertie's in the freakin' snow. I was stone cold (very cold) sober and they were all pissing about taking their sweet, drunken time. We got there and everyone got in except me. I just stood outside freezing my bollocks off. Saying that, I wish I did actually have some fucking bollocks for they might have treated me with a bit more respect if I had! It's a dick's world alright. I was there for ages thinking surely they'll notice I'm not there and come out for me… Twenty minutes went by and I was about to leave when Big Sam came out to see me, but was all like, 'Sorry, Claire...' and went back in. Bunch of wankers the lot of them! It seems that beautiful Dickhead Mike was no better than the rest of them after all.

I didn't see Dickhead Mike again for fourteen years as his family moved abroad shortly after this night. The next time I saw him was at Next Door Andy's wedding in 2016. I was heavily pregnant and Andy thought it would be hilarious to sit me next to Mike. Thanks, Andy. It was fine though. Obviously. We're grown-ups now. We talked about adult things like children, politics and what made a vichyssoise a vichyssoise. Important shit.

I was gutted, sober and frozen. I burst into tears contemplating the walk home in the snow by myself when William of all people comes out. I think Next Door Andy and Big Sam must have said I was outside. I was so relieved to see him. I felt flooded with emotions and in that instant realised he was the only person I wanted to see in the whole world. He wiped my tears away, gave me his jumper and just started walking me home. We didn't really talk. It was just nice to be with him and I think neither of us wanted to ruin it by saying anything.

```
Text to William: Thank you so much for
tonight. You kinda saved the day (night!).
I mean it when I say I've missed you.
```

```
Text from William: Claire, I've missed
you too. Seeing you tonight still proves
how much I care about you but sadly you
still don't want anything. I still love
you.
```

9TH JANUARY 2003
LISTENING TO 'TIMES LIKE THESE'
BY FOO FIGHTERS

Had my first exam today. It didn't go too badly. Shit, I'm nervous about them. I don't feel prepared at all!

I've been hanging out with Big Sam since Next Door Andy and the others have left, and it's awesome. We get on so well. I need more friends like Big Sam.

15TH JANUARY 2003
LISTENING TO 'BROTHER SLEEP' BY JJ72

Woooooo, conditional offer for medical school!

18TH JANUARY 2003
LISTENING TO 'JUSTBOY' BY BIFFY CLYRO

Last night was complete bliss. I had the house to myself and Big Sam came round. We had a curry, drank two bottles of wine and watched *Mulholland Drive*. Big Sam is David Lynch mad, which I love. We are getting on soooo well.

I'm so tired now after only three hours' sleep but on the train to Exeter and going to see Finn – yaay! I just hope I'm welcome as he doesn't seem that overjoyed about the prospect of me visiting this time. It might just be in my head, but things definitely seem different. He's still with his Costa Rican supermodel. I can't compete with that! Life must be so much easier if you look like a supermodel.

21ST JANUARY 2002
LISTENING TO '7TH WAVE' BY JJ72

I'm exhausted and feel heart-wrenchingly disappointed. Things have been so awkward with Finn. When I arrived, things were definitely weird. I was flirting and giggling with him, but I wasn't getting much back. Is this how William and Gael and Skater Chris felt with me?

Finn had 'the ick'.

So anyway I got really drunk. REALLY drunk and then got into bed with Finn. He was all over me and I was so relieved. He was kissing my neck and rubbing himself on me, whispering dirty sweet nothings into my ear. I went to kiss him and he pulled away and looked at me really oddly. He got off me so quickly he practically fell out of bed and said he loved his Costa Rican girlfriend. Fuck! I knew it. I love him and all he's done is fill me up to the brim with false hope. I was just an *amuse bouche* before he had his supermodel main course (literally). He slept on the floor next to the bed and I lay there silently crying for hours. I felt so embarrassed.

After that night, Finn was really off with me and I spent the weekend with his friends cos Finn 'had shit loads of work to do'. Bullshit! But I was happy not to have to see him. I felt half mortified and half fucking pissed off. Thank God his friends were so nice. They took me to the station at the end of the weekend and Finn didn't even say goodbye. I still haven't slept so I've basically had about three hours' sleep in the last seventy. Bollllloooxxxx. I just want to cry, but I'm too tired even for that.

23RD JANUARY 2003
LISTENING TO '27' BY BIFFY CLYRO

I'm so emotional at the moment. I miss Finn and he's not speaking to me. He went from 'Oohh, I'm so tempted by you, you have a great butt, I can't resist you' to completely ignoring me. But before that, he was my friend and I've ruined everything. I'd speak to him nearly every night and now nothing. I miss him. I have sent him an email, a text and some one rings. Nothing.

In other (un-boy-related news), I think I have totally fucked up my prelim exams and Mummy Le Day is not going to be impressed at all. I'm so worried. I might never get to do anything with my life and I'll be left to wallow in the gutter with William and the other losers for the rest of my life. GREAT.

Sorry, William. Incidentally he is fairly successful and very much not in the gutter, having casually just dropped a cool mill' on his new house.

24TH JANUARY 2003
LISTENING TO 'SAN DIMAS HIGH SCHOOL FOOTBALL RULES' BY THE ATARIS

Why am I so miserable? It would take nothing for me to just burst into tears and I don't even know why. Mish is being a right twat at the moment, which definitely isn't helping. He dismisses everything I say and *his* problems are the only problems. Mish chat or no chat. He really fucked me off in chemistry the other day when we were doing a practical together and we got a bit stuck. He asked, 'What do you think we should do?' and I suggested adding some… let's just say water… or something. Wow. This inability to retain ANYTHING to do with chemistry is seriously concerning! Anyway, I suggested adding 'water' and he was like, 'Oh no, that doesn't sound right', whilst looking around to see what everyone else is doing.

'No, really. We definitely need to add water.'

He ignored me and asked Herbert who said he'd added some 'water' and Mish was like, 'Oh, cool. Thanks, mate!', and then just went on and did it as I stared at him in disbelief. God, he pisses me off.

Mish was an askhole.

Askhole (noun): A person who constantly asks for your advice, yet always does the exact opposite of what you told them.

We were chatting on the phone tonight and he told me he quite liked Holly (even though he's been with Lovely Lyla for over a year). What is the deal with Holly? Other than the fact that she looks like Carmen Electra? She's so dumb though! Not Sofia-dumb but pretty fucking ditsy. I think that all the boys just think it's ditsy in a 'cute' way. Is it cos they all feel so macho and clever when they're with her? Mish spends so much time up there on his high horse, judging me, I can't believe he's now got the cheek to tell me he fancies someone other than his girlfriend!

27TH JANUARY 2003
LISTENING TO 'DREAMS' BY THE CRANBERRIES

I've been hanging out with Big Sam way too much. I love his company, but I'm worried I might have fucked up our friendship. He came with me to St Felix's Burns Supper on Friday night. I'd got a table and had Maggie, Charlie, Mish, Lovely Lyla, Gretchen, Jamie, Herbert, Andy 'Lads Lads Lads' Burns and Big

Sam. 'Lads' kept saying that Big Sam and I would make a great couple. None of them really know Big Sam and it was really great of him to step up last minute, but 'Lads' was making things weird. Big Sam's my friend! I don't want to be in a couple with him. Fortunately Andy 'Lads Lads Lads' Burns was smashed and quickly moved on to talking about something totally gross like 'donkey punching'. Standard dinner chat.

Big Sam and I were steaming by the end of the night. We went back to mine and watched a film and then out of the blue, he kissed me. I didn't know what to do so I kinda kissed him back for a minute then pulled away in a 'end of the pull' way rather than a 'I don't want to kiss you' way then put my head on his chest to watch the rest of the film. FUCK! It was nice, but I don't want that from him. I really hope we're ok.

2ND FEBRUARY 2003
LISTENING TO 'JUST THE WAY
I'M FEELING' BY FEEDER

Well, it's been an interesting weekend. I ended up having a massive argument with William. Again. Big Sam and I went to the cinema on Friday night and he saw us later at the pub and was like 'ANOTHER BOYFRIEND AYE?' and mouthed 'slut' at me as he walked away. Fortunately I only gave a small angry shit for about five minutes.

```
Text to William: Why do you always have
to be so unreasonable? Not that it's any
of your business but Sam and I are just
friends. I knew I stopped being friends
with you for a reason you massive wanker.
```

From W: ha ha that's polite but it was me that stopped being friends with you cause you turned into a nutcase but some things will never change you total whore. I can't believe you still think you're better than me. I work harder than you and at least I don't spend all my money on getting drunk — that's just sad.

To W: Ha! I can't believe you chose working hard as your thing. Wow — that really doesn't say much for all the other aspects of your life. If you've worked harder than me, how come ur not able to do anything useful with your life? Enjoy uni… oh no wait… I mean college… oh no… Next time try and come up with something more original than 'whore'. Those 'insults' wear thin.

From W: Like your pussy.

I spat my coffee out laughing at the last bit. Like your pussy… good one, William.

Mish was being an absolute wank on Saturday when I met him for a dog walk. He was endlessly banging on about Holly until he eventually (after I'd tried to come up with some very reasonable solutions to his 'problem') sat down on a rock in the most exasperated way imaginable. Alright, drama?!

'You wouldn't understand, Claire!'

Umm… yes I fucking do. I LOVE a love triangle and eat unrequited love for breakfast! Cheer up! We're all teenagers. We're all heartbroken. We're all stressed. Just snap the fuck out of it! … I wish I'd said. Instead I probably said something pathetic like the good little subservient sidekick that I am.

On Saturday night I went to Holly's 1920s murder mystery night. Mish was a lot cheerier, saying he'd had a long three-hour chat with Lovely Lyla after our walk and he was feeling better about everything. Who gives a shit, Mish?!

The dinner was pretty good fun then I went to meet Big Sam in town dressed like a twat. He was a little bit too handsy and I didn't want to embarrass him so I went home. I'm worried I might have to address this at some point.

5TH FEBRUARY 2003
LISTENING TO 'OUT OF ROUTINE' BY IDLEWILD

Well, I'm feeling a lot happier with my life situation right now. Everything in school feels fairly settled, everyone is being friendly and I'm on top of work. I wish it could be like this all the time. No drama. No fuss.

Lovely.

Gretchen and I are actually friends. For real (I think). I'd never have thought it. She might well be 'friends close, enemies closer'-ing me, but for now I feel like I can relax a bit.

I'm supposed to be seeing Big Sam on Friday, but just don't know how to act around him anymore. Next Door Andy has been gone too long now. He needs to come back from his ski season to fix Big Sam. All I had to do was look after Big Sam while he was gone and I think I've broken him. Or at least dented him.

6TH FEBRUARY 2003

The most horrific thing has just happened. My sister's best friend was killed in a car crash this morning. It's so horrible. Chloe's completely distraught and it's tearing me apart to hear her like this. I just wish I could do something for her – I've never heard her so upset in all my life. I'm just sat in my room listening to her crying. She's actually wailing and it feels like the sound of her breaking. It's causing me actual physical pain hearing it. I can't imagine how she feels, feeling it. I would do anything to make things better for her. I would switch places with her if I could. I wish it had happened to me and not her. I just don't know what to say to her. Does she want to be left alone or should I go in and sit with her? She screamed at my parents to leave her alone, but is it different for me? I just wish I could do something. I've always felt like I could look after her and right any wrong for her, but I'm so helpless right now. I can't even sympathise properly cos I've never even had a friendship like they have. Had. Poor Chlo.

9TH FEBRUARY 2003
LISTENING TO 'TIME FOR HEROES'
BY THE LIBERTINES

I started driving today and it was amazing. I'm finally driving! Yeeeha. It won't be long till I am free to roam the world; just me and my car, wherever I want. Freedoooooooommmmmm!

While I was learning to drive I had a very clear vision of what it would be like to be 'a driver'. It would usually involve slight variations on the theme of road trippin' through the States, smoking Lucky Strikes in a sky blue Cadillac convertible. The Texan sun beating down on me as I held the wheel with one hand and a Stetson in the other, flying through the hot, dusty air. There'd be a very hunky cowboy in the passenger seat chewing on a piece of

straw and calling me dahlin'. Hunky Butch and I would
have a bootful of dollars from our recent big Vegas win
and I'd shout a 'so long, suckers' (to no one in particular)
as we sped off into the sunset. Ahh, the driving dream.

Mish and I are getting on really well at the moment, although it feels like we're dangerously skirting the rim of friendship and… well, something else. We had our usual play fight-y thing in the prefects' room, again, this afternoon. It's totally bizarre. We just roll around laughing and taking turns to straddle each other and 'win'. I just love to feel him pin me down with his strong hands and I guess it's getting increasingly sexual. We definitely both felt 'it' more today. There was a moment when I thought he might kiss me. It was weird and I pretended like nothing had happened and sat back on the sofa and put my feet up on his lap. We were having a general chat about life and he definitely had an erection. I don't know if it means anything or if it's simply that he's a teenage boy who had brief physical contact with a girl and the erection is biology and nothing more.

The play fighting that went on with Mish was really
something only children do when they like each other. It
was silly, inappropriate and a bit 'gropey', but somehow it
seemed like day-to-day friendship stuff at the time.

10TH FEBRUARY 2003
LISTENING TO 'AMERICAN ENGLISH' BY IDLEWILD

God, I fancy Mish. I just don't know if I only fancy him cos I can't have him and if I could, I wouldn't want him. Maybe I only like him cos he blows so hot and cold with me that I'm constantly striving for the hot.

18TH FEBRUARY 2003
LISTENING TO 'F**K HER GENTLY' BY TENACIOUS D

Got an interview for Bristol and Durham coming up... yayy. God, I hope I don't blow it all. Not sure my head's in the game at the moment.

23RD FEBRUARY 2003
LISTENING TO 'I NEVER WANTED' BY IDLEWILD

I think what happened to Chloe's friend put me right and gave me some perspective. I was spending far too much time moping about and moaning about things that, frankly, were not important. It's embarrassing to think it took something like that to make me realise I was so self-indulged.

```
Text from Big Sam: Morning Sweetie, how are
you today? Do u want to go and see tenacious
d in March I can get tix. Also wanted to
say I really do enjoy spending my friday
nights in your company. You're beautiful
and fun to be around (how's this for a nice
message!) can't wait to see you again.
```

2ND MARCH 2003
LISTENING TO 'LIVE IN A HIDING PLACE' BY IDLEWILD

God, last night was awful. The chat wasn't flowing and EVERYONE was coupled up (again!). It's always the same crowd and to start with I was enjoying my drama-free friendship group, but our nights out are all pretty same-y now. Gretchen and Jamie, Maggie and Charlie, Mish and Lovely Lyla… and me. They're all sickeningly smug. We were sat in the pub tonight when I realised that I had either kissed or fancied all the boys around the table. Mish is still very much a real ongoing crush. Charlie was my childhood crush, and Jamie and I obviously have 'surprise bus snog'.

Then when I thought it couldn't get any worse William arrived with his new girlfriend. Gretchen had obviously invited him (thank you, Gretch!). The worst part was that she is completely normal. Normal age, normal attractiveness, normal shoes and good-ish chat. Fuck. I hate seeing him anyway, but seeing him with someone actually palatable was fucking awful.

So I left and got a bus to Big Sam's. We were chilling out listening to music when I went to change the song. That's when I saw an email on his computer from Next Door Andy saying things like, 'Way to go, mate! Happy for you' etc. I looked down and Big Sam had emailed them all basically saying I was his girlfriend. Say what now? I pretended like I hadn't seen, but it's fucked me off. How do I tackle this? Did he think I just wasn't going to find out? What happens when Next Door Andy gets back? DOES HE THINK I'M HIS GIRLFRIEND? Surely not.

9TH MARCH 2003
LISTENING TO 'THE CHAIN' BY FLEETWOOD MAC

I'm such a sad loser. I don't go one day without thinking about William. Is he really going to be on my mind my whole life? GO AWAY, imaginary William, and let me live. I've finally got an amazing group of friends, but I miss William more than I ever thought possible. For someone whose jokes I hate, whose attitude towards life I hate, whose manipulative techniques I hate, whose looks I hate, I do spend an inordinate amount of time thinking about him. Actually, for someone that I have spent most of my adolescence obsessing about, there is very little I like about him.

Big Sam and I are still such good friends, but everything feels a bit weird since the email. I'm worried that by spending so much time with him, I'm giving him the wrong idea. I realised I needed to take a step back when I felt a bit jealous when he was talking about this girl he'd met. Why am I such a sociopath?! I don't want him! I should be happy that he's met a girl! I'm backing off.

15TH MARCH 2003

This page is absolute chaos. It's almost illegible and I have kept it uncorrected just to demonstrate my level of inebriation.

Ok, there's no real print in my writing this – I'm just dubious about how drink I am. It's one of these situations where you don't really just how drunk you are yet don't feel sobe or drunk. Been to this party in Jamie's Crammond with Gretchen, Jamie, Mish and Grumpy Arseface Toby. Toby still cuntface has a girlfriend and love hate Gretchen – fucking hilarious. Party was pretty shite – loads of cheap fourteen-year-old sluts with short skits. Bunch of skanks. William would have heaven. Haha. Pedo. Gretchen told me she didn't hate me anymore. Me too, although still felt pretty nervous that she might turn and kill me one day. Anyway Im drink – felling it now. Don't want to lie down as will be very dizzy. Fuck Mish. Dickhead.

17TH MARCH 2003
LISTENING TO 'HORRORSHOW' BY THE LIBERTINES

I have loads of work on and my mum's on my back all the time, which isn't helping. I actually want to NOT do any work the minute she bangs on about it, but then have to secretly revise or I'm fooked. Mish and I both are. Chemistry is totally hopeless. I've been getting tutoring, but it's not helping. We're both going to fail at this rate.

26TH MARCH 2003
LISTENING TO 'TELL ME TEN WORDS' BY IDLEWILD

Jeeeeez. I am seriously beginning to wonder about my mental health. I can't get William out of my head. I wrote a long letter to him, but after speaking to Mish, decided not to send it. It was definitely the right call. Our relationship was definitely 90% pain, 10% pleasure. I just wish I could convince myself!

Oh, and I got four out of four offers for medicine (Bristol, Durham, Dundee, Peninsula) so I obviously wasn't that bad in my interviews. Now all I have to do is choose... aaaand not cock up my exams. Easy... fuck.

29TH MARCH 2003
LISTENING TO 'TRIBUTE' BY TENACIOUS D

Maggie dumped Charlie today. He'd only just finished telling me how much he loved her and he was going to tell her he was in love with her. But instead of declarations of love, it seems he got the boot. Poor wee lamb. He's devastated.

Apparently Grumpy Arseface Toby has been bitching about Maggie and her size, talking about how gross it would be to have sex with 'a fat mess' like her and can't believe *she* dumped Charlie. He is such a fucking arse-nugget. He is like the white stuff that accumulates round the side of an old man's mouth. But on a cockroach. Total scum.

31ST MARCH 2003
LISTENING TO 'A TOWN CALLED MALICE'
BY THE JAM

I went out with Lucy and the old girls from school at the weekend and it was so shit. I don't know why I keep going back to them. Probably because there's still some needy part of me that likes being accepted by 'the cool girls'. They all spent the entire night bitching about whoever went to the toilet or was out of earshot. Sofia was there, but I don't care anymore. Finally. At one point she came and sat next to me.

'Hey, Claire! It's so nice to see you! We miss you!'

'I'll bet you do...'

'No, really! It's so funny. I was just saying to Lucy – remember what a loser you were and look at you now!'

She's such a dick. The sooner I stop seeing her, the better.

2ND APRIL 2003
LISTENING TO 'CRY ME A RIVER'
BY JUSTIN TIMBERLAKE

What an interesting evening I've had. I met the school crew in The Brauhaus then went to Standing Order, Espionnage then ended up in Garibaldi's (Gari's).

Garibaldi's is one of those places that defies all time and sense. It is 'small family-run restaurant' sized and yet, it has somehow earned the title of 'club'. It has remained unshakably and inexplicably popular for decades. It is the same today as it was the first time I stepped through the looking glass in 2000. Gari's is overcrowded and a bit smelly with averagely priced, average-tasting drinks. The DJ has, for the last twenty years, religiously played old school hip hop and R&B. This manages to trick everyone into believing it's the <insert favourite decade>s and they're still carefree teenagers partying all night with reckless abandon. Regardless of its many faults, people LOVE it. Even to this day it stands firmly on 'Edinburgh's best club nights' list and everyone's buddy, Andy 'Lads Lads Lads' Burns, along with the other diehard lashers, can still be found there, at closing time, every Sunday morning.

I accidentally let slip to Charlie that I fancied Mish. I really hope he keeps it a secret. Anyway in Gari's I bumped into William's new (annoyingly nothing wrong with her) girlfriend. I was trying to be polite and ended up getting stuck chatting to her for ages. She was pretty cool actually, but obviously I hate her (on principle). She was telling me that it wasn't really working with William. I tried my hardest to give her the most neutral responses to everything she said, but it shamefully filled me with joy that it might be ending. Despite my uncontrollable internal reaction, I didn't want to get caught up in it all. She then told me that he treated her like shit and was quite mean to her all the time. Really? William Macleod? Later on, she came back downstairs, clearly upset and crying and said he'd just yelled at her for getting drunk. What? Is this the same William? Did I do this to him? She told me that it was over between them and goaded me into calling him on her phone.

No no no no, please don't call him.

So I rang him and said she had every right to get pissed and who did he think he was telling her what to do?!

Noooooo! What was I thinking? Why was I getting involved? Well, I know why I was getting involved, but I wish I hadn't. I just couldn't help myself. I couldn't resist one more dig.

He was soooooo angry. I just listened to him spewing hatred down the phone at me for ten minutes before he eventually said he wished he could get into his car and run me over. He actually wants me dead.

Well, that was a disaster.

TWENTY-EIGHT

MISH

7TH APRIL 2003
LISTENING TO 'LIFESTYLES OF THE RICH
AND FAMOUS' BY GOOD CHARLOTTE

Mish and I have arrived in Cambridge. We're staying in one of the colleges for an Easter revision course. Losers, I know. It's not exactly our first choice of holiday destination, but at least we're here together. We both completely failed AS mock chemistry (fairly predictably) and our parents have decided to spend our eighteenth birthday money on this course. Otherwise there isn't a sodding chance in hell that either of us will ever get what we need for medicine. I have very mixed feelings about this.

We're staying in catered halls and outside of the 2-1 chemistry tuition in the day, we're free to do whatever we want. We went out to Bar Oz last night for happy hour with two other guys who are staying in the room above Mish. The four of us spent the whole night getting to know each other. I can't believe how different Mish is outside of Edinburgh! He's been the life and soul since we got here! I've watched him relax and he is a joy to be around. He is completely unrecognisable. It must be exhausting being Edinburgh Mish.

When we got back to the halls, Mish ended up coming back to my room and we pulled. It felt weirdly very normal. Like we should have been doing this the whole time. There was a voice in my head screaming, 'STOP KISSING ALL YOUR FRIENDS!', but hey. He spent the rest of the night in my bed and we kissed and chatted till morning. It's amazing that we still have stuff to talk about. We didn't sleep and went straight to breakfast and then classes. I'm embarrassed to say that I didn't even think about Lovely Lyla until now, but surely it's his responsibility not to cheat? Like Skater Chris? And Finn? How responsible am I?

11TH APRIL 2003
LISTENING TO 'WONDERBOY' BY TENACIOUS D

I have no idea what is going on anymore. Everything is a huge blur. Who am I? Where am I? This is probably not conducive to the extremely expensive Cambridge University A-level chemistry revision, but fuck it... I'm down the rabbit hole now.

Mish and I have basically become a couple. It's amazing to be away from anyone who knows us and essentially living together. We're just able to openly be boyfriend and girlfriend. We've got eight hours of chemistry every day, then we go out with the boys then back to Mish's room and stay up all night kissing, cuddling and chatting. He spent about two hours the other night just slowly running his fingers up and down my back as we fantasised about the life we could have together if things were different. It sounds creepy having written it down, but he started it! I think we both know it will end when we go back to Edinburgh (and he's back in Lovely Lyla's arms), so we don't want to waste any of this week sleeping. I'm pretty sure we haven't slept since we got here and we're both getting a little delirious. It is amplifying all the emotions of our 'affair' and it's starting to feel like a bit of a dream. I think I love him, but I also don't know if it's day or night right now so I probably shouldn't trust my feelings too much.

Last night was Mish's eighteenth and it was probably the most hilarious night of my life. I bought a birthday cake and the two other boys made some cocktails. As soon as we finished lessons we went to their flat and started drinking. We'd been playing 'darts' with drawing pins all week so they were all over the floor. I can't remember if it was a bet or what circumstances led to this, but at one point Mish was naked and chasing one of the other boys around the room trying to 'peenie whack' him. I already couldn't breathe, I was laughing so much, when he slipped and fell straight down, embedding hundreds of upturned drawing pins into his arse. He jumped up yelping, 'OOWWWWEEEEEE', with his arse peppered in multicoloured dots. I came as close as I have ever come to wetting myself.

And then I had children. Thank goodness I didn't have my modern-day pelvic floor to contend with. Maybe my modern-day brain wouldn't have found it so funny though. Although I wouldn't want to live in a world where I don't find naked men falling over funny.

When we were lying in bed later I had my head resting on his chest and he was stroking my hair. He held me really tightly.

'I'm so sad this week is coming to an end.'

I sighed and just said, 'Me too, Mish… me too.' My whole body ached with the grief that I was essentially about to endure an enforced breakup AND have to keep it secret. I have loved being Mish's girlfriend. We're so good together. In another world we would have met later in life, at uni, as equals (or at least where he viewed me as an equal), and maybe we'd have fallen in love and lived our fake fantasy life together. I could definitely fall in love with 'Cambridge Mish'. He strokes my back and kisses my neck and tells me I'm beautiful and I'm everything he wants. He tells me that I'm the kind of girl he wants to marry and that I make him happier than he's ever been. He does cute things in public that 'Edinburgh Mish' would scoff at like kiss the tip of my nose in front of lots of people or dance and twirl me around in the street serenading me. 'Edinburgh Mish' doesn't even smile at my jokes if there are other people around. Although maybe things will be different now. Maybe we will actually fall in love.

12TH APRIL 2003

> Text from Mish: Night night sexy Claire. I
> hope you're not too lonely tonight. Thank
> you for the most amazing week. Luv me zzz

13TH APRIL 2003
LISTENING TO 'THE BITTER END' BY PLACEBO

Yup. I've crashed. I am seriously sleep deprived and I think I've gone a bit mad. I'm back in Edinburgh and I'm sooooo miserable. It was such a shock going to bed by myself and I kept waking up expecting to have Mish's arm around me. The only time we spent apart in the whole week was when we went to the toilet and it feels weird now. I was devastated this morning when he wasn't there, cuddled into me, and I realised he probably wouldn't be ever again. I got used to waking him with a kiss. But no. No more. This is basically like going through a breakup, but the whole thing is secret and I can only mourn in private. FUCKKKKKKK I've fallen in love with him. Yes, Skater Chris... I've fallen in love agaaaaiiinnnnnn. It just felt so right.

I have been absolutely sick with jealousy all day knowing he's probably with Lovely Lyla. I wonder if he's the same with her as he is with me? Does he joke around as much? It never seems like they're having fun... but then I guess no one would believe that Mish and I get on so well cos he's so secretive. Does he prefer her company to mine? God, this is torture! She's so lucky. Shit, I like him and he obviously likes me too, but clearly he's ashamed of me. I hate myself for having done anything cos now I can't stop thinking about him. What did I expect? I suppose part of me thought he might leave her for me. Classic mistress mentality. I'm such a fucking cliché. The worst part is I want to tell someone, but I can't tell anyone. If Next Door Andy was here, I'd probably be able to tell him. ARRGHHHHHH. The irony is that I would have been able to talk to Mish about it.

14TH APRIL 2003
LISTENING TO 'THIS YEAR'S LOVE' BY DAVID GRAY

Well, if there was ever any doubt, it's crystal clear now: I am a bad person. I have absolutely no morals. I'm not even sure how much I did have, but they've well and truly been obliterated now.

I met Mish today and he kept saying how terrible he felt about Cambridge cos he loved Lovely Lyla. Oh my God, how jealous am I?! How can he just expect me to go straight back to being the supportive friend? He's talking to me like the 'affair' happened with someone else entirely! Has he just forgotten all that stuff he said to me? Does he not realise I have feelings?! Did he not mean it? I just want him all to myself and I want to throw up when I imagine him with Lovely Lyla. We went for a walk and a pint and before I knew it, we were back in my room and he was kissing me and touching me then he stopped and was like, 'That's it! I feel so bad. This is over!' He left and I'm now sat on my bedroom floor crying. Why can't it be me? Why can't he choose me? He's never going to split up with Lovely Lyla. Why do I keep doing this to myself? I eventually had to tell someone so I spoke to Big Sam, but he clearly didn't want to know. All he could say was that I was 'wanton'. I had to look it up:

```
Wanton. Adj: dissolute or immoral; without
motive; sexually unrestrained.
```

Thanks a fucking bunch, 'mate'!

A fairly accurate adjective for me at the time. Big Sam ended up teaching English.

15TH APRIL 2003
LISTENING TO 'BLOWN IT AGAIN'
BY DANIEL BEDINGFIELD

Jamie's Eighteenth
I. AM. SMASHED. So I won't write much, but I need to get this off my chest. It was Jamie's eighteenth tonight and he had a BBQ at his, which was alright. Maggie and Charlie are back together and they seem happy, but I'm not sure she's back with him for the right reasons. Grumpy Arseface Toby was there and we just

sat death-staring each other all night. I REALLY don't like that boy. I caught him sniggering and throwing a condescending 'yuck' look around the table when Maggie and Charlie shared a snog. If it wasn't such a completely psycho thing to consider, I'd have loved to just stand up, walk round the table and punch him in his stupid grumpy arseface!

Mish walked me home at the end of the night along the Water of Leith. We stopped at the bridge to the Modern Art Gallery and had a sit down. We started kissing and before I knew it he was going down on me. I was only just getting to grips with outdoor action when I was then giving him a BJ! Neither of us was thinking. It's crazy how you can just turn your brain off and do something that, say twelve hours earlier, you wouldn't have dreamed of. I've never done anything like that in public and before tonight, Mish and I had only kissed with some heavy petting. This was a huge step up and we were both so pissed. When it was over I just felt my brain slowly turn back on. Whirrrr bing... WHAT ARE YOU DOING, CLAIRE? Too late, I did it. We sat on the steps in silence and I couldn't figure out what anything meant. We got up and started walking then had a huge chat about how we just 'clicked'. Fuuuuuuuuuccccckkkk, I'm properly worried about how much I like him and that I've fallen in stupid love with him. Am I only attracted to the unattainable?

God, I'm drunk and it's 2am – fuck. I have a chemistry revision session first thing. Really need to get some sleep now.

```
Text from Mish: Hope your mum wasn't too
annoyed and we didn't wake her up. Don't
feel bad about Lyla — that's my problem.
I properly like you and we really do click
on another level. I just need to sort
myself out. Get some sleep now sexy xxx
```

16TH APRIL 2003
LISTENING TO 'SHE'S ONLY HAPPY IN THE SUN' BY BEN HARPER

I spent the morning feeling like I'd just emerged from a decade up a badger's arse. Mish and I struggled through the chemistry session then had a nice lunch in the garden. He kept touching me. He'd brush hair out of my face or put his hand on my back or my arm… it felt wonderful and like he cared about me. I've fallen for him big time. I can't stop thinking about him.

> Text from Mish: You deserve someone amazing and I know the perfect guy is out there for you. You'll make someone very happy one day. I wish it could be me but well you know… I'm soooo tired. Don't want to go and get phone from parents room now. What do you think about going to Toby's tomorrow? If you're not going, i won't either, I rate our friendship so so much. Love urs xxx

17TH APRIL 2003
LISTENING TO 'THE END' (EDIT VERSION FROM THE FILM APOCALYPSE NOW) BY THE DOORS

It was really warm and sunny today and Mish and I met along the river. We lay on a blanket and I had my head resting on his chest, looking up at the clouds and we chatted for hours. I just wanted the world to stop so I could stay there forever. We were only there for each other and because we wanted to spend time together. Nothing else mattered and it felt perfect, except of course nothing is ever perfect. At one point he slowly ran his hand all the way up the inside of my leg; it was torture and I wanted to just give in to him so badly. But I realised I couldn't live in a world where I spent half the time feeling like the only person that mattered in Mish' life and the other, like someone he barely knew. I came to the conclusion that if 'it' continued, it would just end in tears (mine) cos the longer things went on, I was only falling more and more in love with him. He was clearly never going to end it with Lovely Lyla, so I would eventually explode with jealousy and lose one of my best friends (if I haven't already). So I told him all this and he agreed that 'just friends' was the way forward. I am upset about it, but I know that it would only have been worse if I'd left it. I know I've fallen for him, but I'm just going to have to get over him. Bosh. *Juste comme ça.*

18TH APRIL 2003
LISTENING TO 'WITH MY OWN TWO HANDS' BY BEN HARPER

I'm feeling much better today. I've had a good night's sleep and done a tonne of work. I've had the house to myself and so I've sat in the garden, basking in the sunshine, smoking and revising. Mish came round briefly and I feel that over time I'll be able to calm my feelings down. We were friends for years first after all.

I was bursting to tell someone about Mish so I started to tell Maggie, but I had to do a serious 180 and rein the story in when I saw how shocked she was. She was so horrified that I then made out like it was just one drunken kiss when we were in Cambridge. She has no idea about the extent of it all or that anything happened after we got back. Man, I am trusting her with my life now. Shit. I shouldn't have told her. FUCKKKKK what if she tells Gretchen? Oh sweet Jesus. Or anyone.

Just found out Next Door Andy is back on Monday – woohoooo!

20TH APRIL 2003
LISTENING TO 'BABYLON' BY DAVID GRAY

Every second I spend with Mish eats away at my happiness and self-confidence. I leave every encounter hating myself just a little bit more. It hurts so much to be around him, but then every moment without him is filled with jealousy and longing. I'm clearly destined to spend the rest of my life languishing in a cesspool of unrequited love.

> Text from Mish: Thanks 4 this afternoon, had a great time. Ur right — I don't want to go back to school as I want you all to myself. Love Spunky

> To Mish: It's going to be shit. I don't feel like we're as close in school. I feel lucky to have u as my friend but I'm not always sure u feel the same.

> From Mish: you been smoking crack again? I'm the lucky one to have u as a friend. Until I met you, I'd never had such a close friend. Have a good night, ur as close as can be. Xxx

22ND APRIL 2003
LISTENING TO 'WHEN SHE BELIEVES'
BY BEN HARPER

Next Door Andy came back today – yaaaaayyy! I went round to
see him this evening and it was largely 'skiing this, après booze
and châlet girls that'. He spent far too long recounting the rivalry
between snowboarders and skiers…

'Two boards, good. One board, bad.'

Yawn. You had to be there I reckon, but I'm delighted to
have him back and I'm sure the skiing douchiness will subside.

24TH APRIL 2003
LISTENING TO 'EVERYTHING' BY BEN HARPER

Ahhhhh, it's all bollocks. Everything and everyone at school
is bollocks!! I spend hours surrounded by people who are not
themselves, people I've known for years but I'll never truly meet.
Mish is un-fucking-recognisable again. So long 'Cambridge
Mish', my love. Hello 'Edinburgh Mish', you massive wanker. He
acts like he doesn't even know me and I certainly don't know this
arsehole. How could he? After everything?! It's back to school
and I'm geeky, love-struck Sandy after all that *summer (Easter)
lovin*'. Well, I'm not going to change for Mish-the-arsehole-
Zuko. *Grease*: a pathetic, moral void of a film.

What even makes someone popular? Nothing but confidence.
Popularity is just one giant con. Anyone could be Queen Bee (or
King Bee?); it just depends on your first impression and how
much you fling your balls and tits about when adolescence hits.
Once you're established at the top of the food chain, you can say
or do whatever the fuck you like. We all get typecast when we're
still essentially children and we somehow have to carry on in

that vein. Have we learnt nothing from every coming of age/90s romcom ever made?! Never underestimate the underdog. That geeky girl with thick-rimmed glasses and awkward shoes... she always gets the guy in the end. Oh God... I've just realised... like 'Man Shoes'! Man Shoes *She's All That*-ed me!

27TH APRIL 2003
LISTENING TO 'SLIDE' BY GOO GOO DOLLS

4pm: I'm not feeling very sociable right now. I'm on the biology field trip in a cottage in the Highlands and I feel so low. I've been really struggling to hold back the tears all weekend until a few minutes ago when I just cried in front of Charlie. I'm so pathetic. He was talking about Mish and Lovely Lyla being the perfect couple when out they popped: big, fat, ugly, weakling tears. PERFECT COUPLE?! Are they fuck! Charlie's really suspicious that something has gone on between Mish and me now, but I don't really care anymore. Mish is back to being a complete arse since we got back to school. He's so paranoid about someone finding out about us that he is extra cold with me. It's like we're not even friends anymore. Fucking bastard. I'm so angry at him right now.

6pm: I just told Holly about what happened with Mish. We went for a walk down into the gorge and I was having a cigarette when I thought: *Fuck him.* Why should I be tortured with his secret and he gets to do whatever the fuck he likes and then behave like a class A wankpuffin?! Holly then said that when Mish had a crush on her he kept telling her that the two of them 'really connected/clicked on another level', which is exactly what he keeps saying to me and that she was 'his best friend', which is also what he says to me! The fucking shit! When did I get so gullible?

Urrghh, I can't believe I cried – how embarrassing. I'm hoping not too many people noticed. I feel so angry and hurt and betrayed. I was clearly never anything special to him – just a way of getting his end away cos Lovely Lyla is holier than thou and probably won't even touch him. He just casts out his charming bit of chat and hopes someone will bite. ARSEHOLE! I just can't believe I took the bait. God, I feel so stupid. ARRGHHHHH, I'm fuming. He's just in the next room and the two of us said we'd cook dinner for everyone in the cottage tonight, but I would rather die than spend another second with him right now. FUUUUUUCCCKKKKK.

9pm: Soooo, dinner was awkward. We cooked spag bol and the whole time he was like, 'What? Are you angry at me? What's wrong?' I couldn't really put it all into words so I was mostly grumpy and monosyllabic. I couldn't exactly just start screaming at him…

'I LOVE YOU! I'VE LOVED YOU FOREVER. I FEEL INSANELY JEALOUS THAT YOU HAVE A GIRLFRIEND AND FEEL THAT WE'D BE BETTER TOGETHER SO I THINK YOU SHOULD DUMP HER! I ALSO FEEL USED AND MANIPULATED NOW THAT I REALISE YOU'VE GIVEN THE SAME 'YOU'RE MY BEST FRIEND/WE CLICK ON ANOTHER LEVEL' CHAT TO OTHER PEOPLE! I THOUGHT WE HAD SOMETHING SPECIAL. PLEASE LOVE ME!'

Nope.

So I opted for a 'I'm fine. Stop asking, you weirdo.'

1am: After we went to bed he came and got me and asked if I wanted to go for a midnight stroll. We went for a walk in the woods and had a long chat. He tried to reassure me and said I was his best friend and that it can't be compared to Holly. He said he clearly can't give me what I want though and that maybe we should be spending a bit less time together.

There's the gut punch. Oomph.

Jesus, I've just realised I'm William. This is me and William but in reverse. Fuck. Have a big tasty bucket of karma, Claire. Choke on it.

TWENTY-NINE

THE WITCHES OF ST FELIX'S

28TH APRIL 2003
LISTENING TO 'DIAMONDS ON THE INSIDE'
BY BEN HARPER

This has been one of the most disastrous days of my existence.

How would I have coped without lashings of hyperbole?

I was so fucked off when we got back from the field trip that I told Maggie everything that happened with Mish. I'd told Holly, and Charlie basically knew so the cat had very much clawed its way out of the metaphorical bag already anyway. Maggie has since been in a grump with me because:

A. 'I can't believe you did that, Claire!'
B. cunty bitchface Gretchen is in a huff with *her* now for not sharing *my* secret.

When I saw Gretchen this morning, I told her it wasn't any of her business and surely she can't blame Maggie for not telling her, but she gave me the usual, 'I've got loads on my plate – I don't need this. I couldn't give a shit about your B-side "problems".'

Classic Gretchen. She then spent the whole day turning on the waterworks at will for everyone, and somehow this was all my fault! I had a few:

'What have you said/done to Gretchen, Claire?!'

Maggie managed to make sure everyone knew there was an almighty secret she was keeping, but kept it all the same time 'cos she's such a good friend'. Come on! So the girls kept coming up to me all day asking what had happened and 'you can tell me, I won't tell anyone, I promise'. Fuckety fuck fuck fuck. I spent most of the day praying it would just burn out, but before I knew it, everyone knew. Andy 'Lads Lads Lads' Burns just came up to me and shook his head disappointingly.

'Jesus, Claire… Mish?!'

It was only going to be a matter of time before Mish found out I'd squealed like a little piggie. Oh God… I'm going to be banished. I bet Maggie told Gretchen and she jumped with glee before distributing leaflets:

`Claire's a whoring slutbag!`

I'm going to have to tell Mish before someone else tells him, or worse, someone tells Lovely Lyla.

Maggie and Holly just keep saying that Mish was using me and treated me like shit and he wasn't even a good friend to me. They said that what happened over Easter wasn't special and could easily have happened with anyone (they clearly mean Holly). They're telling me that Mish has 'brainwashed' me and how could I not see that?

I realised after dinner that I had to tell Mish that the whole bloody school knew. I called him and said we needed to talk and he wasn't going to like it. I told him everything and by the end I was sobbing. I felt so guilty and overwhelmed. I was mostly scared that I was about to lose him and that I had just spoken to him for the last time. Surprisingly though, he said it was bound to happen and it wasn't my fault and we were still friends. I was so relieved, but also knew deep down that everything was going to be different from now. He told me he was going to have to speak to Lovely Lyla, but needed some time. I feel so bad, but actually don't regret what we did. Does this make me a bad person? I reckon bad people don't realise they're being bad. I just regret having ever told a soul. I'm going to miss him so much. I'm completely in love with him and now I won't even be able to have him as a best friend cos of my big fucking mouth. FUCK. Lovely Lyla is going to be heartbroken when he tells her and it'll all be my fault. I properly hate myself.

I spoke to Maggie afterwards and it seems she's slipped straight back into Gretchen's pocket.

'I feel so sorry for Lyla. She's so lovely, she doesn't deserve to be treated like this. How could you do this to her?! I feel like I have a duty to tell her.'

(Err, no you fucking don't!)

'Mish will tell her when he's ready. Remember all those times Gretchen cheated on Jamie and you never felt a "duty" to tell him.'

'That's not even a bit the same, Claire! God! It's totally different! You just don't get it, do you?! I'm not sure I can be friends with you until you grow up, sort your life out and stop blaming everyone else for your mistakes!'

'WHAT?!'

'Oh, just fuck off, will you!' she screamed before slamming the phone down on me. Alright, defensive? What the hell was that about? It's almost like Gretchen had passed her a crib sheet to read from.

About half an hour later Holly called. Oh great! They're ganging up on me now, are they? Marvellous. Holly told me that Maggie, Gretchen and her have decided that I'm 'a shit friend'. I supposedly treat them like 'doormats' and that I'm a 'fucking disillusioned loser' for saying 'we' when referring to Mish and I. She laughed so hard and with so much venom when I said that Mish was my best friend.

'You and Mish are in your own little bubble and it's only a matter of time before that pops now. We've been good friends to you, Claire, and it seems you've now chosen to isolate yourself by choosing Mish over your *real friends*.'

'Oh! Real friends like Gretchen, you mean?! Pah!'

She then just spoke in this evil snarl. It was deep and dark and demon-y. It made the hairs on the back of my neck stand up.

'We won't be there to pick up the pieces when he shits all over you. You've changed and become the biggest bitch alive. William and Jane [Psycho Jane] warned us about you, but it wasn't until now that we can see the real you. I can't wait to watch your life blow up in your face and when it finally happens we probably won't even care enough to laugh cos you're such a meaningless, pathetic mess. You're totally irrelevant. I can't wait to watch you drown in your own shit.'

How lovely. Which is it, Holly? You care about seeing me suffer or you don't care about me? I didn't get a word in edgeways through the barrage of abuse before she eventually hung up on me. Wow. I felt a bit shaky, but miraculously didn't cry. I can't quite believe how mean Maggie and Holly have been. I'm not even quite sure I know what I've done to deserve this from them. Holly just yelled at me, but why exactly are they all mad at me? I mean, Gretchen doesn't count. She's been lying in wait for something like this to happen. It's a miracle that she's kept a lid on the crazy for so long. I just can't believe I've been so stupid as to give her all this Mish-related ammo. But the other two... what exactly have I done to them?! I know what I've done isn't great, but I'm hardly proud about it. I shouldn't keep being surprised by the immense capacity that girls have for cruelty. I'm dreading school tomorrow. The three of them are going to work super hard on making me miserable. Urgh, they're probably all plotting together right now.

11TH MAY 2003
LISTENING TO 'SUPERMAN' BY GOLDFINGER

I've got so much on my plate at the moment and I feel so overwhelmed that I keep bursting into tears. I've properly lost all the girls as friends. I tried to make up with Maggie (even though I wasn't really sure what I was apologising for) by just saying 'I'm sorry' loads, but she just threw it all back in my face. She told me to go fuck myself and it was too late to make up for having been such a bad friend. For doing what exactly? Arrrggghh! I don't really care about the other two, but I'm hurt that Maggie was so quick to let herself be led. Gretchen has been up to her old tricks again, spreading nasty little rumours through the school about me. It's mostly about me sleeping with people who I don't even know or saying horrible things behind people's backs. It's all bollocks and I'm not even aware of most of it. By the time I do find out, they're so in keeping with the other lies about me (and some truth!), that no one believes me when I say they're not true. I mean, Gretchen would never lie, she's such an honest person. God – she's a fucking psychopath. It's not just Gretchen's shit storm though, I do think some people are actually disgusted with me because of the Mish thing and I guess that's (half) on me. Jamie scowled at me when I said hi this morning and when I looked hurt he turned to me with a look of pure revulsion.

'Don't play the victim. I can't believe you said that about me. I thought we were friends...'

'What have I said?'

'You know.'

'For fuck's sake. I don't know. I haven't said anything.'

'Liar.'

I give up. I can't win. If I get the choice of where I go to study, I think above all else I will make sure I am the farthest away possible from Gretchen. No doubt whatever I study or wherever I go, I'll arrive at my halls of residence to discover I'm sharing a room with her.

Everyone is obviously still friends with Mish though. He's the one who fucking cheated, but you'd think I'd forced him to sixty-nine me! Have people just chosen to ignore that he is also in the wrong? Or am I just such an easy target? There's not even a sideways glance for Edinburgh's golden boy, but what is to become of me? The clichéd mistress who fell in love with her best friend? I've been outcast while Wanker Mish sits back smugly, basking in the knowledge that he had a bit of fun and got away with it. He is socially untouchable with a backboneless girlfriend who's blindly forgiven him for licking out his best friend. Next she'll be packing him away for a boys' weekend away with egg and cress sandwiches, a flask of sugary tea, a multi-pack of ribbed condoms and some strawberry-flavoured lube. Have fun, dear!

Fortunately some people have been paying no attention to everything going on. Herbert, for one, seems completely oblivious and is proving to be a rock solid friend. Phew. I don't know if he's in his own little world of maths and music or if he can see through the rumours and doesn't want to get involved. Either way, I'm grateful. It's such a relief to hang out with him and just talk about normal (non gossipy) things. Well. Normal for Herbert.

I'm also spending a lot of time with Next Door Andy. School is so stressful – I'm on high alert all the time. It is not an entirely bonkers possibility that someone will literally stab me in the back one day. Actual knife and everything. Well, probably not literally but… och, who knows? Gretchen is fucking crazy after all. So I finally get to the end of the school day, take a deep breath, walk home chain-smoking Marlboro Lights and go to Next Door Andy's. We just sit up on his roof, have a beer and smoke cigarettes. It's so peaceful and it's somewhere I can let my guard down. I know what my dad means now when he talks about 'the comfortable silence of friends'. We have that and I'm so thankful for it.

Exams are constantly hanging over my head and I've never been so terrified about anything in my life. I'm trying really hard to focus, but I'm worried that I'm getting too distracted by everything else going on.

I'm so disappointed in Maggie. I can't believe she's willing to give up our friendship over… I'm not even sure what!

Text to Maggie: Maggie, please. Can you at least just tell me what you think I've done?!

I got the ever helpful reply.

Text from Maggie: You know…

She's still friends with that fucking adulterer of course. What have I done to deserve this?

13TH MAY 2003
LISTENING TO 'WANNA BE' BY NINE DAYS

There's too much going on at the moment. I'm drowning. The Witches of Eastwick are continuing to pour all their energy into turning the school against me. They're trying to pick my friends off one by one. Real nice girls. I hate them so much. Sometimes I find myself white-knuckled and grinding my teeth at the mere thought of them. Thank God there are quite a few people taking no notice of them now. I wish this was a film cos I'd at least know it would end well. I'd *Carrie* their asses. Although that didn't end brilliantly and it's obviously way too fucked up... and impossible given my distinct lack of superpowers and murderous impulses. Ok, terrible analogy. I'd *Karate Kid* their asses!

Got an email from Sexy Laurent today telling me he was going out with Marie again. What? I just don't understand anyone anymore. Everyone's gone mad.

THIRTY

HERBERT

Well, my life has turned around. Maggie and Holly decided 'they couldn't be bothered' falling out with me anymore. They treat me like they can just pick me up and put me down, but I haven't got any energy anymore so just said, 'Yeah, friends.' So that's two out of three sorted and I'm hoping it will take the sting out of Gretchen's tail to lose her lackeys. It also means I have been 'reinvited' to Maggie's eighteenth and we're going to see *The Magic Flute*, which I was really looking forward to, so that's good. Maggie dumped Charlie again too. Hopefully that's that now.

I had a dream last night that Herbert asked me out. I was so disappointed when I woke up this morning and realised it hadn't happened. It's weird. I didn't realise, but I think I fancy him… but not in a sex way. In fact the thought of having sex with him is super weird. I can't even really imagine it. Does that mean I don't fancy him? Or do I just fancy his mind? Is that a thing?

Mish and I are back to being friends, but in a boring, normal way. Lovely Lyla has been predictably lovely and forgiven us. She should hate me and tell him he's not allowed to be friends with me. I'd totally understand. No wonder he loves her and not me. I'm the shit version of her. Actually, no. I'm not a *version* of her at all.

20TH MAY 2003
LISTENING TO 'IGNITION REMIX' BY R. KELLY

I had the most hilarious night last night. I was invited to a dinner at Herbert's house with Mish and the rest of the A-level French class. It was a completely ridiculous evening, but the goofiness felt like some much needed light relief from the last month. We played football in the garden, and Herbert and Mish played with their trousers round their ankles because 'we're just too shit hot at this otherwise'.

Herbert was cooking dinner when he got bored and before I knew it, the boys were all wandering around with their boxers stuffed with various household items in order to play some elaborate (slightly dodgy) guessing game. Herbert had a pepper grinder and a whole loaf of bread tucked down his Calvins.

Posh boy bants. How many middle-class clichés can I mention in one night? Pretty sure we played Ibble Dibble too.

313

THE DIARY OF A TEENAGE DIRTBAG

We'd just finished dessert (Herbert had rather impressively made raspberry soufflés!) when Mish suddenly threw a full, open bottle of red wine at Herbert, confidently explaining that 'the centrifugal forces will keep the wine in the bottle'. Not only was this unlikely to work in the first place, but he threw it bottom end forward. Red wine went everywhere and the bottle smashed on the flagstone flooring. It literally took hours for us to get the bits of glass out the floor. Part of me loves their immaturity and carefree stupidity, but it's such a pain sometimes too. They always break stuff. ALWAYS. I've lost count of the number of dinner parties where I find myself trying to superglue something back together at the end of the night. I'm seriously considering making superglue part of my leave-the-house checklist... phone, fags, finance, keys... superglue. Check.

The night continued in the same vein with Mish and Herbert racing to see who could eat their entire raw garlic bulb and onion the quickest. The loser had to streak down the road. It was well into the early hours of the morning and we were all pretty drunk when we played sardines. Herbert and I were hiding in the shower when it was turned on by some joker. There was a moment after the screaming when he held his hand out, helped me out the shower and wrapped a towel around me that I thought about kissing him. I chickened out though, which is weird. It should have been so easy; we were drunk and wet and he already had his arms around me. Am I just making this something it's not?

I can't even remember most of the silliness, but happily sat back and laughed all night. I'm annoyingly not able to shift my Herbert crush. It has helped me get over Mish though. Mish being a wanker with a gaping black hole where his morals, humility and virtues should be has also helped.

Not bitter at all. Totally fine. Don't care about it at all anymore. Cool cool cool.

25TH MAY 2003
LISTENING TO 'GIRLS & BOYS'
BY GOOD CHARLOTTE

We all went for Mamma's pizza on Saturday night then back to mine to watch a video. I was squidged against Herbert on the couch and I swear our hands were touching. AHHHH. I would have done anything for him to just turn and kiss me.

I am stressing so much about exams now. I feel sick every time I think about it. I'm utterly terrified. I'm not quite sure why Herbert is on my mind allllllll the time, he's nothing like the kind of guy I go for, but maybe that's a good thing...

Maggie came round this evening and we just smoked and drank gallons of homemade chocolate milkshakes... I feel so sick now.

28TH MAY 2003
LISTENING TO '99 RED BALLOONS'
BY GOLDFINGER

Next Door Andy has recently turned into a bit of a tosser. He's got a new friend who sounds like such a druggie-rentboy-bellend and thanks to this new 'really cool' friend, Next Door Andy is going through a drugs phase and it's so fucking boring. I went round today and he was all like, 'I'm Andy and I'm so cool and hard. I take loads of drugs. I was so fucked last night. I took this and that and drank this much and did this stupid thing...' I DON'T GIVE A SHIT! It's literally the worst chat from him. THEN he started telling me about this amazing girl who is sexy and funny and beautiful and intelligent and takes loads of drugs and blah blah blah.

'She's called Jane and goes to your old school. Actually, I think you guys used to be friends.'

Yup. Fucking Psycho Jane. Next Door Andy has been hanging out taking drugs with my ex best friend (and world-class nutjob) and has a fucking crush on her. Major eye roll. Of course he does.

I was telling him about going to see *The Magic Flute* for Maggie's eighteenth tomorrow and how I was really excited about it.

'Opera? Fucking hell, Claire, what kind of geeks do you hang out with? Doesn't sound like any kind of eighteenth to me! You're supposed to get shitfaced at your eighteenth, not piss about at the opera.'

Well, fuck him. I'm really looking forward to pissing about at the opera. Go and snort some shit with Jane, you impressionable bawbag.

31ST MAY 2003
LISTENING TO 'GIRLFRIEND'
BY DANIEL BEDINGFIELD

Maggie's Eighteenth
Last night was weird. My dad picked Herbert up on the way and my God he looked bloody good in a suit. We all had drinks at Maggie's then went to *The Magic Flute*. It was amazing. When I'm old(er) and rich (actually earn more than my part-time babysitting income) I'm going to buy all the albums I want, drink champagne at least once a week, be dressed in the coolest clothes and go to the opera all the time.

Not quite, but it's a lovely vision.

We went out for dinner afterwards, but the chat wasn't really flowing. There was too big a mix of people, with some utterly smashed and some not even drinking. Herbert and Andy 'Lads

Lads Lads' Burns were sat next to each other and I swear they were talking in different languages. Poor Herbert looked stressed and confused. 'Lads' had just finished explaining 'teabagging' and he was moving on to how to do a 'dirty sanchez' when I jumped in to try and rescue Herbert. Unfortunately I found it difficult to follow on from 'Lads'' dinner chat and Herbert and I had absolutely nothing to say to each other. We just sat there uncomfortably flitting between silence and small talk. Why do I even like him? We have nothing in common. Am I just in awe of his talent?

We went out to The Brauhaus afterwards and bloody William Macleod was there. We said 'hi' to each other and then kept our distance. I still feel like I have a rock in the pit of my stomach every time I see him. I wonder if that'll ever leave me? Why does he not seem to have this? He's clearly completely over me and I am nothing to him anymore. Herbert walked me to get a taxi and I really wanted to tell him how I felt, but I didn't have the guts and seeing William somewhat threw me. I was trying to summon the courage when the taxi arrived. Weird night.

1ST JUNE 2003
LISTENING TO 'I DON'T LIKE MONDAYS' BY THE BOOMTOWN RATS

I went to Next Door Andy's tonight and met his new skinhead-druggie-rentboy friend. He looks like a fucking convict. The only thing missing was a swastika face tat. Other than that he was nailing the track-marked, track-suited, grey-skinned and grey-toothed look perfectly. Where on earth did Next Door Andy find this guy? Big Sam and I do not approve. He is such a bad influence on Next Door Andy and he's clearly going to get him into some serious trouble. Then he said that Psycho

Jane might pop round too. I went home pretty sharpish after that. I have no interest in seeing her. I can only imagine what the drugs have done. No thanks. Jane was a fucking lunatic before months of pharmaceutical abuse. I do not need more Gretchen in my life right now and I was sick of all the drugs banter anyway.

5TH JUNE 2003
LISTENING TO 'I LOVE YOU ALWAYS FOREVER' BY DONNA LEWIS

Fuck it. The not knowing is killing me.

~~Nothing worth having is worth fighting for.~~ No, that's not right. ~~Everything worth having?~~

Anything worth having is worth fighting for. There it is.

```
Text to Herbert: I'm just going to text
it cos Ill neva have the guts 2 say this
2 ur face. Do u think anything could ever
happen between us?
```

Still no reply from Herbert and it's been about eight hours and definitely delivered. Shit. I've clearly been KB'd.

8TH JUNE 2003
LISTENING TO 'THE ANTHEM' BY GOOD CHARLOTTE

I'm so embarrassed by my Herbert text. I can't believe he hasn't replied. I think I can now categorically say that nothing will happen.

11TH JUNE 2003
LISTENING TO 'SEND ME ON MY WAY' BY RUSTED ROOT

I'm such a wreck at the moment. I'm not sleeping enough and stressing out about six exams next week. My revision is intense and I don't feel like there are enough hours in the day. I'm sooo tired, which is just making me stress, which is stopping me from sleeping and so the vicious cycle continues...

I wish Herbert had just said he wasn't interested so I can snap out of this inexplicable infatuation. I'm sure I just started liking Herbert to get over Mish, but now I've actually convinced myself I really like him. In fact, I don't think I even liked him until I had that dream about him asking me out... Is that what this is? A fake dream crush? Did I just fall for him because dream-Herbert (who no doubt looked like Ben Affleck) swept me off my feet in the most un-Herbert way possible?! ARGH, stop thinking about boys and REVISE REVISE REVISE. Please please please can I get what I need for medicine next year. PLLLEEEAAAAASSE.

17TH JUNE 2003
LISTENING TO 'GET BUSY' BY SEAN PAUL

Well well well, who'd have thought it. William and Claire – friends again. After years of pain, hurt, betrayal, lies, love and hatred we have decided to put it all behind us. Too good to be true? Probably. There really is a very thin line between love and hate. I'm not saying I love him, but I certainly miss him when he's not in my life. Maybe we are meant to be? I went to his this afternoon, we watched a film, made some lunch and had a good ole catch up. It was like no time had passed and nothing's changed. He's definitely made me see all the colours of the emotional spectrum and there's something psychologically unhealthy that happens to me when I'm with him, but I can't help myself. My actions around William are probably the only thing I have absolutely no control over. Whenever I'm near him, I can feel how much he loves (loved) me and it's soooo addictive. I know it's fucked up but I crave his attention more than anything.

18TH JUNE 2003
LISTENING TO 'BRING ME TO LIFE' BY EVANESCENCE

I have NEVER worked so hard in my life. Working till midnight and up again at 6am and working. Breaking only for exams and dinner. I feel like I'm going to go mad, but it's the final push!

19TH JUNE 2003
LISTENING TO 'HALLELUJAH' BY JEFF BUCKLEY

I felt unbelievable sorry for Next Door Andy today (an emotion I never thought I would have towards him!) after discovering that he's just spent three days and nights in a police cell. He must have been absolutely terrified and he looked bloody awful when I saw him earlier. He was a really funny greeny-grey colour with huge bags under his eyes. He was hunched over and skittish. His normal arrogance and general punch-in-the-face bravado were nowhere to be seen. Oh, how the cocky have crashed... I've never seen him look so vulnerable and... small... like a beaten puppy. This was of course thanks to his new arsehole-druggie-rentboy friend. Surprise surprise. I bet he looked right at home with his fellow inmates. God, what a twat.

So anyway, it turns out they'd been out getting high when his friend climbed up a wall and jumped down into a courtyard. Next Door Andy (being the idiot sheep that he is) followed. They then tried a back door, which was unlocked, so his friend went in and Andy, to his credit, was apparently protesting at this point, but not enough to not actually go in as well. Unfortunately they'd found themselves in the Crown Court chambers and there is then CCTV footage of his druggie friend trying on wigs etc. Luckily for Next Door Andy, he did nothing (on camera), but by the time they exited the building, it was surrounded by police. Anyway he was in court this lunchtime and proved 'not guilty'. Phew. Home safe and sound now.

He learnt his lesson after this. We never heard of his druggie friend again and Next Door Andy behaved himself... ish... more? He got all his rebellions out the way before he was twenty. After that, even keeping him out post-10pm was hard work. He took over his father's company, goes to bed early, wakes at dawn to wild swim (before everyone started wild swimming) and spends his weekends walking up Monroes with his dog. I still can't quite believe how wholesome he is now. We joke that from 2001 to 2004, Next Door Andy never greeted me with anything other than 'I'm so hungover, Claire.' It wasn't a joke though. EVERY TIME. I have images etched in my brain of Next Door Andy in terrible states. He'd regularly be found rolling on his bedroom floor clutching his face after snorting bottle caps of whisky before heading out. When I last saw him, he was sober, living in an enormous house in Fife, growing his own vegetables and training for yet another Iron Man. NO ONE can party forever.

20TH JUNE 2003
LISTENING TO 'THIS PICTURE' BY PLACEBO

Mish is pissing the hell out of me (agaaaiiiiinnn). He's so rude to me and so desperate to prove me wrong all the time! It's like he wants to make me feel (or rather seem) stupid. I'm not stupid. In fact I reckon I just pip him on the intelligence scale and he doesn't like it. He thinks he's the alpha, but then has to ring me every night to ask for help with his chemistry.

We were all (Mish, Maggie, Charlie, Herbert, CuntFaceGretchen etc) sat in the prefects' room today talking about the leavers' match. The school had put on breakfast for us during the exam period so most people were in.

The leavers' match is based on an eighteenth-century Scottish ball game. It is played with wooden bats (which are like giant wooden spoons) and involves the whole year group in fancy dress, hitting a tennis ball around the forecourt. When the game finishes, everyone has their bat signed in place of a traditional yearbook. Here's some of what was written on mine:

```
Mish: Hello Cheeky. Let the good times
roll. Captain Spunky xxx
```

```
Herbert: Vegetables are good for you.
Herbert
```

```
Maggie: I'm not worried about missing you
because I'm going to see you every weekend.
It has been good and life would certainly
not have been the same without you. Love
you so much. Big snogs, Maggers xxx
```

Charlie: Dearest Claire Bear. You've been such a good mate to me. I can't thank you enough for everything although there's been a distinct lack of nooky. Gutted. Love u.

Dan Jeffries: Good Luck Claire! Blow them away! Lol.

Gretchen: Good Luck with everything. I hope everything goes exactly as you want it to. Take Care. Don't be a stranger. Love Gretch xxx

Was it all in my head?

Andy 'Lads Lads Lads' Burns: Claire, ure like the sister I never had. Thanks for providing the entertainment. Burnsie x

Holly: Hi Claire: it's been a bit of a rollercoaster but it all turned out… well! I'll miss our chemistry chat. Love Holly xxx

Jamie: Hey Claire. Thanks for my 'surprise'. Mine's still in the mail… love Party Boy

Grumpy Arseface Toby: Toby

So when chatting about the leavers' match, Mish said everyone was thinking of dressing up as cartoon characters.

'Oh really?' I said. 'That's a shame. I'd already made a costume… although I'm sure I can probably adapt it…'

Mish then turned to me in front of everyone and snorted, 'Oh no, sorry, Claire, I meant the prefects, not you. No offence.'

Errrrm, MASSIVE offence taken. Then he looked around the room in this really annoying exaggerated way.

'Actually you probably shouldn't even be in the *PREFECTS' room* because... well... you know.'

He put his hands up to the sky, shrugged his shoulders and said, 'Sorry. Not my rules, but those *are* the rules...' My jaw literally dropped and I felt my eyes start to sting. It was so humiliating. Everyone was looking at me in a half shocked/half pity way. Except of course for Gretchen who couldn't hide her wretched smile. I came so close to saying, 'Oh, *now* it matters that I'm in here? You didn't ask me to leave on the multiple occasions we made out on that sofa. Or do the rules not apply if you have your hand down my top and you're dry-humping your pre-cummed boner all over me?'

ARSEHOLE! Who the hell does he think he is? I left in silence and burst into tears the second I'd passed the school gates. I'm sat at home trying to revise now, but my eyes keep filling with tears.

23RD JUNE 2003
LISTENING TO 'YOU DON'T CARE ABOUT US' BY PLACEBO

Well, ladies and gentlemen, I am well and truly fucked for tomorrow's exam, but I don't care anymore. I'm spent. Last one! Hallelujah!

THIRTY-ONE

POST-EXAM
EUPHORIA #2

27TH JUNE 2003
LISTENING TO 'LATIN GIRLS'
BY BLACK EYED PEAS

5am: Oh my God. Everyone's gone mad. Everything is weird
and crazy and God knows what the fuck is going on anymore…
post-exams recap:

Tuesday 24th: I finished my last exam late morning and
spent the whole afternoon in the pub. I got super drunk then
we went out to Bar Oz, Standing Order, Jekyll & Hyde then
Garibaldi's till closing. It was messy.

Wednesday 25th: I failed my driving test in the morning.

*Well, that's not totally surprising. Booking my driving test
the morning after I finished my A-levels was certainly
a significant scheduling error on my part. I failed with*

countless minors, four majors and a dangerous. Most
people haven't even heard of 'a dangerous'. I basically
crashed the car and the test ended rather abruptly after
that. Not a proud moment.

Maggie and I then spent the whole day drinking in the sunshine
(drowning my driving licence sorrows). It was amazing. We
both got stupidly sunburnt, but we didn't care. We were young
and drunk and free. Then I met up with William and we went
for a sunset walk up Arthur's Seat for old times' sake. On
reflection it was a bizarrely romantic and nostalgic activity to
choose considering how much time we've both spent trying not
to love each other. We sat and watched the sun set in silence and
I wanted to cry when I thought about 'us'. I reckon I'll always
feel something for him, although I'm pretty sure I'm over the
worst of it now. The problem is when we're together we seem
to quickly fall back into our old ways. It's like we're either going
to have a punch up or start ripping each other's clothes off. He
told me he'd always love me and felt that we'd probably end up
together one day because like it or not we were soulmates. Maybe
one day. We were then being really flirty and this DANGER
DANGER DANGER alarm was going off in my head so I put a
stop to it before anything happened and we said our goodbyes.
Part of me wonders how amazing it would have been to have sex
with William, up Arthur's Seat, at sunset during midsummer.
Oh well. I'll never know.

I then made my way to The Watershed to meet Mish and
Jamie and then back in Gari's till closing. I have no idea what
happened in Gari's as it has blurred into every other Garibaldi's
night out.

Thursday 26th: Mish and I have kinda made up and I spent
the day with him feeling hungover in the sunshine. We had a
picnic and it felt like old times again… before 'the affair', before

he threw me under the bus, before his favourite pastime became publicly humiliating me… I tried to forget about all that and focus on the present. It was such a lovely afternoon. We had a few beers and we were simply content with being in each other's company. He did utter a quiet 'I'm sorry' at one point. So he fucking should be. I went straight from our picnic to the A-level French dinner and I felt like I was just continuing to top up on the last few days of boozing. We went to Rev and it was MENTAL. It felt like everyone I've ever met was there.

- Tom Southall had a little dance with me. His smile still punches me in the face. It's so goddamn beautiful, but he looked a bit ill and off his face. God knows what he's up to these days, but it feels a bit *Trainspotting-y.*
- Aussie Jason was there with his stupid Aussie mates. They were behaving like total dicks as per usual, flashing their arses to everyone and shouting total nonsense. I suspect they got chucked out before I got a chance to say hi.
- William and Angus were there too and we all had a final goodbye shot together. William and I had a slightly too long (and too tight) hug goodbye. I pressed every bit of me into him. Oh, William.
- Maggie pulled Charlie again.
- Mish told me he still had feelings for me and I think I tried to kiss him, but I'm not sure anymore. Did I kiss him? Yeesh! How do I not remember?!

It was like a weird dream and then I walked home. It's all a massive blur. I seriously need to get some sleep now.

I actually do remember this strange night very clearly, but it took sixteen years for me to read my diary and realise that it was real. I had always believed it to be some bizarre hyper-

realistic dream. It felt a bit like the goodbye scene in the film Big Fish where all the fictional characters and impossible figures from the storyteller's past turn up to say goodbye.

LISTENING TO 'PURE MORNING' BY PLACEBO

6pm: I need to calm down a bit. What feels like endless days of drinking, sunshine and not sleeping are starting to take a toll on me. Charlie and Maggie came round today and I have just felt weird and tired and hungover. They brought round some beers, but I had one and I couldn't even finish it. I'm tapping out. It's like I'm on some massive trip and watching myself in the third person. No more booze today and I need to eat properly. Have I eaten anything today? Did I eat anything yesterday? Jeeez. Get it together, Claire, and go to bed.

28TH JUNE 2003
LISTENING TO 'ENGLISH SUMMER RAIN' BY PLACEBO

Leavers' BBQ
It was so much fun. We played drinking games all evening and at the end of the night, I went and lay down on the grass with Herbert and had a cigarette (*I* had a cigarette). I was doing all the talking and he was completely silent. Classic Herbert. We were just lying back, looking up at the sky and I told him I really valued our friendship, but couldn't bring myself to say anything else. I know I sent him that text and he never replied, but it really does feel like he quite likes me. He's just different from the others and I really wanted something to happen and I thought about just kissing him, but I just lay there completely silent and

motionless. It really felt like we were just waiting for the air to ignite between us, when he put his hand down right next to mine, his finger flickered against mine and he sighed and said, 'You're a good friend, Claire.' God, he's so frickin' awkward.

When we went back inside, Herbert went home and I went to the pub with Mish, Jamie, Andy 'Lads Lads Lads' Burns, Grumpy Arseface Toby and the rugby boys. Everyone was so ridiculously drunk. I definitely couldn't be an alcoholic. It's so exhausting and I would almost definitely end up depressed. I'm only five days in and can't hack it anymore. I feel so low and bloated and shit and tired. I have this weird paranoid anxiety that I know is all in my head and booze blues related.

29TH JUNE 2003
LISTENING TO 'DON'T KNOW WHY'
BY NORAH JONES

Charlie's BBQ
I just spent the day eating and said a big fat NO to booze today though. Maggie spent the whole day telling me that she fancies Charlie again. She said she was nervous about how he'd react and then eventually asked me if I could have a word to say that she wants him back. So I took him aside and told him she wanted to try again and after weeks of heartache, he just lit up. He was resuscitated, his skin changed colour, his eyes twinkled and he smiled in a giddy child-like way. I've never seen anyone so happy. He hugged me so hard, kissed me on the cheek and did a little joyful jig. Lovely Charlie. I thought there was going to be a happy reunion between them, but no. She changed her mind about two minutes after I told him. Fucking biatch.

Mish was there without Lovely Lyla, but he still semi ignored me with Jamie, 'Lads' and Grumpy Arseface Toby about.

I went home and Charlie came round for a walk after everyone had left his. He just cried the whole time – totally heartbroken. I felt so awful for him. He told me there was nothing worse than loving someone who didn't love you back. Ouff, I agree, mate, I agree. There was nothing I could do to make it better. He loves her and she has crushed him (again!). Poor bugger.

30TH JUNE 2003
LISTENING TO 'HANDS UP' BY BLACK EYED PEAS

Leavers' Ball
Tonight was decidedly average. I had people round to mine for drinks before the ball and Herbert looked absolutely unbelievable, but 'I'm a good friend'. Whatever. We walked to St Felix's and the first person I saw standing outside having a fag was William. He doesn't smoke! It looks ridiculous on him. Why was he even there anyway? Why is he everywhere?! I feel like I'll never be free. I'll be forever restrained by his emotional shackles. I try not to care, but I'll always care a bit. Fuck! I smiled at him as I walked past and he tipped his invisible cap to me, but we didn't speak for the rest of the night. I just realised when I got home that it was his birthday. He didn't really seem himself tonight (as far as I could tell from a distance). I hope he's ok.

Mish was being an arsehole all night. He was obviously there with Lovely Lyla so didn't want to talk to me. She may be lovely, but she looked absolutely ridiculous in a white meringue wedding dress, a huge diamante tiara and white satin mary-janes… like a blown-up flower girl. So I was having my internal bitchy monologue about how she looked when she came up to me and gave me the most sincere-feeling hug ever. She was obviously utterly lovely to me.

'Oh, Claire, you look amazing! Do you know where you're going next year? It'll be a shame if you're far away and we can't hang out anymore! I hope we can put what happened behind us as I always thought of you as a friend. Oh, your shoes are awesome! I could never pull off something like that...'

It sounds sarcastic having written it down, but it really wasn't when coming out of her mouth. She makes me instantly squirm with guilt. Is she faking or is she genuinely that lovely? Is anyone really *that nice*? Why am I not like that? I need to try and be more like Lovely Lyla, just maybe with a better dress sense.

I believe Lovely Lyla really was (is) that nice. I tried to find her on Facebook recently to see what she's up to, but it doesn't look like she's on any form of social media. I suspect she's working for a non-profit/relief/aid-type organisation saving children and chimps from famine or deforestation (likely both). Here I am, totally absorbed, typing up my fickle teenage romances while Lyla's lovely hands are probably building an orphanage whilst simultaneously bottle-feeding abandoned chimp babies.

Anyway, it was classic ball chat then home. Everyone went into town, but I wasn't up for yet another 'last orders' night in Gari's. I needed my bed.

4TH JULY 2003
LISTENING TO 'PAINTER SONG' BY NORAH JONES

Leavers' Lunch at School
What an emotional day. I've hardly loved St Felix's, but the nostalgia factor associated with leaving this whole section of my life behind is turned right up to eleven... *cos these go up to eleven**. Ha.

*Quote from 'This Is Spinal Tap'. If you weren't communicating in film quotes, you were nobody.

The drink was flowing and I freaked out that I might never have the guts to tell Herbert how I felt and I'd forever be damned to wallow in limbo and wonder, *What if…*

I wasn't. Herbert wasn't interested and even if he had been, we were horrifically matched… like cheese and fish. (If you think this is ok whatever you do don't go to Italy and grate some parmigiano on your spaghetti vongole. For out of nowhere will appear an incensed Italian to slap you across the face with a salami.) I can't even remember how it felt to fancy Herbert and I question how real this fascination with my friend really was. But I had convinced myself that I liked him and I was stubbornly going to persist until it came to some kind of definitive conclusion. I believed all those sickening motivational slogans like 'better to have loved and lost…' or 'you'll sleep when you're dead'. I'd constantly spout some rubbish about it being better to die young and free of secrets rather than to be left rotting away, regretful and unfulfilled in your beige, warden-controlled flat. As it happens, I did in fact turn into a fearless speaker. 'An open book' is the polite version; 'unfiltered' is getting a little warmer. This is a trait I have inherited from my father who has managed to insult everyone he has ever met with such ferocious audacity that it makes me smile with pride.

So at seventeen, I was already convinced that there was nothing worse than a lifetime filled with regret. I was naively under the impression that this would be avoided by telling my friend (who I'm fairly sure I didn't fancy) that I really fancied him.

After umming and ahhing all afternoon, I decided that I had to tell Herbert how I felt. I kept running through the scenarios in my head and things weren't ending well with one of two likely outcomes.

Outcome 1: He has been secretly in love with me this whole time and hiding it (very well). I'd declare my love and he'd sweep me up in his arms, we'd kiss aaaaannnd I'd leave Edinburgh a week later after having spent eighteen years living round the corner from him. Unlikely. But that would be utterly devastating.

Outcome 2: (The more likely outcome) He's managed to pretend (right up until I unveil my 'secret' feelings to him) that he hasn't noticed my enormous crush. He'd have no choice but to tell me he doesn't like me back. We'd both be embarrassed and our friendship would be ruined. Also a shit option.

So that's decided then. I'll tell him I fancy him.

Later that night, Maggie, Charlie and Herbert came back to mine. Maggie said she's been talking to Herbert and he said he wasn't a 'lunger', but he definitely wouldn't pull away if I did (lunge). My heart went mental! I decided that this was essentially an invitation and I should go for it! The night dragged on and every five minutes I kept saying to myself, 'Ok… now! Kiss him now, Claire!' But I couldn't do it. When did I get so spineless? It's not like I've ever had any problems kissing people before.

Quite.

5TH JULY 2003
LISTENING TO 'THE PERFECT YEAR' BY DINA CARROLL FROM *SUNSET BOULEVARD*

6pm: Tonight is my last chance! He's coming to watch a film. Herbert is mine. I'm going to lunge.

LISTENING TO 'PAIN IN MY HEART'
BY OTIS REDDING

11.45pm: Well, I blew it. We watched a film and he was sat so close to me all night, but I just sat there statue-still. I was too nervous to even breathe too deeply. What the hell is wrong with me? I think we may have brushed knees at some point. Hot stuff! Then before I knew it, he was going home… slowly putting his jacket on… giving me a long, lingering hug goodbye… (kiss him kiss him!!)… letting me go… out the door… walking down the path and I shut the door. I was instantly flooded with regret. I stood in the hallway for a minute before I opened the door and ran after him in my socks. He was about to drive off when I waved him down. I must have looked like such a raving lunatic. He wound down his car window and I said, 'Kiss, please', as I pecked him on the lips. If only I'd held it a bit longer, but the coward that I am pulled away and walked off. It's unclear if he 'pecked' me back. I texted him later and we've arranged to meet for breakfast. Right. Tomorrow. I'll do it tomorrow. It really will be my last chance.

6TH JULY 2003
LISTENING TO 'THE BOOGIE THAT BE'
BY BLACK EYED PEAS

Herbert and I went for breakfast this morning and then for a long walk into town. We just chatted. I was clearly not going to pounce in broad daylight after a breakfast of *huevos rancheros*. So that was that. We'll never know. We said goodbye, enjoy your summer, good luck with results and have fun at university. I was gutted. I'll never know if he would have kissed me back.

Text to Herbert: Thanks for breakfast. It's been great hanging out with you so much recently. Sorry I was a bit quiet today. I think I wanted something to happen between us but never had the guts to find out. I know it's stupid as we're both leaving. Hopefully we can keep in touch. x

And he never replied. I'd forgotten that that's how we'd left it. My weird crush dissipated soon after I left Edinburgh and by the time I visited him in Cambridge, a couple of months into our first term, I'd forgotten all about it. The thought that I ever fancied Herbert feels nothing short of wrong and incestuous now. We've remained friends and have enjoyed a periodical catch-up ever since. We used to meet up whenever I was in London and we would invariably get very carried away. We were fun, young and obnoxious, spending money we didn't have on extortionate drinks we didn't need. Well, money I didn't have. Herbert was (is) LOADED doing something wanky and banky. He bought a two-bed flat on the King's Road in his early twenties when I was still doing the weekly Saturday night 'food OR wine?' dance at the supermarket.

Herbert went from awkward, hopeless academic to successful, charming Lothario. He married an utterly beautiful and talented woman, had exceptional children and aged marvellously.

I was of course afflicted with a spectacular bout of 'revertigo' at Herbert's wedding.

(Revertigo: an emotional and physical regression that occurs when nostalgic sentiments are triggered by people

or places. A term coined by the hit American sitcom How I Met Your Mother.)

I arrived giddy with excitement as we had just left our six-month-old with my parents in a hotel in Chelsea. We were freeeeeeeeeee for the first time since she was born and my husband and I were desperate not to waste the opportunity for fun. So I arrived sober, thirty-one years old, a parent, a professional and if proof was needed that I had hit peak 'adult', my bag contained plasters, tissues, paracetamol and flats. Within seconds of being surrounded by my old school friends (who have never known me to be any of these things), the revertigo spell was cast and POOF, I was transformed back into my dickhead seventeen-year-old self. I proceeded to sink at least three bottles of champagne and behaved in a way that would have made my teenage self proud. It wasn't long before I was on the front deck of the wedding boat, sailing down the Thames and slurring to Herbert's sister, with a badly made rollie hanging out of my mouth, that I used to fancy Herbert 'big time'. Goddamn revertigo.

Herbert and I never talked about my schoolgirl crush. I'd actually almost forgotten about it until writing this book. I really hope he's forgotten too, but sadly his brain is much bigger than mine and he was drinking significantly less than me at the time. Soz for the awkwardness, Herbie. x

7TH JULY 2003
LISTENING TO 'COLD COLD HEART'
BY NORAH JONES

I'm feeling really sad about leaving my Edinburgh life behind. Especially my Maggie and Charlie. Good riddance, Gretchen, though, you fucking basketcase. Whenever I feel nostalgic about leaving I remind myself that I never have to see Gretchen again and it makes me want to sing in the streets and click my heels. Hooray!

I'm so terrified about my exam results though. I'm talking brown pants scared. My next level fear is that even if I do get in, what if I don't make any friends? I am banking on it being better than school, but what if it's not?! Oh God, what if there's a Gretchen at uni?

There wasn't. People like Gretchen don't exist in the adult world. They're either institutionalised or they've, rather boringly, just grown up.

Please please PLEASE make my results be ok. I know Mish has been a bit of a willy with me but please can he get into medicine. Please can Maggie and Charlie be happy (together or not). Please can my parents stay in love. Please can Chloe stay happy and carefree. Thanks for listening.

Am I praying? Who am I talking to? God?! What the deuce! I am a steadfast atheist. How did this happen? Amazingly, all my prayers were answered. So… thank you. I guess?

10TH JULY 2003
LISTENING TO 'THE SCIENCE OF SELLING YOURSELF SHORT' BY LESS THAN JAKE

And breathe. I'm finally in the South of France after a rough couple of days. We were travelling yesterday and I thought I was going to die. I was so shivery and feverish with horrendous stomach cramps, vomiting and diarrhoea. I spent the whole flight in the toilets and it was hell. Things have got better since I arrived, but I have such a sore throat now. Mum says I don't deserve any sympathy as it's probably because I've been partying too hard. I feel so ill and I'm in so much pain. I'm supposed to be seeing Sexy Laurent and Marie tomorrow. Great. I'll probably look like arse.

11TH JULY 2003
LISTENING TO 'LET'S GET RETARDED' BY BLACK EYED PEAS

I've just got back from a pretty shitty night. I went down to Nice with Sexy Laurent, Marie and some of their friends. Marie was all over Laurent – it's like she had to prove to me that he's hers now. Honestly. It was embarrassing to watch. She'd just start snogging him when he was mid-sentence. Although I guess it worked. Point made and I have to admit I was a little jealous watching the two of them. He used to kiss me like that. He's playing along with her 'point-proving' game and doing everything to show he doesn't fancy me anymore. Although that's not hard right now as I look like crap after a month of partying and this new mystery illness to boot. Sniff sniff. It's so unfair. I seem to have spent most of the last year fancying people who either don't fancy me back (Herbert, Dickhead Mike, Grumpy Arseface Toby) or people in a relationship with someone else (William, Skater Chris, Finn, Mish and now Sexy Laurent). What is wrong with me?

13TH JULY 2003
LISTENING TO 'MY IMMORTAL' BY EVANESCENCE

All is well in the world. Papie (*my grandfather*) just told me I reminded him a bit of a young Brigitte Bardot. Love him!

I was definitely trying to channel a 1960s Bardot at the time, but it was a pretty indulgent statement, even for him.

My lovely papie.

I adored my grandfather and because I shared his love of sailing, I grew up feeling like we were the only two allowed in the best club in the world. We had our own childish code of sneaky looks at the dinner table as I hid his greens. He was my buddy.

For nearly a decade I would get up before dawn and spend my summer days out on the boat with him. I almost definitely have a romantic memory of what was actually a lot of wet, miserable days at sea being shouted at by a man who viewed me as an incompetent skipper and not his seven-year-old granddaughter. In between the shouting though, we shared some beautiful moments eating jambon fromage sandwiches and boxes of chipsters.

Much to my regret, I swapped days sailing with my papie for boys and lie-ins when I turned into your garden variety soulless teenager. There are countless things I did as a teenager that I wish I had done differently (a whole book's worth, some might say), but the thing that breaks my heart the most is the day I told my papie I didn't want to go sailing with him anymore. He was one of my favourite people in the world and I'd cut off a limb to have just one more day on the boat with him.

My last memory of him was about a week before he died. It was a slow decline and the struggle to the dining table eventually became too much for him that he resided in his bed, his appetite elusive anyway. As a fabulous eater, this felt like the moment we had all been dreading.

It was over. No more suppressed sniggers across the table…

French palliative care still left a lot to be desired and my mamie was still under strict instructions to prohibit sugar because of his diabetes. It felt ludicrous, when he was dying, to deny him some real (non-diabetic ice cream). He had been deprived of this as long as I had known him, always left to sulk over a bowl of sugar-free sorbet. Well, not on his deathbed! I was getting him some real ice cream goddamnit. 'Mission Carte D'Or' became the most important thing in the world to me. I was one step away from commando rolling from the freezer to his bedroom. I snuck him daily bowls of the stuff and he dutifully ate every spoonful. I wonder, in retrospect, if his apparent enjoyment was forced for my benefit, but that wink, as I brought him ice cream in bed, was simply perfect.

14TH JULY 2003
LISTENING TO 'COME AWAY WITH ME' BY NORAH JONES

I'm *still* ill. I asked my mum if she thought I should see a doctor cos I was still ill and she said, '*Non. C'est ridicule!*' I then said I wondered if I could have glandular fever and she laughed and said, '*Probablement!*' Nice.

20TH JULY 2003
LISTENING TO 'THE BRIGHTEST BULB HAS BURNED OUT' BY LESS THAN JAKE

I went clubbing last night with Sexy Laurent, Marie and their friends. We went to Le Grand Escurial Club and I had two TGVs on arrival.

*Le TGV is of course well known as France's superior train
network, but it is also a disgusting 'cocktail' of tequila, gin,
vodka and blue curaçao. Bleurgh! CHOO CHOO, it's the
speedy train to chundertown!*

It was so hot in the club everyone was instantly sweating the
second we went in. I decided I was just going to let my hair
down, enjoy myself and ignore Sexy Laurent and Marie. I was
having the best time, shimmying frantically in my own world
of sweat, drink and music. I literally did not care what I looked
like. This is the way you're supposed to dance. It was bliss. Then
I noticed a hot guy dancing near me and I was snapped straight
back into the real world. He smiled at me and I smiled back…
Well, hello there. We were both absolutely dripping with sweat.
We danced together for the next few hours and then pulled at
the end of the night. Ahhhh, it was amazing. All the Mishs and
Herberts and Williams disappeared and I felt like myself again.

21ST JULY 2003
LISTENING TO 'SWEETNESS'
BY JIMMY EAT WORLD

I'm finally feeling a bit better. Was that all I needed? A random pull?

THIRTY-TWO
EWEN LE PERVERT

27TH JULY 2003
LISTENING TO 'SHOOT THE MOON'
BY NORAH JONES

Woooo! I'm finally on the train for Brittany! I am beyond excited, but it doesn't look like I'll see the old gang as much as normal.

- Gael is working so I probably won't see him much this summer. It's sad that we're not as close anymore, but I need to stop being so greedy and expect friendship from anyone who might have loved me. It is so selfish and attention-seeking… Oh, don't stop loving me just cos I don't love you anymore. Pathetic. It is not a transferable emotion from relationship to friendship. William is a case in point. Dump them and leave them be, Claire, you total knobhead.
- Les Marseillais and the twins aren't sure if they're coming at all this year. It feels like the end of an era already.

- François and Yannick are working about half an hour away so I'll still see them in the evenings and at weekends, but it won't be the same.
- Marc is working at the port as *le passeur* (the ferryman) so at least we'll be able to hang out a lot.

Marc's 'job' was nothing more than a social exercise in getting to know the local boating community and accepting their tip-based offerings of booze, fags and the odd croissant. I spent the next three summers by his side, come rain or shine, with only one constant: we were drunk. We were an absolute disgrace and I wince when I think back to the state we would get ourselves into. We would rock up every morning (tide dependent of course), straight from a night out, steaming and arrogant to a queue of eager yachtsmen. I'd somehow repeatedly managed to convince Marc to have 'encore un…' in exchange for promising to suffer the morning hangover on the boat with him. He never took much convincing and whenever I flagged, he took the reins as prime booze motivator. So we'd sit there swaying, sweating and queasy in the morning sunshine, feeling overwhelmed by the stench of engine fumes and dried, hot sea water. We fuelled ourselves with black coffee and cigarettes. Barf. Marc and I spent most of the next three summers on that boat, metabolising a frightening amount of alcohol and occasionally ferrying people to their boats. The embarrassment makes my skin crawl now.

We developed a kind of friendship akin to eating several packets of Tangfastics in one sitting. You know it's bad and it hurts, but it's fun and addictively naughty. We spent every waking moment together and saw each other at our absolute worst. Marc has seen the most degrading and exposed version of me. He has seen the sort of things that, if I had become an alcoholic, I would talk through at AA meetings. We were teenage drunks and we enabled and encouraged each other into oblivion. But it felt wonderful at the time. I guess that's how we justified this inebriated 'folie à deux' to ourselves. Reading it back now gives me a terrifying insight into a potential future where we'd end up as depressed alcoholics clinging onto the memories of when it was fun and when we had a choice. I used to resent his wife for having been such a bore and 'taking' one of my best friends away from me, but she may very well have saved him and, more worryingly now I think about it, saved me.

31ST JULY 2003
LISTENING TO 'MOTOWN NEVER SOUNDED SO GOOD' BY LESS THAN JAKE

Well, Ewen is such a fucking chancer! Just got home from a bit of a nightmare night with him.

Ewen was Marc and Gael's friend who I met at his (weed and saucisson) dinner party who threatened to 'shit himself' if he went out with me. Even Marc, who sees the good in everyone, called Ewen 'un enculé'. If only I'd listened.

When the bar closed tonight we were the only two still kicking about and neither of us really wanted to go home.

I NEVER wanted to go home. My desire to party was a little bit out of hand at this stage and it felt like there was always something in my system, furiously trying to get out.

I would go to bed, after even the most debaucherous of nights, thinking that there was still room for improvement.

Something used to happen to me when I arrived in Brittany during my teenage summers. I don't know if it was the sea air, but something enchanted me and made me go completely wild. I fell in love with the limitless summer nights that allowed me to discover this secret moonlit world. It was a world where everything was more beautiful and people would suddenly start to open up under the cover of darkness and drugs. I craved deep and douchey conversations with stoners at 6am, watching the sunrise with a joint and a bottle of rum. I wanted to feel like I was making profound connections with people when the rest of the world was asleep. I didn't want to miss anything and I believed that all that was important and authentic happened just before dawn.

The bars would call last orders and I'd instantly feel the familiar panic that the night might be over. I believed that every night had the possibility to turn into THE biggest night of the summer; the one that we'd remember forever and repeatedly reminisce over as grown-ups. I'd start every evening full of hope that I'd finally scratch that itch; but the clanging of the bell felt like all the night's promise was being ripped out from underneath me. The bars would close and I'd then be found desperately seeking an afterparty or rallying up a crew of wasters for a fire on the beach. I'd delegate out all the jobs... booze, weed, people, drums. (Yes, drums. Djembes to be precise. Give me strength.) I'd find myself creeping round the back of sleepy cottages nicking firewood from unsuspecting log stores. I wanted to keep going after the afterparty – constantly convincing everyone that the fun wasn't over yet! They couldn't go to bed. I was forever chasing this elusive, impossible high. More more more! My thirst for revelling into the night and making endless meaningless memories was unquenchable.

Ewen and I had pulled briefly the other night after he'd given me a lift home from the bonfire. Part of me still wondered if it was ok from a Gael point of view, but Ewen was so charismatic, I was drunk and I just wanted a bit of fun. We both hung around outside the bar to see if someone would come up with a party, but nothing. He asked if I fancied a night cap at his so we went to the place he was renting. We were smoking a spliff and kissing when he asked if I wanted the same thing as him? Ummm, and what exactly is that? Oh! A no-strings-attached purely sexual relationship for the summer? Just a bit of fun? Errr, no thanks, you fucking pervert! (And I think I 'jokingly' used words to this effect.) Then he pinned himself on top of me and started grabbing my tits and in between my legs. The tone of the night changed within a split second. I was trying to push him off me as he tried to pull my clothes off, but he was so strong. He was kissing me so aggressively that I couldn't even turn my head away. I started feeling really panicky cos he was so forceful and just kept saying, 'Shhhh shhhh', when I was shouting at him to stop. I managed to wrap my leg round him and kick my heel into the back of his calf. He jumped and it gave me a few seconds to wriggle out from underneath him. I told him he was an *'enculé'* and tried really hard not to cry as I grabbed my bag and went to leave. He got really angry saying, *'Je ne pensais pas que tu étais aussi coincée!'*, and that the nunnery might be recruiting. He shouted after me that he was so annoyed that he'd wasted a whole night on me for nothing! Was I definitely not up for a quick shag, *non*? Err, *NON*! What a fucking arsehole. He screamed, *'Pétasse!'*, at me as I shut the door and ran home.

'*Coincé*' literally means '*stuck*' but if someone is a bit '*coincé*' they are uptight or frigid.

'*Pétasse*' means bitch.

Well, that made for slightly uncomfortable reading. I don't think I truly appreciated what had happened at the time. More worryingly I don't really remember it. It's amazing, however, that I was perfectly capable of legibly writing it all down when I got home. I don't even remember this having much of an impact on me at the time. It's shocking that as a generation we were so accepting of this kind of behaviour. What would he need to have done for me to see this assault for what it was? Would he actually have raped me? I never told a soul about this and I'm still not sure if it was because I felt guilty and responsible or because seventeen-year-old me genuinely didn't attribute much meaning to it. As far as I was concerned it was a near miss and nothing technically happened. I'm still not sure if I had a need to process it at the time. Would acknowledging it and talking about it have affected me positively or negatively? It was a time when I definitely didn't feel like I had much self-worth and I'm sure there was still a part of me that was flattered that Ewen Le Pervert even fancied me and wanted to have sex with me. I felt that I didn't deserve any better. I was the 'slut' that broke hearts and cheated. I was the eternal mistress, never worthy of having someone's whole self… only allowed the physical part while the true love was reserved for their real girlfriends. I find it disgusting that my adolescence essentially culminated in a total indifference to what was, unquestionably, a sexual assault. That chubby, bullied, *unpopular fourteen-year-old was still in there craving any attention or lechery available. I wish now that I had at least spoken to someone about it.*

Oh! The internet tells me that Ewen Le Pervert is a police officer now! Yikes.

2ND AUGUST 2003
LISTENING TO 'SEVEN YEARS' BY NORAH JONES

Yesterday was one of those utterly fantastic nights that I'll always remember and cherish. We all went to Gael's parents' house for a party to celebrate his birthday. It was weird setting foot in that house again. I can't believe how different I am now. I do worry sometimes that it's not different in a good way...

I sat in his garden smoking spliffs and drinking Pastis with Marc, Yannick and Gael until the sun came up. I had the best time! Everyone had gone to bed apart from the four of us and I was sat on the bench, under a blanket with Marc. It must have been about 5am and I looked round at the three of them and wanted to cry with happiness.

Fortunately Ewen Le Pervert wasn't there and I didn't tell anyone about what went down the other night. I feel so embarrassed about it and that I even let myself get into that situation in the first place.

THIRTY-THREE

VIKING GOD MAX

10TH AUGUST 2003
LISTENING TO 'FLAKE' BY JACK JOHNSON

We went island camping last night and it was such a blast! There were about thirty of us, but it was a bit of a drug-heavy crowd for my liking. It's all a bit of a blur, but I remember laughing. A LOT.

At some point before the sun started coming up, I went for a wee in the dunes and Marc cornered me when I was making my way back to the fire. He just sat down, lit a fag and passed it to me as he lit another. So I sat down with him in the pitch black. He then (out of nowhere) confided in me about being repeatedly beaten and emotionally abused by his aunt throughout his childhood. It was seriously graphic – I couldn't believe some of the things he was saying. He just blurted it all out. It led to him wetting the bed for years. I thought back to him sleepwalking and pissing in the wardrobe at Mattie's and felt so guilty that Gael and I had made fun of him. He told me he still has nightmares about it now and he was shaking as he was telling me. Jeez. I can't believe I've known him for so long and he's never even hinted at a difficult childhood. It's crazy what some people have had to deal with. And yet Marc is the happiest, friendliest, most caring and loving guy I've ever met. How can something like that not haunt you and fuck you up forever? Although I guess it has a bit if he's still having nightmares about it. And he probably drinks too much. I mean, we all do, but Marc usually takes it to another level. Oh God! Is that why? Am I encouraging this dreadful coping mechanism? I didn't know what to say so I said something about her sounding like a massive cunt (using the English word) and then just put my arm around him and we just sat there like that for about an hour as he cried. I'd kinda lost the party vibe after that, so Marc and I went to bed in his tent and I just stroked his hair as he just sobbed. It broke my heart.

The walk back this morning was rough. I was carrying three bin bags full of empty beer bottles and half of François' weight cos the twat's probably broken his ankle. He was doing a lot of backflipping (his new trick) and absolutely caned himself landing like a drunken prat this morning. Marc was really quiet. I'm not sure I'd make a good counsellor as he definitely seemed worse after he got all that off his chest. The walk back took nearly two hours and my back and shoulders have been absolute agony all day; I can hardly move my arms anymore. I must have been moaning about it a lot because on the beach today Viking God Max offered to rub them. He must have rubbed them for an hour and I was like melted chocolate by the end. I just wanted to marry him and his big strong Viking hands then and there.

Unsurprisingly Max looked like a Viking. His head was about 99% white blonde hair and 1% visible features including the palest, glacier blue eyes imaginable. At twenty-one Max was an incredible human specimen with a genetic make-up that was completely wasted on him being a total bum. He was born a Hercules, but then discovered weed. He is sporting a serious dad bod now with his mane thinned, receded and dry. He seems exhausted by the constant army of mini blonde Viking children running circles around his tired, saggy, balding body. A before and after photo of Max would make a wonderful anti-drugs campaign. He was truly mesmerising to look at and he seemed to just sit back, peacefully contemplating everything around him. This quietness was similar to Grumpy Arseface Toby's complete inability to say anything, but Max was more smouldering than grumpy. As it turned out though, Max was just as much of an arseface. For years before the summer of 2003, I used to just catch myself staring at him with a dreamy, half-smile plastered on my face. I suppose I imagined him a thinker, a philosopher, all knowing and tranquil. I realised during this summer that the silent staring was largely down to the fact that he was permanently stoned... and he was an idiot... the complete opposite to the god-like Aristotle I had imagined.

11TH AUGUST 2003
LISTENING TO 'TURN ME ON' BY NORAH JONES

Score! Pulled Viking God Max tonight! We'd been at the bar with everyone and he asked if I fancied joining him for a spliff on the beach. We were sat on the beach and he put his arm around my shoulders and said that he thought I was *'cool comme fille'*. Then he turned his head and slowly kissed me on the cheek, staying there until I turned my head to meet him. I just wanted to collapse into him. I reckon he could lift me up with one hand.

He's just a big dreamy ball of muscle and hair. God, he's hot. I never thought he'd be interested in me. Why does he like me? He's a solid ten and realistically, on a very good summer's day, I'm an eight (at a strong push). 'Winter Claire' has to fight it out with the other fives and sixes in the middle of the pack, pulling out the good chat that is only reserved from October to May. Meanwhile, 'Summer Claire' talks out her arse and gets a lot of what she wants with a smile and a flash of skin. This is clearly Summer Claire here – talking grade-A bullshit.

Marc didn't have anything to drink tonight, but seemed ok. It was weird so I took him aside and asked if he was alright. He nodded and thanked me for listening the other night and said he actually felt better but didn't want to drink tonight as it had brought so much up the other night. Fair enough.

12TH AUGUST 2003
LISTENING TO 'FORTUNATE FOOL'
BY JACK JOHNSON

Woooo! Viking God Max is my boyfriend. François doesn't approve. He says I shouldn't be hanging out with such a 'druggie'.

I can't even remember the last time I had a boyfriend. Mish was with Lovely Lyla, Skater Chris with Steph, Finn had his Costa Rican supermodel. Can I count the twenty-four hours when I thought I was Dickhead Mike's post-blowjob girlfriend? Was it Aussie Jason? That still feels like a long time ago. I was still accidentally slipping and falling into bed with William then. Oh, William Macleod. That feels like a lifetime ago. I wonder what he's doing now? I wish I could talk to him. I would be able to tell him about Ewen Le Pervert and he would hate him for me. Although he would HATE Viking God Max and we'd probably end up shouting at each other about that. Never mind.

14TH AUGUST 2003
LISTENING TO 'SO FAR AWAY' BY STAIND

4.30am: OH DEAR LORD! Five and a half hours until my exam results. PLEASE PLEASE PLEASE be ok. I don't think I'm going to be able to sleep until I get my results. I've just got home from an amazing night. I'd organised a sunset apéro for Annie's birthday tonight. She's this new English rose that all the boys seem terribly interested in. She's quiet and pale and mysterious. The opposite to me basically. She's hung out with me all week cos her French is ropey and she doesn't really know anyone. François and Marc have spent the whole week treating me like their own personal translator/dating agent… *What did she say, Claire? How do you say 'chaude' in English? Does she like me? What did she say? Is she wearing a thong?* I love them both to bits, but they are ridiculously predictable the minute there's a new girl on the scene. She seems sweet though and I really like her; it's just a bit annoying to watch Marc and François turn into slavering idiots the second she's within a two-mile radius of them.

So I set up all the drinks and snacks on one of the picnic tables round on the west side beaches. Everyone was there and we all got seriously fucked. I was sat in the dunes having a spliff with François when I realised that if my results go down the pan, this could be my last night with my current potential future. This may be the last time in my life when I can say *I'm going to be a doctor when I grow up.* If I don't get what I need, I think I'll emigrate to Cuba and become an artist living in a one-bedroom studio above a rum bar.

This is still my backup life if it all goes wrong. I have always believed that everyone needs a fantasy plan if 'the unthinkable' happens. 'The unthinkable' changes with time and with each person, but it's a 'fuck it' contingency for when your life is turned upside down. In this disaster future, damaged and dependant-free me would wake up just after midday, smoke Cubans for breakfast and then drink toxic local rum for the rest of the day as I paint until dawn. I'd probably be sporting some white trash dreadlocks, a perma-tan and salsa dance with the passion and flair of a pro. I'd just flounce about being dark, arty and poor. It's a world away from my lucky life. I look pale as fuck, I haven't painted in years, I can't dance and my hair is boring and mumsy, but I'm otherwise pretty healthy with my veg boxes, moderate alcohol intake and ex-smoker status. I'll probably live much longer now too instead of the rather macabre gamble of 'which organ will kill me first?' Lung, liver or skin?

Viking God Max and I scuttled off for dinner at the restaurant. It was so nice just sitting with him and chatting. I say chatting, but I was doing most of the talking. I can't tell if he's a bit slow or if he just sits back and takes things in without always feeling the need to make noise all the time. That's fine though. I talk plenty and I've had my fill with the heart-on-my-sleeve talkers of the world. So dinner was really scary. What? SORRY – I stopped thinking for a minute and kept writing. Ha… is that my subconscious? Was I scared? No. Right, focus. Ouff, I don't think I should smoke any more weed. My brain is turning to mush. Maybe that's what has happened to Viking God Max? So annnyyyyway, dinner was *fabulous* and then we went back to his. We sat there for hours smoking and listening to Radiohead's *OK Computer*. It does slightly remind me of William though, which is annoying. So we got a bit carried away and I ended up sleeping with him. IT. WAS. AMAZING… like having sex with the Greek god of… Vikings? Sex? Weed? A god anyway.

4.45am: Oh God, five hours and fifteen minutes left. Pllllllleeeeeeeeaassssssse.

LISTENING TO 'SUNCHYME' BY DARIO G

9.50am: Jesus Fucking Christ this is unbearable. Ten minutes to go. I just don't know what to do with myself. I'm trying so hard not to think about it so I'm going to write about last night's frolicking. At first when I looked at *it*, I thought it was pretty small, but actually not at all! It must have been the perspective in relation to his MASSIVE body. Urgh, no this isn't working. Going for a five-minute run.

I can run?

15TH AUGUST 2003
LISTENING TO 'FREE' BY ULTRA NATE

Well, thank fuck for that! I'm eternally grateful and I BELIEVE! Well, not really, but just in case – THANK YOU!

French A, biology A, chemistry B. God knows how I managed. Now, the day I got my results will truly be one to remember.

It really was.

As soon as I got my results I had a celebration breakfast with Mum and my grandparents. I rang Mish to see if he got what he needed, but Mrs Binky-jolly-bloody-hockeysticks-Allison answered the phone.

'Oh, I'm sorry, Claire, Hamish is busy right now. I'll see if he wants to call you back later.'

I thought that sounded a bit ominous. Also: see if he wants to?! Why the fuck wouldn't he?! I shot him a quick text:

```
Hey Mish. How's it going? Did you get
what you needed? Your mum didn't make it
sound great. Let me know when you're free
for a chat and I'll go home to ring from
landline. Big love x
```

And Nothing. I never heard from Mish or saw him ever again. It was so strange. Just like that, with a puff of smoke, he vanished from my life and I never found out why. Maybe he was embarrassed about his results? I found out that he didn't get what he needed, but the school was able to 'negotiate' a rugby scholarship-type deal and he squeezed in. Maybe he never liked me in the first place and waited for school to end to cut ties completely? Maybe he loved me? I'll never know, but it hurt for a long time afterwards. It still hurts a bit now, actually. We'd gone through so much and the ease with which he cut me from his life made it feel like nothing.

In a weird twist of fate I recently found out he lives about twenty minutes from me in rural Devon. What are the chances? I keep expecting to bump into him at the local Co-op. I'm embarrassed to say that this thought is always in the back of my mind when I nearly leave the house without a flick of mascara. Just in case, I think. I wish I didn't care anymore. It's so petty, I know, but I never got to say my piece to Mish and I never got an explanation for his disappearing act. Not to Americanise the hell out of it but I never got 'closure'. I have spent decades fantasising about what I'd do if I saw him. It usually involves obscenities and violence, but with me somehow coming out of it as the bigger, better person... and hot. I'm obviously always hot as

I say something poignant and clever before smacking him in the chops. So if this chance encounter does ever happen, forgive me, but I want to look my best. The last sixteen years of partying, sunshine, smoking and children have not been that kind to me, so there's no harm in a bit of makeup.

After breakfast I went to meet François, Marc and Ben. We went and had a *café calva* then played volleyball on the beach for the rest of the morning. I think it was the happiest morning of my entire life. I'M GOING TO MEDICAL SCHOOL!

Ah yes, le café calva, the breakfast of French alcoholic champions.

16TH AUGUST 2003
LISTENING TO 'BUBBLE TOES' BY JACK JOHNSON

I feel completely away with it and I haven't slept properly for four days and now Viking God Max hasn't called or texted all day, which has put me in the worst mood. I've also not heard back from Mish AT ALL. What's going on? I texted him loads and I rang again a couple of times, but his mum is continuing to be evasive.

'I'll let him know you called, Claire…'

I was about to go to bed when François came round and asked if I fancied going for a quick drink. Go on then. Better than staring at my phone all evening. So we went out and VG Max was there, absolutely shitfaced. He was really pissing me off being super arrogant saying it seemed like I was always just doing things for him rather than because I wanted to do them for me. He sobered up a bit later and apologised. I went back to his, but it was still a bit weird. He went down on me and we had a quick shag, but I wasn't really feeling it after what he'd said tonight. I'm nervous about letting my guard down and getting too attached. I'm clearly more into him than he is me and I'm leaving in ten days, so what's the point? I've fallen in love in half that time in the past though and then what? Another broken heart for me? MUST NOT FALL IN LOVE with Viking God Max.

18TH AUGUST 2003
LISTENING TO 'BROADWAY' BY GOO GOO DOLLS

So Viking God Max is not turning out to be much of a Romeo. I hosted drinks at mine for everyone on Saturday to celebrate my results. We went out to Le Cabanon then I stayed the night at his and had sex for most of the night. It was really good, baby.

> *Eep. I'm flinching at the sleazy Austin Powers-esque use of the word 'baby'.*

Then he told me he was going to go on a last-minute golf trip with some of the guys till Thursday (including Ewen Le Pervert, urgghh). I'm only here until Saturday! I said that was a shame that we wouldn't be able to spend my last week together and he said he needed some space and he's not good if he feels suffocated. Nice. Everyone just loves being the suffocating girlfriend!

19TH AUGUST 2003
LISTENING TO THE 'THE GHOSTS OF ME AND YOU' BY LESS THAN JAKE

5.30am: All is well. Everything is fine with Viking God Max. Sex was great and all is fabulous. There was a bit of a nightmare after we finished tonight though. We were lying in his bed when suddenly he said, 'Where's the condom?' Ummm, say what now?! We looked everywhere when it suddenly dawned on me where it might be... Shit shit shit. I managed to retrieve it, but not only was it hugely embarrassing, it's also a little concerning. Is that basically like having used no protection? Oh God. This would be a fairly catastrophic time to get pregnant... or syphilis. Although I don't think there is ever a good time for syphilis.

LISTENING TO 'FLAVOUR OF THE WEEK'
BY AMERICAN HIFI

8.30pm: Well, he left and I honestly can't say he looked too bothered at all. I'm starting to think I've made a BIG mistake and I've been taken advantage of. Whenever VG Max and I are with other people, I don't even seem to exist, but when we're alone (having sex), well, he's Prince-fucking-Charming. Ahhhh shit. I fell for it. He doesn't give a toss about me. I'm such a stupid hopeless romantic. I need to get my head out of my fairytale arse.

21ST AUGUST 2003
LISTENING TO 'WHERE IS THE LOVE?'
BY BLACK EYED PEAS

I had some people round for drinks last night as the family had gone to the cinema. It was all going fine until we started playing Ring of Fire. I got the fourth K two games on the trot. Out of eight people! Needless to say I was royally fucked by the time we all headed out. About midnight Mum called.

'Rentre à la maison immédiatement!'

Well, I shit myself. It's been years since I've heard that tone of voice and when I hear it I need to be scared. Very scared. Turns out when we'd left the house, I'd left all the lights on and the door wide open. Oopsie. So I went home shitfaced with my tail between my legs and let her scream at me for about an hour. It wasn't so bad after all cos it meant I had an early night and a good sleep for a change.

I can't believe this used to qualify as an early night. I spiral into a whole new realm of panic if I'm still 'out' past 10pm now. And drinking games? Ohhhh hell no.

23RD AUGUST 2003
LISTENING TO 'GIRL ALL THE BAD GUYS WANT' BY BOWLING FOR SOUP

2am: It was my last night in Brittany and I think it's made it into the top five worst nights of my life. Marc had an apéro and dinner at his house with me, François, Yannick, Ben and the twins. It felt like the old gang back together again and everyone was being super sweet saying it was my last night and they were really going to miss me. François and Marc told me that I was like their little sister and they loved me. I love them! I got a bit pissed and then Yannick was driving everyone to Le Fennec. I said I wouldn't go cos I was a bit strapped for cash, but François then offered to pay for me to go to the club (18€). I said no, I couldn't possibly accept, but I mostly declined cos I wanted to spend my last night with Viking God Max. In retrospect herein lies my error. I should have gone clubbing with my friends. Bros before Viking hoes and all that.

When I got to the bar, VG Max wasn't there. I rang Gael cos he'd just finished a sailing competition with Ewen Le Pervert and Viking God Max in Saint-Lunaire and I couldn't get through to VG Max. They all sounded totally wasted, and Gael said they were all staying there and I could join them 'if I really wanted to'. Great. How the fuck was I supposed to get there and back tonight? Plus it didn't really sound like I was that welcome and I didn't want to see Ewen Le Pervert. Has he told them anything about what happened? Probably some twisted truth that makes me sound like a stuck-up slapper. Urgh, I bet the three of them could share some delightful stories about me. I couldn't believe that Bastard Viking wasn't even going to come and see me for my last night. Then twenty minutes later I saw him arrive with Gael. Jesus… did one of them drive? In twenty minutes and in that state? They're going to kill themselves one day…

I was in such a bad mood by this point that I ignored them. VG Max came over and just said he was going home so bye and safe trip home. Oh, thanks. How kind. Bye then.

I sat thinking, *Was that really it?*, when this girl who'd driven us to the club a few nights ago came over and started screaming at me that I'd left her car open and all her stuff got nicked! What? I was thoroughly confused as I'm pretty sure I jumped out when she was still in the car. She just yelled at me for ages and then started accusing me of having stolen it myself. I honestly couldn't believe it. Everyone was looking at me and this was the last straw and I felt tears stinging my eyes. I just felt so sad and overwhelmed. This was my last night and I wasn't spending it with anyone I wanted to. No one was there and it was all my own fault. I walked home alone and I'm now lying in bed feeling sorry for myself. Ohhhh fuck. I've just realised I lost my camera tonight with all of my photos from this summer. Wonderful.

23RD AUGUST 2003
LISTENING TO 'ROCK YOUR BODY'
BY JUSTIN TIMBERLAKE

3.30pm: I'm on the plane heading back to Edinburgh. The summer went by really quickly and I'm feeling a bit weird about it all. Viking God Max turned out to be a real shit. I sent him a goodbye text and the fuckweasel didn't even have the decency to reply. So much for a summer romance. There was nothing romantic about it. More like summer fucking. God, it makes me so angry. I feel really gullible and cheap about it all. Anyway, I'm excited to see Maggie and Charlie tomorrow. All day and night with them. Yes!

THIRTY-FOUR

GOODBYE EDINBURGH

25TH AUGUST 2003
LISTENING TO 'PLUG IN BABY' BY MUSE

I've had the most fantastic day with Maggie and Charlie. We just messed about all day in Charlie's garden, in the sunshine, drinking a bottle of champagne my mum had given us for our exams. I've missed them so much this summer. It seems like they're just friends now too – it's a relief that that saga is over.

We went to the pub and then met Finn (he's back in Edinburgh for the end of the Festival) and his friend in Beluga. After a ridiculous night of shots, drinking games and dirty dancing, Finn walked me home. We sat and chatted with a film on and we finally pulled about 6am. He's still such a great kisser. He's just left and I heard my dad getting up for work about thirty seconds after I got into bed. Close one.

28TH AUGUST 2003
LISTENING TO 'BREATHE'
BY SEAN PAUL FT. BLU CANTRELL

I've just spent the past couple of days with Finn and it's made me realise that I really didn't feel anything for Viking God Max. I should change his name now. He doesn't deserve it. Viking Buttface Max. Argh, I regret sleeping with him so much! I stayed with Finn and his friend in their flat last night. I stayed in a bed with Finn, but we just pulled. God, he gives me butterflies like Viking Buttface Max never managed to, but I haven't completely forgotten Costa Rica/abandon-me-in-Exeter Gate. But he's like an enormous Claire magnet and I'm completely powerless to his charm. I really could just fall in love with him with the click of his fingers.

30TH AUGUST 2003
LISTENING TO 'SURRENDER' BY LESS THAN JAKE

I spent last night with my beloved Maggilicious. She was completely hammered – I love her. I can't believe after all this time I've found my bestie and now we're leaving. We started in the Southside Steamie and loads of the boys from school came and joined us. Mish wasn't there and I asked Jamie if he'd heard from him and he was like, 'Errr, yeah. He's fine.' I asked if he knew why he'd cut contact and he was really vague and just said stuff like, 'Oh, has he? Yeah, I don't know. Maybe… oh no, I don't know.' It's so annoying! We all then went to Opal Lounge. Gretchen came and joined us, but I've mentally blocked her from my life now and we were both able to pretend we didn't exist. It was great.

I met up with Maggie again tonight and we went to Bar Kohl, Beluga and then met some of the others at the fireworks before having a dance in Frankie's. Grumpy Arseface Toby was there. Urgh. He normally doesn't go out so I don't have to see him, but there he was, in all of his thundercunt glory. I told him, 'You should really buy me a drink with the winnings from your bet, you arsehole.' He looked a bit sheepish and just about squirmed through a 'fuck off'. Ha.

I looked round Frankie's and realised it was my last night out before university and I was spending it in Frankie's of all places. It's been three years (almost exactly) since I first set foot in Frankenstein's on opening night, when I had my first test tube shot with Tom Southall, and what an epic ride it had been since. What a weird place…

Then I said bye to Maggie. She's off to uni tomorrow and I don't know when I'll next see her. After she left I saw William at the bar. I felt such a sadness seeing him; maybe one day that will pass. I nearly went to say hi, but decided against it. It never ends well. I looked around at everyone dancing and decided to leave. I didn't say goodbye to anyone – I don't think I'll keep in touch with anyone from school except for Maggie and Charlie. Looking back, I'm not really sure I was that happy there.

6TH SEPTEMBER 2003
LISTENING TO 'LAVA' BY SILVER SUN

I'm feeling so lonely. It feels like I'm just waiting to go to uni now. I've been making compilations all day to take with me cos I couldn't possibly take all my music. I'm feeling completely overwhelmed by it all. I can remember what I was doing, who I was with, how I was feeling… even what I could smell etc the first time I heard all these songs.

I will always think of William with Ben Folds Five, Foo Fighters, Everclear, Feeder and Less Than Jake. Wheatus'

'Teenage Dirtbag' makes it all come flooding back... I can smell Hugo by Hugo Boss... I can feel his hands stroking my hair and my cheek on his chest... I can hear us 'harmonising' together. The first few chords of 'Evaporated' make all the love, the hurt and the nostalgia bubble right up in the middle of my chest. Oh, William.

I can smell the hot pine trees in the South of France and think of Sexy Laurent when I hear Otis Redding.

Merzhin will always make me think of the night at Mattie's when Gael first said, '*Je t'aime*', when I was having my obligatory and clichéd post-coital fag out of the moonlit window. I can feel his rough, sunburnt lips on mine and his beautiful curls tickling my cheek.

I can taste the stale sandwich and salty tears that accompanied my train ride from Skater Chris' when I hear 'Place So Near'.

Placebo will make me remember the pain I felt when I got back from Cambridge and realised it was over with Mish.

The emotions and songs are endless... So many boys... so much love.

14TH SEPTEMBER 2003
LISTENING TO 'AWAY FROM THE SUN'
BY 3 DOORS DOWN

I am so drunk and stoned, but more than that – I am the WORST person in the world! I thought I was past being a monster. I thought I was nice now. But nooooo. I'm the villain. Deep down I'm Gretchen. I was the bitch all along! It's like the end of *Fight Club* and I've just realised I'm Tyler Durden.

Charlie and I hooked up at Jamie's party tonight. Oh shit oh shit. Just having written it down now has made it real and I want to shred this page, bury my head in my pillow and pretend

it was all a big bad dream! Maggie must never find out. Fuck…
she really was better off with Gretchen. Gretchen would never
have done this to her. I'm such an awful friend to her AND to
Charlie! What have I done? How did this happen? We both got a
bit stoned and then it turned into a weird frantic pulling frenzy
for nearly an hour. Oh God, I feel sick just thinking about it. I
suddenly had a moment of clarity and recoiled in horror at what
I'd done before bumbling out the door. It felt like incest. Before I
left he said, 'I wish we'd done this earlier – we should have gone
out.' Urrrrrghhhh. I made him promise he wouldn't tell anyone
(especially Maggie!).

> *This is what eventually caused my friendship with Maggie
> to disintegrate. I kept it a secret for another three years,
> but selfishly felt the need to offload my guilt and confess
> over lunch one day. We had both lost touch with Charlie
> after leaving school, but he remained her first and I was
> supposedly her best friend. She was calm and I stupidly
> made it out to be nothing. No biggie. I assured her it was
> meaningless and that I had simply neglected to tell her
> rather than purposefully kept it from her. The betrayal was
> blindingly obvious and we both knew I'd fucked it. It was
> a bit of a biggie. I tried to keep calling/texting and seeing
> her, but she made it so difficult that I eventually gave up
> after about a year. I don't think she was able to forgive me
> and never spoke to me again. She is now happily married
> with a gorgeous little boy and back to being besties with
> Gretchen. I had my chance and I fluffed it.*

I just need to go to uni, start afresh and pretend this never
happened. I've learnt the lessons I need to learn. I need to draw
a line underneath my teenage life and be the person I want to be
when I get to university. I want to be able to like me. I'm going

to step out the car on my new turf and I will be confident and friendly and kind and loving. I'm not just going to snog and shag everyone. I'm going to be better than that. I AM better than that.

16TH SEPTEMBER 2003
LISTENING TO 'BOY WONDER' BY SPEEDY

Well, I failed my driving test again – argghh.

17TH SEPTEMBER 2003
LISTENING TO 'LIKE GLUE' BY SEAN PAUL

Ohmigod! I just found out that Charlie shagged Man Shoes just five minutes after I left the party the other night. MAN SHOES?! I am speechless. No words can describe how I feel. I bumped into Gretchen in town today and she told me.

'Did you hear about what Charlie did at Jamie's party? Poor Maggie. I don't know if I should tell her…'

I was obviously pooing myself thinking she knew about me and Charlie, but then she slapped the fakest concerned face on and put one hand on my shoulder.

'Oh, you don't know? Maybe I shouldn't tell you… but he had sex with Sarah [Man Shoes].'

I hate that she was the one to tell me! I obviously couldn't conceal my disgust and she couldn't hide the amount of pleasure she got from seeing me suffer. She was ecstatic! FUCKING GRETCHEN! WHY IS IT ALWAYS FUCKING GRETCHEN?! But also Charlie! I am so hurt and feel so cheap. Jeez, Maggie better not find out about this night. Wow. FUCK Charlie. THE SLUTFUCKING MEGADOUCHE! I bet they were both naked albeit her disgusting man shoes. Well – that's an image that will remain etched in my brain forever... Charlie, Man Shoes and her man shoes. Bleurgh!

18TH SEPTEMBER 2003
LISTENING TO 'HE'S ON THE PHONE'
BY ST ETIENNE

I'm leaving for uni in the morning. It's actually happening. I'm all packed up and my new life starts tomorrow. I'm lying in bed thinking about the last few years and keep coming back to William. Are you always haunted by your first love? Even if it wasn't the right person for you, are they always there? I hope he finds someone and I hope that one day we might even be friends. We'll probably have to be married (not to each other) and have gone through a ten-year (at least) cooling-off period. Then maybe. But for now it's goodbye, old life. Goodbye, William. Goodbye, dirtbag Claire.

> Text to William: I'm off to Uni in the morning and just wanted to say goodbye. Sorry things got so sour. Cheers for the laughs — you really were very special to me. See ya around x

And off I went!

THE DIARY OF A TEENAGE DIRTBAG SOUNDTRACK

'Teenage Dirtbag' by Scott Bradlee's Postmodern Jukebox
'Better off Alone' by Alice Deejay
'Unpretty' by TLC
'Sing It Back' by Moloko
'Kiss the Rain' by Billie Myers
'I'm Kissing You' by Des'ree
'Drinking in LA' by Bran Van 3000
'Little Discourage' by Idlewild
'If I Could Turn Back the Hands of Time' by R. Kelly
'There She Goes' by Sixpence None the Richer
'9pm (Till I Come)' by ATB
'Disco 2000' by Pulp
'Beautiful Ones' by Suede
'Santeria' by Sublime

'That Don't Impress Me Much' by Shania Twain
'You've Got It Bad' by Ocean Colour Scene
'You're Gorgeous' by Babybird
'Save Tonight' by Eagle Eye Cherry
'Flying' by Cast
'Tubthumping' by Chumbawamba
'Son of a Preacher Man' by Dusty Springfield
'Moving Too Fast' by Artful Dodger
'Born Slippy' by Underworld
'Steal My Sunshine' by Len
'Under Pressure' by Queen and David Bowie
'Livin' on a Prayer' by Bon Jovi
'Imagine' by John Lennon

'Wonderwall' by Oasis

'Barber's Adagio for Strings' by
William Orbit

'Little Green Bag' by George Baker
Selection

'Breakfast at Tiffany's' by Deep Blue
Something

'You Never Can Tell' by Chuck Berry

'Pride' by No Use For a Name

'These Wooden Ideas' by Idlewild

'Rise' by Gabrielle

'Kiss Me' by Sixpence None the
Richer

'Pure Shores' by All Saints

'Push' by Matchbox 20

'Dancing in the Moonlight' by
Toploader

'Have You Ever' by The Offspring

'Miami' by Will Smith

'No Scrubs' by TLC

'Iris' by Goo Goo Dolls

'She's So High' by Tal Bachman

'Whole Lotta Love' by Led Zeppelin

'I Guess That's Why They Call It the
Blues' by Elton John

'Sullivan Street' by Counting Crows

'Dancing in the Dark' by Bruce
Springsteen

'Life is a Flower' by Ace of Base

'Welcome to Paradise' by Green Day

'All Star' by Smashmouth

'Round Here' by Counting Crows

'It's My Life' by Bon Jovi

'Ramp! (The Logical Song)' by
Scooter

'The Real Slim Shady' by Eminem

'Set You Free' by N-Trance

'Stand By Me' by Ben E. King

'Scar Tissue' by Red Hot Chili
Peppers

'Somebody to Love' by Queen

'Rhythm is a Dancer' by Snap!

'Oliver's Army' by Elvis Costello

'I Want to Break Free' by Queen

'Heroes' by David Bowie

'Freestyler' by Bomfunk MCs

'Rhythm of the Night' by Corona

'7 Days' by Craig David

'Hitchin' a Ride' by Green Day

'Good Riddance (Time of Your Life)'
by Green Day

'Lady Hear Me Tonight' by Modjo

'36 Degrees' by Placebo

'Church on Sunday' by Green Day

'Mr Jones' by Counting Crows

'Muscle Museum' by Muse

'Warning' by Green Day

'Stan' by Eminem ft. Dido

'Pretty Fly (for a White Guy)' by The
Offspring

'Re-rewind (The Crowd Say Bo
Selecta)' by Artful Dodger ft.
Craig David

'There She Goes' by The La's

'Affirmation' by Savage Garden

'Demons' by Fatboy Slim ft. Macy
Gray

'Lust for Life' by Iggy Pop

'Video Killed the Radio Star' by Ben
Folds Five

'Philosophy' by Ben Folds Five

'Sugarhigh' by Coyote Shivers

'The Day Brings' by Brad

If You're Gone' by Matchbox 20

'Doll' by Foo Fighters

'Brick' by Ben Folds Five

'Like a Prayer' by Madonna
'Evaporated' by Ben Folds Five
'Try a Little Tenderness' by Otis
    Redding
'Dancing with Myself' by Billy Idol
'Wonderful' by Everclear
'Kryptonite' by 3 Doors Down
'Kate' by Ben Folds Five
'Tiny Dancer' by Elton John
'Teenage Angst' by Placebo
'High' by Feeder
'Next Year' by Foo Fighters
'Shining Light' by Ash
'Black & White People' by Matchbox
    20
'Fit Boy + Faint Girl' by 3 Colours
    Red
'Monkey Wrench' by Foo Fighters
'Walking After You' by Foo Fighters
'You're My Evergreen' by Feeder
'Bed of Lies' by Matchbox 20
'The Kids Aren't Alright' by The
    Offspring
'It Wasn't Me' by Shaggy
'All The Small Things' by Blink-182
'Armatage Shanks' by Green Day
'Chasing Rainbows' by No Use For
    a Name
'A Little Respect' by Wheatus
'Sometimes' by Nine Days
'DND' by Semisonic
'Teenage Dirtbag' by Wheatus
'Not Your Saviour' by No Use For a
    Name
'Bat Out of Hell' by Meatloaf
'Born to Run' by Bruce Springsteen
'Blinded by the Light' by Manfred
    Mann's Earth Band

'Sweat (A La La La La Long)' by
    Inner Circle
'Brown Eyed Girl' by Van Morrison
'Piano Man' by Billy Joel
'As Cold as Ice' by M.O.P.
'New Way Home' by Foo Fighters
'Angel' by Shaggy ft. Rayvon
'Rendez-Vu' by Basement Jaxx
'Help!' by The Beatles
'Porcelain' by Moby
'Maxwell's Silver Hammer' by The
    Beatles
'Californication' by Red Hot Chili
    Peppers
'Up in Arms' by Foo Fighters
'Parallel Universe' by Red Hot Chili
    Peppers
'Dumpweed' by Blink-182
'Otherside' by Red Hot Chili Peppers
'A Woman's Worth' by Alicia Keys
'Teardrop' by Massive Attack
'February Stars' by Foo Fighters
'Road Trippin'' by Red Hot Chili
    Peppers
'Castaway' by Green Day
'Arms Wide Open' by Creed
'Misery' by Green Day
'Les Nains de Jardin' by Merzhin
'1979' by Smashing Pumpkins
'My Hero' by Foo Fighters
'Basket Case' by Green Day
'Drops of Jupiter' by Train
'Castles in the Sky' by Ian Van Dahl
'The Space Between' by Dave
    Matthews Band
'Absolutely (Story of a Girl)' by Nine
    Days
'Everything' by Dumdums

'Buck Rogers' by Feeder
'Father of Mine' by Everclear
'Thunder Road' by Bruce
Springsteen
'Here Comes the Sun' by The Beatles
'I Will Buy You a New Life' by
Everclear
'She's On Fire' by Train
'I Think We're Alone Now' by Tiffany
'Sugar in Your Gas Tank' by Less
Than Jake
'Crazy' by Nine Days
'Bitter' by Nine Days
'Rush Hour' by Joyrider
'Fast Car' by Tracy Chapman
'Story of a Lonely Guy' by Blink-182
'October Swimmer' by JJ72
'Undercover Angel' by JJ72
'3am' by Matchbox 20
'Saturday Night's Alright for
Fighting' by Elton John
'Girl Like That' by Matchbox 20
'There Must Be an Angel' by
Eurythmics
'Talkin' 'bout a Revolution' by Tracy
Chapman
'Cigarettes and Coffee' by Otis
Redding
'Every Time I Look For You' by
Blink-182
'Vertigo' by American Hi-Fi
'Always Getting Over You' by Angela
Ammons
'Be Like That' by 3 Doors Down
'Oxygen' by JJ72
'Smooth Criminal' by Alien Ant
Farm
'Smokescreen' by Flying Blind

'Cheating' by Jettingham
'Phoebe Cates' by Fenix TX
'Learn To Fly' by Foo Fighters
'Fallin'' by Alicia Keys
'Raining in Baltimore' by Counting
Crows
'Seven Day Mile' by The Frames
'Because I Got High' by Afroman
'Don't Stop Me Now' by Queen
'Breakout' by Foo Fighters
'If I Had $1,000,000' by Barenaked
Ladies
'California' by Rufus Wainwright
'Gotta Get Thru This' by Daniel
Bedingfield
'Underground' by Ben Folds Five
'Friday I'm in Love' by The Cure
'Just a Day' by Feeder
'Smile' by The Supernaturals
'Boys Don't Cry' by The Cure
'Narcolepsy' by Ben Folds Five
'Love Has Passed Away' by The
Supernaturals
'Addicted to Bass' by Puretone
'Tomorrow' by James
'Always on Time' by Ja Rule ft.
Ashanti
'Lucky Denver Mint' by Jimmy Eat
World
'Lullabye' by Ben Folds Five
'Walk Away' by Ben Harper
'True Love Never Dies' by Flip & Fill
'The Middle' by Jimmy Eat World
'Hey Baby' by No Doubt
'Waiting on an Angel' by Ben Harper
'Breakin' Down' by Ben Harper
'All My Best Friends Are Metalheads'
by Less Than Jake

'The Blower's Daughter' by Damien Rice

'Fake Plastic Trees' by Radiohead

'How You Remind Me' by Nickelback

'Zombie' by The Cranberries

'Flowers in the Window' by Travis

'Mama's Got a Girlfriend Now' by Ben Harper

'Underneath It All' by No Doubt

'You Held the World in Your Arms' by Idlewild

'Jah Work' by Ben Harper and The Innocent Criminals

'High and Dry' by Radiohead

'Gold to Me' by Ben Harper

'Dreaming' by Blondie

'Burn One Down' by Ben Harper

'Vegetable' by Radiohead

'Mess' by Ben Folds Five

'Beer' by Reel Big Fish

'Anyone Can Play Guitar' by Radiohead

'American Girls' by Counting Crows

'No Surprises' by Radiohead

'Why Don't You Get a Job?' by The Offspring

'Nancy Boy' by Placebo

'Hot in Herre' by Nelly

'She's Got a Way' by The Smithereens

'Steal My Kisses' by Ben Harper and The Innocent Criminals

'Wherever You Will Go' by The Calling

'Rain King' by Counting Crows

'Suzie Blue' by Ben Harper and The Innocent Criminals

'The Zephyr Song' by Red Hot Chili Peppers

'Universally Speaking' by Red Hot Chili Peppers

'Heaven' by DJ Sammy ft. Yanou & Do

'By the Way' by Red Hot Chili Peppers

'Place So Near' by Rootjoose

'Black-Eyed' by Placebo

'Slave to Wage' by Placebo

'James Dean (I Wanna Know)' by Daniel Bedingfield

'Special K' by Placebo

'On Mercury' by Red Hot Chili Peppers

'Complicated' by Avril Lavigne

'Karma Police' by Radiohead

'Come Home' by Placebo

'Let Down' by Radiohead

'Dilemma' by Nelly ft. Kelly Rowland

'I Saw a Prayer' by JJ72

'Just' by Radiohead

'The Ballad' by Millencolin

'Nameless' by JJ72

'The Scientist' by Coldplay

'Formulae' by JJ72

'Blurry' by Puddle of Mudd

'Like I Like You' by Justin Timberlake

'Sk8r Boi' by Avril Lavigne

'You're a Superstar' by Love Inc.

'Half Three' by JJ72

'Eddie Walker' by Ben Folds Five

'I Won't Spend Another Night Alone' by The Ataris

'Everlong' by Foo Fighters

'Times Like These' by Foo Fighters

'Brother Sleep' by JJ72

'Justboy' by Biffy Clyro

'7th Wave' by JJ72

375

'27' by Biffy Clyro

'San Dimas High School Football Rules' by The Ataris

'Dreams' by The Cranberries

'Just the Way I'm Feeling' by Feeder

'Out of Routine' by Idlewild

'Time for Heroes' by The Libertines

'American English' by Idlewild

'F**k Her Gently' by Tenacious D

'I Never Wanted' by Idlewild

'Live in a Hiding Place' by Idlewild

'The Chain' by Fleetwood Mac

'Horrorshow' by The Libertines

'Tell Me Ten Words' by Idlewild

'Tribute' by Tenacious D

'A Town Called Malice' by The Jam

'Cry Me a River' by Justin Timberlake

'Lifestyles of the Rich and Famous' by Good Charlotte

'Wonderboy' by Tenacious D

'The Bitter End' by Placebo

'This Year's Love' by David Gray

'Blown It Again' by Daniel Bedingfield

'She's Only Happy in the Sun' by Ben Harper

'The End' (edit version from the film *Apocalypse Now*) by The Doors

'With My Own Two Hands' by Ben Harper

'Babylon' by David Gray

'When She Believes' by Ben Harper

'Everything' by Ben Harper

'Slide' by Goo Goo Dolls

'Diamonds on the Inside' by Ben Harper

'Superman' by Goldfinger

'Wanna Be' by Nine Days

'I Can't Read You' by Daniel Bedingfield

'Ignition Remix' by R. Kelly

'Girls & Boys' by Good Charlotte

'99 Red Balloons' by Goldfinger

'Girlfriend' by Daniel Bedingfield

'I Don't Like Mondays' by The Boomtown Rats

'I Love You Always Forever' by Donna Lewis

'The Anthem' by Good Charlotte

'Send Me On My Way' by Rusted Root

'Get Busy' by Sean Paul

'Bring Me to Life' by Evanescence

'Hallelujah' by Jeff Buckley

'This Picture' by Placebo

'You Don't Care About Us' by Placebo

'Latin Girls' by Black Eyed Peas

'Pure Morning' by Placebo

'English Summer Rain' by Placebo

'Don't Know Why' by Norah Jones

'Hands Up' by Black Eyed Peas

'Painter Song' by Norah Jones

'The Perfect Year' by Dina Carroll from *Sunset Boulevard*

'Pain in My Heart' by Otis Redding

'The Boogie That Be' by Black Eyed Peas

'Cold Cold Heart' by Norah Jones

'The Science of Selling Yourself Short' by Less Than Jake

'Let's Get Retarded' by Black Eyed Peas

'My Immortal' by Evanescence

'Come Away With Me' by Norah Jones

'The Brightest Bulb Has Burned Out'
    by Less Than Jake
'Sweetness' by Jimmy Eat World
'Shoot the Moon' by Norah Jones
'Motown Never Sounded So Good'
    by Less Than Jake
'Seven Years' by Norah Jones
'Flake' by Jack Johnson
'Turn Me On' by Norah Jones
'Fortunate Fool' by Jack Johnson
'So Far Away' by Staind
'Sunchyme' by Dario G
'Free' by Ultra Nate
'Bubble Toes' by Jack Johnson
'Broadway' by Goo Goo Dolls
'The Ghosts of Me and You' by Less
    Than Jake
'Flavour of the Week' by American
    HiFi
'Where is the Love?' by Black Eyed
    Peas
'Girl All the Bad Guys Want' by
    Bowling For Soup
'Rock Your Body' by Justin
    Timberlake
'Plug In Baby' by Muse
'Breathe' by Sean Paul ft. Blu Cantrell
'Surrender' by Less Than Jake
'Lava' by Silver Sun
'Away from the Sun' by 3 Doors
    Down
'Boy Wonder' by Speedy
'Like Glue' by Sean Paul
'He's on the Phone' by St Etienne

ABOUT THE
AUTHOR

Claire describes her life as being completely ordinary. She works as a doctor, living in Devon with her husband and two children. *The Diary of a Teenage Dirtbag* is Claire's first self-published book.

.